C Programming Techniques
for the Macintosh

Zigurd R. Mednieks
Terry M. Schilke

Howard W. Sams & Co.
A Division of Macmillan, Inc.
4300 West 62nd Street, Indianapolis, IN 46268 U.S.A.

International Standard Book Number: 0-672-22461-5
Library of Congress Catalog Card Number: 86-61450

Acquiring Editor: *James S. Hill*
Cover Art: *Gregg Butler*
Composition: *The Publisher's Network*

Printed in the United States of America

Trademark Acknowledgments

Contents

QuickDraw is the basis of all activity on the screen.

The Event Manager controls user interaction with Macintosh programs.

The Window Manager organizes the display of information, and generates events to keep the display up-to-date.

The Dialog Manager provides high-level tools for conducting a dialog with the user.

The Memory Manager allocates and organizes space in heaps.

The Menu Manager controls the content of pull-down menus.

The Control Manager provides high-level tools for creating buttons, scroll-bars, and other graphic interfaces.

Preface

This book is designed to break down barriers for a new breed of Macintosh user: the power user. Many power users reach a point at which it is no longer satisfying to be an expert user. If you are familiar with the Macintosh as a tool, and want to go beyond using the Macintosh to programming the Macintosh, you have reached that critical theshhold. If you want to start programming your Macintosh, this book is intended to get you started faster and to greatly improve the chances that your first program will work well and be easy and enjoyable to use.

The Macintosh has earned a reputation as a challenging machine to program. This is due, in part, to the Macintosh Toolbox. While it provides powerful routines for creating user interfaces, it also requires the programmer to be knowledgeable of and sensitive to the way Macintosh programs are written. Where as other machines are just a hardware vehicle for programs of almost any kind, the Macintosh is a highly integrated hardware/software system. If you are not programming for a living, and even if you are, you cannot afford to spend time making uninformed design decisions and painting yourself into corners. This book provides a clearly marked path for new Macintosh programmers:

- You will find how to convert you knowledge of other computer languages into expertise in C.
- You will be able to learn C quickly from this book if you already know Pascal or another block-structured langauge.
- If you already know C, your knowledge of the features of C commonly used in Macintosh programming will be strengthened.
- You will find out how the Macintosh graphics and windowing environment is put together.
- Your programs will not "sit on top of" the Macintosh Toolbox routines. There is interplay between your programs and the rest of the Macintosh system. This book shows where your programs fit in and what the Macintosh will take care of for your programs.
- No program is flawless, and Macintosh programs can be challenging to debug as well as write. You will learn how to use a debugger in the Macintosh environment and what the commonest bugs and their symptoms are.

This book, unlike other reference books, presents a complete guide to programming the Macintosh. Beginning with the C language, continuing through the Macintosh development environment, and culminating in a detailed study of a complete Macintosh application, you will find all the information a programmer with some experience with other computers needs to program the Macintosh.

The second part of the book contains reference material on the portion of the Macintosh Toolbox required for applications programming. This reference section, which is written using C syntax, expands on the reference material that comes with most C compilers. In addition to the parameters and return values for the Toolbox routines, brief descriptions of the actions and side effects of these routines are provided. This departs from a three-tiered form, which provides preliminary discussions, detailed descriptions, and summaries for each Toolbox manager; our reference section is in a concise handbook format. Information about each Toolbox routine is found immediately after that routine's name and parameters.

Together, the two parts of this book speed up learning and programming. By enabling Macintosh programmers to get to work sooner and by giving them reference material in a convenient format, the barriers to taking advantage of the Macintosh Toolbox are lowered. This book is a way of accelerating the progress of new Macintosh programmers.

Because of the focus on speeding up the learning process, it is impossible for this book to cover all aspects of the C language and Macintosh programming: If you have never written a program before, this book should be read after, or in conjunction with an introductory C programming book. This book does not cover Macintosh systems programming, networking, file system utilities, or device drivers, nor does it cover reference material related to systems programming.

This book's technical accuracy and readability rest heavily on the contributions of the kind people who have given their time to review parts of the manuscript: Steve Golson and Herb Philpott; Bill Harrington of GARDé; Charles von Rospach of Sun Microsystems; Burt Sloan and Gill Pratt who have our best wishes for success in their studies at MIT and beyond. We are forever in debt to David Eyes of Apple Computer for getting us into book writing and for his experienced hand in creating the framework of this book. Without David we would not have known where to begin.

of the kind people who have given their time to review parts of the manuscript: Steve Golson and Herb Philpott; Bill Harrington of GARDé; Charles von Rospach of Sun Microsystems; Burt Sloan and Gill Pratt who have our best wishes for success in their studies at MIT and beyond. We are forever in debt to David Eyes of Apple Computer for getting us into book writing and for his experienced hand in creating the framework of this book. Without David we would not have known where to begin.

How to Use This Book

Compilers Used in Example Programs

Two compilers were chosen for use in the examples in this book: Aztec C by Manx Software and LightspeedC by Think Technologies. They are both excellent compilers. They translate C into efficient sequences of instructions for the Macintosh's 68000 processor to run. They both implement the C language very correctly. Most important is the fact that they both remain close to the Pascal development environment Apple provides for the Lisa in the way that they interface to the Macintosh Toolbox. This means that you can read documentation published by Apple and, with a little effort, apply that documentation to your work in C.

Differences Between the Compilers Used

Since neither of the two compilers we have selected embellish the Toolbox interface, they are also very compatible with one another. The only significant difference in programs written using these compilers is in the names of the header files that are included in C programs to access predefined constants and macros. At the head of each example program in this book is a preprocessor symbol that can be used to indicate which compiler is being used. It should be named the same as the compiler you are using.

Aztec C and LightspeedC are also very different. The differences are not readily apparent from the example programs because the differences lie in the way programs are prepared for compilation under these two compilers. Compilers, especially those for the Macintosh, come with their own development environments through which the program is written, edited, compiled, linked, and tested.

Aztec C provides an environment somewhat like the UNIX "shell." The shell is a command-langauge interpreter that lets you set up scripts to compile, assemble, and link your programs. An editor that resembles the UNIX "vi" editor is also provided with Aztec C. The advantage Aztec C has is that Manx Software has published versions of this compiler for many different machines. If you want to use roughly the same development environment on a wide range of computers, Aztec C is a very good choice. Those experienced with UNIX-based program development will find the Aztec shell environment familiar.

Lightspeed C provides a highly integrated development environment that takes good advantage of the Macintosh user interface to make compiling, assembling, and linking, even for novices, painless and easy. All the phases of compiling a program are rolled into one program – even the program editor is integrated into the LightspeedC environment. This degree of integration provides two advantages: If a syntax error is discovered in your program, the file in which the error occurred is placed right there in an editor window, with the cursor in the offending line of code, ready for you to fix. The other advantage of LightspeedC is speed. Lightspeed C is the fastest available C compiler on any microcomputer. If used with a hard disk, it is faster than compiling on all but the fastest mini and mainframe computers.

How to Select Your Compiler

Compilers that insulate you from the Macintosh Toolbox or that attempt to maintain UNIX programming idioms in the Macintosh milieu make it much more difficult to tap the technical information available in Apple's documentation, technical journals, and user's group newsletters. Insulating you from the "native" Toolbox interface also takes code, which increases the size of your applications without increasing their power.

If you are considering using a compiler not specifically mentioned in this book, you should look for one that has the fewest embellishments over and above the standard Macintosh Toolbox interface. New compilers are appearing all the time, and it is certain that some of the new compilers will be at least as good as those used in this book. Sometimes selecting a compiler is a difficult judgment to make. Contact your local user's group if you need technical information on which to base your decision.

Part I

Tutorial on Macintosh Programming in C

Chapter One

Beginnings

In this first chapter you will find:

- The origins of UNIX and C.
- The path that C has traveled in UNIX and other systems.
- The path that you will travel in the course of reading this book.

The Macintosh is unlike any microcomputer that preceded it. C, on the other hand, has a long history on more traditional computers. This chapter traces the history of C up though the point where it has become the most popular language for professional developers of Macintosh software. If you are choosing a language for your first major Macintosh program, you may want to know the reasons for C's popularity and the facts behind its suitability for Macintosh programming.

Origins

Nearly every book that discusses C and/or UNIX begins with a brief history of these two intertwined pieces of software. This has led to a large body of apocrypha that would have one believe that UNIX was written as a prank to support a space war game, or that it was all part of AT&T's highly coherent plan to become a significant player in the computer industry, or that Dennis Ritchie and Ken Thompson were fed up with the size and complication of the Multics system and wanted to show the world that something simpler would be better.

When Ken Thompson, one of the original principal authors of UNIX, gave a lecture at MIT in the spring of 1985, he responded to the usual questions from the attendees about the origins of UNIX and gave answers that shed some light on the actual circumstances and motivations that led to the creation of both UNIX and C. Part of what Thompson said could be expected: UNIX wasn't part of a grand design – neither AT&T's nor his own. Thompson and his colleague Dennis Ritchie had been working on the Multics project. Multics began as a huge project involving MIT, General Electric, and Bell Labs. Although flawed, Multics was far ahead of any other operating system of its time and is still possibly the best software system for very large computers. So when Bell Labs withdrew from the Multics project, Ritchie and

Thompson found themselves back in the computing stone-age, where they had to submit batch jobs on decks of punched cards and wait a few hours or perhaps until the next day to see the results.

Thompson went on to describe how he and Ritchie tried to get their own computer that they could use interactively whenever they wanted to. Initially they wanted to buy a Digital Equipment Corporation PDP-10, a fairly large machine. In the end they got a PDP-7, a smaller machine – a "minicomputer." How different history might be had they succeeded in procuring the PDP-10, a machine with 36-bit words, 9-bit bytes, and 18-bit addressing, yielding an address space of 256k 36-bit words! How odd this machine seems compared to the processors that are prevalent today. Yet, at the time, there was no accepted bytesize, no expectations of a large address space, and usually nothing that deserved to be called an operating system available from the manufacturer of a computer. Not only did UNIX spawn C, the prevalence of hierarchical file systems, command processor shells, and numerous other software design concepts, it also helped solidify the 8-bit byte as the atomic unit of addressing.

Implementation and Implementation Languages

UNIX was first written in assembly language. Even before C was created, UNIX had been ported across members of DEC's minicomputer line. Still written in assembly language, it arrived on the PDP-11, DEC's last 16-bit computer. Eightbit bytes, general registers, and memory-mapped I/O are etched into the face of the UNIX kernel code. Although UNIX grew up portable, it did pick up some of the design philosophy of DEC minis. Partly because of UNIX, the DEC PDP-11 is the architecture that almost every 16-bit microprocessor is patterned after.

The first application the UNIX environment found was the continued development of UNIX. Self-hosting, in which UNIX kernel development was done on UNIX systems, greatly sped the development of UNIX. The importance of self-hosted development cannot be underestimated. Systems without strong self-hosted development environments usually die from a lack of applications software. With self-hosted development on UNIX, the community of co-workers that UNIX supported could be a community of UNIX developers, not just UNIX users. The appearance of C compilers on the Macintosh means that the Macintosh is now self-hosted for developing Macintosh software. The developer no longer needs two or more machines, and no longer needs to wait for downloading to write Macintosh software. Self-hosted development also means that user–programmers can use the same tools that professional developers use.

UNIX development was self-hosted before C existed. The important UNIX concepts of a hierarchical file system, devices as nodes in the file system, block and character devices, and the like, were already implemented in the assembly-language versions of UNIX. These concepts and the interactive nature of UNIX were attractive enough that the initial community of UNIX users began clamoring for a high-level language – they wanted a "FORTRAN."

Here we have it, the origin of C, straight from Ken Thompson's mouth: C began as an effort to produce a dialect of FORTRAN for UNIX. But one thing saved us from having just that: the address space of the machine UNIX ran on allowed each program to occupy 64k bytes for both data and program instructions. There wasn't enough room to take into account all the special cases and features that FORTRAN has. So Ritchie began pruning and simplifying, so that all the things he really needed in a language could fit. The result is a spare language that relies on a standard library of routines where other languages would have things such a transcendental functions and I/O built into the runtime environment. Given these rigid constraints on the size of the compiler, it is remarkable that C does not leave out any significant feature in the areas of flow control, data abstraction, or data-structure definition. The completeness of C and its complete adequacy for nearly any programming task is illustrated by the fact that we are now in an era where C and Pascal are by far the two dominant languages in which new programs are written.

Capabilities

A complete set of capabilities is a key characteristic of C. Some computer languages, such as Pascal and BASIC, hide the way the variables in a program are stored. C makes no attempt to *enforce* the abstraction of the computer your program is running on. Practically, this means that when you *must* reach right down to the hardware to turn on a bit in a peripheral controller, you have all the capabilities of C at hand. You can use bit fields, data structures, defined data types, symbolic constants, and so on, to make the parts of your program that "touch" the hardware as readable, maintainable, and easy to write as the rest of your program, even while you are engaged in the down-and-dirty of bit twiddling. Of course, for most programming tasks, you can remain completely oblivious to where the compiler has set aside storage for your variables and subroutines. Few other languages give both the ability to ignore the hardware and hide it beneath abstractions and, alternatively, to manipulate hardware while retaining all the power of high-level language: typechecking, data structuring, and readable notation.

The availability of C to its initial user community at Bell Labs spurred the development of the full set of 300 or so UNIX utility programs such as cat, ed, sed, grep, and awk. To be applied to the task of developing programs in the UNIX toolbox, C had to generate fast code and have very little in the way of a runtime environment so that these programs could be invoked quickly and run quickly and would not displace all the other programs running concurrently in the UNIX environment. The ultimate test of C as a well-honed tool was the reimplementation of UNIX itself in C. In transcribing UNIX into C, C became proven as a system writing tool. C remains the only alternative to assembly language for writing programs for micros, where performance is critical. UNIX was transformed from a toy Multics into a versatile system that one person could come to understand totally in a couple months time.

Wherever C Goes, There UNIX Is

C and UNIX thus became intertwined and thrive together to this day. This is due in part to the popularity of UNIX. C has also become more popular than any other implementation language for microprocessor work; it is more popular than languages such as PL/M that were created for that purpose. C has become a *lingua franca* among computer science students. When you work in C you are assured of a steady supply of assistance from colleagues, of clever pieces of code to be culled from computer magazines, of compilers, debuggers, subroutine libraries, and so on.

The popularity of C and UNIX qualifies as a genuine groundswell, rather than the result of a well-executed marketing plan. Because AT&T was prohibited from selling computers before the local phone companies were spun off, UNIX was either given away to schools or sold "as is" for a fairly exhorbitant price to ensure that UNIX would not compete against other operating systems. Even though UNIX was officially a nonproduct, both UNIX and C were flattered by imitation. C compilers were written for the Z80, the 6809, and other microprocessors. UNIX begat Uniflex, OS-9, and other operating systems that touted their resemblance to UNIX.

C and Microcomputer Software

Even MS-DOS is an imitation of UNIX. That C is a very popular language for writing MS-DOS programs is not suprising. C lets MS-DOS programmers easily port UNIX programs to the IBM-PC and other MS-DOS machines, and, because C allows access to low-level entities like peripheral controller registers, those programmers can also take advantage of PC-specific hardware capabilities without resorting to assembly language. Microsoft, the publisher of MS-DOS, is strongly committed to C and develops virtually all its products in C.

The popularity of C among Macintosh programmers is something of a puzzle, though. It caught Apple Computer's Developer Relations department by suprise. According to a survey taken by developer relations, about half the respondents are using C, a proportion that was expected to be much lower. It is easy to see why C is so popular for the IBM-PC: MS-DOS is overtly intended to be a scaled-down UNIX and the 8088 is in many ways similar, especially in its addressing scheme where the program may occupy up to 64k bytes and the data another 64k bytes, to the PDP-11 that UNIX "grew up" on. But the Macintosh could not be further from the design philosophy of both UNIX and MS-DOS!

Partly, this popularity can be explained by availability. When the Macintosh came on the market, the prevalent use of the 68000 was in UNIX supermicros. In its own way, the 68000 is also a descendent of the PDP-11. Many C compilers had already been written and exhaustively tested in the various UNIX ports and derivatives running on 68000-based machines, so C compilers for the Macintosh can be expected to produce good code. C can also be more convenient for the developer who does not want a Lisa soley for writing Macintosh programs in the Lisa-Pascal cross-development environment. The Macintosh *allows* the choice of a minimal language like C that has no built-in facilities for modular or object-oriented programming, unlike the Lisa which pretty much required the use of Clascal, an object-oriented Pascal, as an applications-writing language.

And partly, C on the Macintosh is a popular development environment due to the use of the Macintosh in universities. Students at universities where the use of a Macintosh is encouraged (or required) do not, in general, even have the choice of using the Lisa Pascal cross-development system. Because UNIX is very popular among universities, students are predisposed to C. At Stanford, the university's long exposure to UNIX manifested itself in "SUMACC"– the Standford UNIX Macintosh C Compiler, a Unix-to-Macintosh cross-compiler for C.

Lastly, C is a wonderful and productive language with no artificial constraints, no excess baggage, and all the significant features needed to create readable, debuggable, and maintainable programs. C is an excellent choice on its own merits.

Breaking Down Barriers

If the 68000 is the modern equivalent of the PDP-11, if C works so well on the 68000, if the Macintosh represents the next wave in microcomputing, and if about half the professional developers of Macintosh software have already decided that C is the best development tool for their work, what problem remains? What obstacles lie between the Macintosh and a large following of user–programmers?

In short, the answer is unfamiliarity. The engineer who used a PDP-11 in his or her lab in college might find the 8088-based MS-DOS computers more familiar. The Z80 microcomputer veteran will certainly find the 8088 instruction set and the notion of a ROM-BIOS more familiar than the Macintosh's Toolbox. The UNIX programmer will have to get used to an environment that encourages a combination of big, heavily used, and highly interactive applications the user might keep running for hours on end and desk accessories that can be quickly invoked to do quick operations of a short duration, whereas the UNIX environment he or she is familiar with is based almost entirely on programs that start quickly, run for a short while, and then give way to the next command the user types.

Where to Go Now

The rest of this book addresses the nature of the Macintosh; it tells you why the Macintosh is the way it is, how to take advantage of it, and how to carry any knowledge of C programming in other computing environments over to the Macintosh environment. Overcoming this unfamiliarity is important to creating software that doesn't chafe against the interface style Macintosh users have come to expect from experience with the Finder, MacWrite, and MacPaint.

By the time you are done with this book you will know the mechanics of programming in C in the Macintosh environment. You will also know how to make design decisions in harmony with the decisions made by the designers of the Macintosh. As a result of knowing both these disciplines, your programs will look just as beautiful and stylish as the programs written by Microsoft or Lotus and without significant extra work on your part. Giving every program that you, the user–programmer, write a professional level of polish is not practical in any other computer system – not UNIX, not MS-DOS, nor any other popular system.

Mastering the Macintosh means more than overcoming the differences between Macintosh and the microcomputers that came before it. It means becoming completely comfortable with the design decisions that went into the Macintosh. It means *being* inside Macintosh.

Points to Consider

1) The following computers are all very successful: Macintosh, IBM PC, Apple II, IBM 370, DEC VAX. Why are they successful?

2) In this group of successful computers, only two occupy roughly the same position in the market. Which two? Why?

3) You may have at some time used a computer system that has fallen into disuse and is now forgotten. Why did that product fail?

4) Users are demanding more and more ease of use and polish in the programs they are willing to use. What does this mean to the small software developer?

5) Of GEM, Microsoft Windows, and Topview, which do you think will become the standard IBM PC window system? What is the effect of the lack of a standard user interface on MS-DOS and UNIX software?

6) UNIX gained popularity because it was given away to universities, and UNIX became a widely cited example in computer science courses. With the University Consortium, Apple has established the Macintosh as the leading microcomputer in many important universities. As you read this book and learn more about the Macintosh, keep asking yourself, "How can the Macintosh be used as an example of good engineering?"

Chapter Two

C and Other Languages

In this chapter you will find:

- How C is related to other computer languages.
- How C is different.
- How to transfer your experience in other languages to C.
- Why everyone ends up putting features of the C language in their language.
- Why Pascal has no advantage over C for Macintosh programming.

Where You Are

If you are approaching this book knowing some language other than C, you may be wondering just what C is, what C programmers think it is, and where C fits in the spectrum of languages.

Where You Are Going

We will take a broad approach to the question of the nature of C. C is not very different from other block-structured langauges like Pascal, **ALGOL**, SPL, *Ratfor*, and PL/1. If you know one of these languages, stepping into C should not be difficult. If you are an assembiy-language programmer, you can think of C as a convenient notation for structuring data, calling functions, and specifying arithmetic operations and control flow. Only if your experience in programming was aquired in an interpretive language like LOGO, APL, or BASIC will you have to learn some really new ways of working to use C effectively.

What You Will Need to Get There

If you are a member of the group of people coming to C from an interpretive language environment, you may want to read a tutorial on C before going on. If you have experience in a compiled, block-structured language already, you may want to have at hand a C reference. And if you are a C programmer, you may want to brush up on function pointers, pointers to pointers, and defined data types, because these are all heavily used in Macintosh programming.

Familiar Tools and New Tools

Computer languages are like tools in a toolbox. You may have already chosen C as the tool you will be using to program the Macintosh. If you are not an experienced C programmer, that decision was made without complete knowledge of what you are getting into. A computer language is just a tool and is inherently less important than the job itself. You may be tempted to just get to work and use C syntax with the style and conventions you used in Pascal or whatever language you are familiar with. Certainly no one cares whether you push or pull on the handle of a wrench, whether you grip a screwdriver overhand or underhand. But in programming, style is important if anyone other than yourself is going to comprehend your programs. C is particularly susceptible to quirky programming since style rules are not built into the language.

The rest of this chapter compares the facilities other languages provide for writing good programs with the facilities provided in C.

Abstraction

Abstraction is the ability to hide the details of an operation from the programmer. Because of the abstraction built into Pascal, Pascal is widely thought to be a superior language for the programmer who is not going to make a career of programming. Standard Pascal, as it was concieved by Niklaus Wirth, can be taught to a student as a set of rules. Students of Pascal can become proficient without knowing what a register is, whether structures are passed on the stack below a certain size and passed indirectly if they are larger than that size, how a data structure is laid out in memory, and so on. If you follow the rules of Pascal, your programs will work and you will not need to know *how* the machine is actually doing it.

For instance, if a Pascal programmer wants to write a procedure with a side effect, he or she would declare a "VAR" parameter, a parameter that is passed "by reference." So when an assignment is made to that parameter in the routine, the variable "passed by reference" to the routine will reflect the result of that assignment. In contrast, a C programmer would have to be aware that in order to have a procedure modify a variable local to its caller, the procedure will have to take a pointer to that variable as a parameter, and all the modifications will have to go through that pointer. This is one case where Pascal provides an abstraction, and C provides a general mechanism for achieving the same result.

The following code fragments show the way a "VAR" parameter is used in Pascal and an equivalent procedure coded in C. This is an example of Pascal abstracting and C requiring the programmer to specify an action explicitly. Both routines do exactly the same thing. First the Pascal version:

```
procedure Assign (VAR to : INTEGER; from : INTEGER);

  {Assign the value of "from" to the variable "to."}

  begin {Assign}

    to := from;

  end {Assign}
```

And the C version of the same procedure:

```
/* Put the value of "from" into "to." */
assign(to, from)
     int *to;
     int from;
{
     *to = from;
}
```

In this case the C programmer has to know that, to change some nonlocal value whose location is not globally known, the procedure has to have a pointer to that location passed as a parameter. The Pascal programmer can achieve the same effect knowing only the following rule: If you want to "permanently" change the value of a parameter, you have to declare it "VAR."

The Cost of the More General Approach

It is impossible to become an expert C programmer without knowing that you cannot, in general, find the address of a register, that strings are conventionally null terminated, that data structures are laid out in the order they are defined, that odd addresses can only point to 1-byte objects on machines based on the 68000, and so on. It is hard to write good C programs without being an expert. Fortunately, C, like Pascal, is a small, simple language. It is not much more difficult to become an expert at C as it is to become proficient in the rules of Pascal programming.

Some other languages, like Pascal, were designed to hide the details of data storage and access, C was not. If you are familiar with a block-structured language that abstracts more than C does, you will find handy a C reference manual that details the way data storage and scope are handled in C. Even if learning C syntax is easy for you, you will want to know what is really going on: what the data structures look like in memory and the size of data objects. By learning about the way C programs function, the semantics of C, you can become accustomed to the lesser degree of abstraction in C.

Hiding Data

If you are writing a large program and you want to avoid naming conflicts or if you are working with other programmers on a large project, you will want to hide data from code that should not be modifying that data.

C provides about the same facilities for hiding data as the typical assembler and some additional capability that lets you hide variables inside procedures. Like most assemblers, you can declare a data object *external*, meaning it is defined in some other file. The linker resolves references to external objects. You can also declare global variables *static*, which means they will never be touched by code in another file. If a local variable is declared static, it will not be allocated on the stack when the procedure it is declared in is called. Instead, it will be allocated in the global data area of the program, but only the code in the procedure it was declared in will be able to access it. Static local variables retain their value across invocations of that procedure, and they always occupy space, even when the procedure they are declared in is not being executed. Procedures can also be declared static, in which case they cannot be directly called from outside the file they are defined in.

Normal local variables are allocated on the stack and disappear when the procedure they are declared in returns. These variables are only directly accessible from code in the procedure they are declared in.

The following code fragment illustrates C's data-hiding capabilities:

```
static int this_file_only; /* Available only to this file */
extern int somewhere_else; /* Defined in some other file */

/* call a routine that accumulates values to accumulate two
 * numbers, then call it with a value of 0 and put the return
 * value in the variable "total"
 */
main()
{
    int a_local, another_local, the_total;

    a_local = 1;
    accumulate(a_local);
    another_local = 4;
    accumulate(another_local);
    the_total = accumulate(0);
}

/* A routine callable only from code in this file */
 static
accumulate(value)
{
    static int accumulator = 0;

    accumulator += value;
    return accumulator;
}
```

C does not have the elaborate scope rules of ALGOL, where, in certain cases, variables in a routine's caller are available, along with local and global variables. But by using the static storage class and by dividing large programs into separately compiled modules, you can do an effective job of organizing your program's data and hiding data from code that has no business modifying it.

Program Structure

C programs are generally organized top-down, no matter what order they are written or designed in. When you look at a listing of a C program, you will generally see the "main" procedure near the top, the high-level procedures next, and the lowest-level procedures either following the higher-level procedures they support or at the end of the listing. This is exactly the opposite of the way most Pascal, ALGOL, and APL programs are organized. In these languages, the lowest-level procedures come first, conventionally or compulsorily before the procedures that call them.

Languages that promote bottom-up order in listings do so because their development environments may provide an interpreter that needs routines defined before they can be called or because they have no way of declaring return values other than in procedure definitions. In some languages there may be no real need to order programs bottom-up, it may just be customary.

C does not require any particular order. C compilers can determine the data type of return values either from procedure definitions or from declarations. Whether or not there is some intrinsic value to top-down program organization, most C programmers expect programs to be organized this way. If you want to take advantage of the advice of experienced C programmers, it is a good idea to lay out your programs the way they would.

In addition to this stylistic convention, you only need to follow common sense and the requirements of the language in laying out your programs. You have to define data structures, variables, and preprocessor macros before you use them. Preprocessor macros are used throughout the file, so they ought to come at the very beginning (this is a flexible maxim, and if common sense dictates defining a macro near the other entities it refers to instead of at the top of the file, follow common sense). After the preprocessor macros come the data structure definitions, the enumerated constants, and the defined data types. They must precede the global data declarations where their definitions are used. Following the global data declarations, the procedures that make up the program are defined.

Structuring Data

The data-structuring capabilities of a computer language are a major determining factor in the expressive power of that language. Roughly speaking, there are low-powered languages like BASIC and FORTRAN at one end of this spectrum; C, Pascal, ALGOL, PL/1, and other block-structured languages in the middle; and Lisp, Modula-2, Smalltalk, and the granddaddy of modular languages, Simula, at the high end of the data-structuring spectrum. Because C is found in the middle of this spectrum, as is Pascal, C can replace Pascal as a programming tool without too much disruption, kludges, or violation of language rules.

C data structures are bit-for-bit equivalent to Pascal records. The differences amount to that C provides bit fields and Pascal has a more convenient way of expressing multiple interpretations of the structure of the same piece of memory. That C and Pascal structure data in about the same way is a very fortunate circumstance: it means that all the data structures that the Macintosh Toolbox uses can be defined and accessed in C without any tricks or hacks whatsoever. Because of this, it is possible to write C programs for the Macintosh that are every bit as enmeshed in the Macintosh environment as any Pascal or assembly-language program.

The languages that fall below C and Pascal in data structuring capability, such as BASIC and FORTRAN, prevent programs written in those languages from taking full advantage of the Toolbox software. Conversely, languages that offer a great deal more data-structuring power than C either make it difficult to do low-level "bit-twiddling," or require a cumbersome runtime environment, or have no way of specifying structured data such that it has a predictable layout in memory, or some combination of these hindrances.

Number Crunching

C is not the best language is for number crunching. It isn't bad if all you need are double-precision floating-point numbers. But single-precision floating point is all but useless in C, because such numbers are converted to double precision before any operations are performed on them. Thus there is no performance gain to be had by using single-precision floating-point numbers, even when they are sufficient for the application.

Some C compilers violate the C standard and provide completely single-precision operations or IEEE standard floating-point numbers, or both. Adding floating-point data types is a fairly innocuous way of fudging the C standard because C programmers can define new data types themselves. If you plan to use a lot of floating-point arithmetic, you may want to look for a C compiler that has additional floating-point data types.

The Toolbox software provides fixed-point arithmetic, but the cost of calling a routine to do a single fixed-point operation is greater than the cost of executing the in-line code for double-precision floating-point arithmetic.

Extensibility

C provides two forms of extensibility: new data types may be defined, as in Pascal, and new types of constants may be defined. C also has a macro preprocessor that should *not* be used to extend the language. Although it is true that you could make C look a lot like Pascal through creative use of preprocessor macros, you should not expect anyone but yourself to be able to read such code!

Although C and Pascal have virtually identical capabilities for defining new data types, C programmers use that facility much less than Pascal programmers. While every pointer used by Toolbox software has a defined data type associated with it, C programs seldom have data types defined for pointers, since C notation for declaring pointers is so simple and terse. In the examples in this book, we will use the defined pointer types provided by the Toolbox, because all the Apple documentation and other Pascal-oriented documentation refers to those data types. For pointers to objects of our own creation, we will follow the usual practice of omitting to define new data types for pointers and structures.

Macros

Unlike most other languages, C has a macro expander associated with it. The macro expander is a completely separate step in compilation, so you can be sure that all macro expansion is done before any C expression parsing has taken place. The C preprocessor is a token-oriented macro expander, which means that it operates on the same chunks of characters that the C parser does.

C's token-oriented macro expander can be contrasted with the string-oriented macro expander "m4," which comes standard with most UNIX systems. m4 can be used to glue tokens together and pull them apart, something that can't (well, shouldn't) be done with the C preprocessor.

The C preprocessor is used to associate names with constants, so when you write

```
#define FOO 5

bar = 3 + FOO;
```

the C compiler proper sees

```
bar = 3 + 5;
```

because the preprocessor has substituted the token 5 for the token FOO.

Most Macintosh C compilers use the preprocessor for Toolbox constants because most C programmers do not use enumerated constants, and because preprocessor symbols can stand for all types of C tokens. (And some compilers do not have enumerated types.)

Why Macintosh Programming Really Ought to Be Done in C

Because Apple had to extend Pascal to include features that are part of standard C (most notably casting operations), the Pascal used to develop Macintosh applications has lost its advantage of hiding the facts of life about data storage from the programmer. One consequence of these extensions is that *Inside Macintosh*, Apple's reference manual for Macintosh programmers, has to cover the nonstandard extensions to Pascal and their use in Macintosh programming, in addition to being a reference document for the Macintosh Toolbox. Programmers who have learned standard Pascal or some other extended variant of Pascal will need to learn the language features added to Macintosh Pascal. Also, Pascal manuals and tutorial books do not cover these added features.

The result of these extensions is a Pascal that can do most, not all, of the things C can do, without any advantage left in hiding details of data storage from the programmer. When you cast one type to another, you have to be aware of how those data types are stored. So instead of keeping track of data storage as part of the rules of C, you have to keep track of a set of violations to the rules of standard Pascal. On the Macintosh, there is no substantial difference in the effort expended of the part of the

Pascal programmer compared with that expended by the C programmer. Programmers might as well take advantage of the added features of C (although, to be fair, the extensions in Macintosh Pascal are quite cleanly designed and do not detract from the readability of programs).

Since Macintosh Pascal is not standard Pascal, the amount of help available to the Pascal programmer from tutorials and other books on Pascal is diminished. On the other hand, in a well-designed C development system for the Macintosh, you will not have to learn new language features. You will have to change the way you think about program design, and you will find yourself using some features of C that are seldom used in other environments. In Macintosh programming, the rules are the same, but the style of the game is different.

Points to Consider

1) Why did you choose C for programming the Macintosh?

2) What obstacles did you foresee in using C?

3) How does C differ from other languages you know? Is the difference greater or smaller than you expected?

4) What other languages would you consider using? Why?

Chapter Three

Knowing C, Thinking C

In this chapter you will find:

- Whether you can learn C in one chapter.
- A description of the C language.
- What is good C style.
- How to read Pascal and think C.

Ready?

To keep this chapter manageable, we do not attempt to do what others do in an entire book. You will need to ask yourself whether you can learn C in a single chapter, or whether you should augment this treatment of C with a tutorial book aimed at teaching C. If you are familiar with a block-structured language, and if you have written enough code in that language to have faced the following issues, you can probably pick up C from this description of the language. Here are the issues you should have faced:

- Calling procedures written in other languages: the practical implications of "call by value" and "call by reference."
- Defining data structures to match structured data from external sources such as networks, data files produced by other systems, or data structures used by library procedures written in languages other than the one you use.
- The scope and visibility of local variables.
- The use of bit-masks.
- Formatting your programs according to accepted practice.

If you are experienced (or at least well versed) in these issues, you can probably go on to pick up C from the rest of this chapter. If you feel you might be left adrift by a description of the C language that omits extensive tutorial examples and exercises, there are many books that teach C in depth and with tutorial assistance.

Which C ?

This description of the C language is derived from the draft ANSI standard for C. This is the subset of that standard that is compatible with the current AT&T Unix C compiler. We will be presenting C in three parts. First, the C preprocessor will be described: it is what gives C constants and macros. Then the C language proper will be decribed in terms of its data types and operators.

The Preprocessor

The C preprocessor is a language in itself. In some implementations of C, the preprocessor is made available in stand-alone form so it can be applied to files in languages other than C. In all implementations, the preprocessor can be considered a separate pass. The compiler only sees code after the preprocessor has finished operating on it.

The language of the preprocessor enables you to specify that some token in a program be replaced by some other token(s). One function of the preprocessor is the creation of symbolic constants ("equates," in assembly language). Most symbolic constants in C programs are preprocessor constants; these are replaced by numeric constants before the C language parser sees them. In Pascal, symbolic constants are part of the language itself. There is little practical difference between these two approaches.

Preprocessor statements have two parts. The left side of a preprocessor statement specifies a token or a macro with a list of parameters. The right side specifies what will replace the left side. Preprocessor statements generally end at the end of the line. When more than one line is required, a back-slash placed at the end of the line indicates that the next line is also part of the preprocessor statement.

Simple Preprocessor Statements

This is the syntax of preprocessor statements:

#define identifier [any-token...]

The basic preprocessor statement associates an identifier with one or more tokens. Before the C parser sees the tokens that make up the C program, the preprocessor will have replaced the identifier that names the preprocessor macro with the tokens to the right of it. If no tokens are given, the identifier token is removed from the program.

A program with the following statement in it would have all instances of the token FOO replaced with the number 3:

#define FOO 3

Preprocessor Statements with Parameters

In addition to an identifier that names a preprocessor macro, a macro can have a list of parameters, enclosed in parentheses, following the macro name. If these parameters are used anywhere in the body of the macro definition, they will be replaced by whatever tokens appear in the parameter list when the macro is used.

#define identifier (identifier [, identifier...]) [any-token...]

Macro parameters are like procedure parameters. When a macro is used, the parameters of the definition are replaced by actual parameters. A macro that looks like a procedure call can replace procedure calls with in-line code, increasing the efficiency of critical sections of programs.

The Opposite of a Macro Definition

#undef identifier

This preprocessor directive causes the preprocessor to forget about the identifier.

Including Files

#include <name-of-file>
#include "name-of-file"

These two statements cause other files to be included in the file being processed. The first form includes files from a predetermined list of directories, the second uses only files found in the local directory.

Conditional Compilation

#ifdef identifier
#ifndef identifier
#if constant-expression
#endif

These are the preprocessor's conditional statements. Lines between an opening conditional statement and a closing "endif" statement are conditionally included in the file being processed. The first two forms of preprocessor conditions test for the existence or nonexistence of preprocessor macros. The identifier may be the name of a macro with no right side (no tokens that would replace occurances of the identifier in the file). The third form of condition includes the entire constant expression syntax of

C. If the expression has a nonzero value, the condition is true. This facility of the C preprocessor corresponds to the conditional assembly facility of most assemblers.

#else

This preprocessor statement divides conditionally included lines into two groups: The lines before the "else" remain in the file being processed if the condition of the conditional inclusion statement is true. The lines following the "else" and before the "endif" are included if the condition is not true.

Support for Program Generators

The "line" statement is not properly part of the preprocessor. The purpose of the "line" statement is to inform the compiler's error-notification system of what line the real source code is on. Preprocessors like the C preprocessor, m4, YACC, LEX, or any of the other macro processors and program generators that are commonly used in conjunction with C often change the number of lines the compiler sees after the source code has been processed. These preprocessors insert line statements so that the compiler does not report incorrect and confusing line numbers when compiling preprocessed code.

#line integer [name-of-file]

These program-generating programs insert "line" statements in their output; seldom would you have any reason to type in a line statement yourself.

Preprocessor Example

The following code fragment is an example of conditional compilation:

```
#if DEBUG_LEVEL > 3

/* Some highly detailed debugging code... */

#endif
#if DEBUG_LEVEL > 2

/* Some less detailed debugging code... */

#endif
```

The Syntax of C: What the C Parser Sees

The rest of this chapter describes the syntax that the C parser recognizes. Whether a particular compiler is implemented this way or not, you can think of a C program as being free of preprocessor statements by the time it reaches the C parser.

While reading this description of C, you may want to keep your thumb on a page with a sample program on it to see examples of the syntax being described. A small sample program appears at the end of this chapter, and later chapters contain much larger examples illustrating Macintosh programming.

Simple Variables: Storage Classes and Data Types

A fundamental part of many computer languages is a facility for setting aside space for variables. Using the following syntax, you can set aside space in units fundamental to C:

```
[storage-class] [data-type] identifier
    [= initializer] [, identifier [= initializer]...];
```

Storage classes determine how a variable is stored. *Data types* tell how the bits in a variable are used and the size of the variable. The *identifier* gives the variable a name. The *initializer* determines the initial value of the variable. Any number of variables or the same type and storage class can be declared, setting aside storage for them, in a single statement.

The following storage classes are available:

static

If this storage class is specified for a global variable, the variable is made unavailable outside the file it is declared in. If the static storage class is specified for a variable local to a procedure, then that variable will be allocated in the *global* data area of the program, and the variable will retain its value across invocations of the procedure it is local to. Because the variable is local to a procedure, no other procedure will be able to access it. Procedures can be declared static as well, hiding them from other files. The static storage class is used to make programs more modular and to avoid naming conflicts among global variables.

extern

The extern storage class tells the compiler that storage for this variable has been allocated elsewhere but that its data type is the one specified with the name of the variable. The extern storage class is used when the compiler needs to know the size and/or type of a variable whose storage has been set aside in some other module of the program.

auto

The auto storage class signifies that a variable is to be allocated automatically, on the stack, when a program block is entered, and deallocated when the block is exited. This is the default storage class for local variables.

register

The register storage class advises the C compiler to place variables local to procedures in the registers of the processor. Using register variables can greatly speed up the execution of a program.

The following data types are predefined in C:

int

The int (integer) data type is the fundamental data type in C. Integers are meant to reflect the architecture of the machine the compiled program will run on. In the case of the Macintosh, integers are 16 bits wide.

short

The short data type is never bigger than an integer, but it can be smaller. The choice of size for a short is up to the compiler implementor. On the Macintosh, shorts are not too useful; if you need an 8-bit quantity, use a char because all compilers have an 8-bit char data type. On machines where integers are 32 bits wide, the short data type provides a way of working with 16-bit integers.

long

The long data type is 32 bits wide on the Macintosh. It is never smaller than an int data type. On most 32-bit machines, it is the same size as an int.

char

The char data type is used to reflect the unit of storage used to hold characters on a machine. On a Macintosh, and most other machines, it is 8 bits wide. Arithmetic operations can be performed on char variables in the same way as on int, long, and short types.

unsigned int

Unsigned integers have no sign bit and so can hold numbers twice the magnitude of signed integers.

unsigned short

Just like a short, but with no sign bit.

unsigned long

Just like a long, but with no sign bit.

float

The float data type may sound as though it is the fundamental floating-point type in C, but it is not. All float variables are converted to double before being operated on. Unless you are storing floating-point numbers in arrays big enough to cause a space crunch, using the double type will make your programs execute faster.

There are no standards specifying sizes or even relative sizes for floating-point types in C. Some Macintosh C compilers use Apple's Standard Apple Numerics Environment, a library that conforms to the IEEE floating-point standard, and some do not. Some compilers omit floating point altogether. Some compilers allow the programmer to specify that float types are not to be converted to double before arithmetic operations.

double

This is the fundamental floating-point type in C. On the Macintosh, a double typically occupies 10 bytes.

An Example: Simple Declarations

The following declarations create simple variables:

```
/* Double-precision X and Y velocities are initialized to 0 */
double x_velocity = 0, y_velocity = 0;

/* The local variable in this procedure retains its value across
 * calls, and is zero before the first call to this routine.
 */
int running_total(add_in)
{
    static subtotal = 0;              /* Initially zero */

    subtotal += add_in;
    return subtotal;
}
```

Data Structures and Arrays

Data structures and arrays are the two means of aggregating variables in C. Arrays can have multiple subscripts, but they are always contiguous in memory. Subscripts are always integers. Negative subscripts indicate a negative offset from the beginning of an array. On a Macintosh, you can use subscripts to access elements of one-dimensional arrays of 2^{15} items or less. To deal in tracts of memory larger than this, you will just have to do the pointer arithmetic yourself.

Array declarations have a syntax that is a minor variation on that used for simple variables:

```
[storage-class] [data-type] identifier[[bounds]][[bounds]...]
     [= initializer][, identifier [= initializer]...];
```

Array bounds can be expressed as any constant expression. C does no bounds checking, and bounds are optional for one-dimensional arrays. Omitting array bounds or ignoring preestablished bounds can be useful for working with variable-length arrays.

Data structures are a way of grouping declarations under a single umbrella declaration. In Pascal, the equivalents of structures are called records.

This is the syntax of C data structures:

```
struct [identifier] { declaration; [declaration;...] }
     [identifier];
```

Data structures are like cookie cutters, and memory is like a sheet of dough: if you leave off the last optional identifier you have made a cookie cutter, but no cookies. If you include the last identifier, you have made a cookie cutter and one cookie. If you plan to use a data structure cookie cutter elsewhere, you will have to name it by including a name just after the struct keyword.

Named structure definitions can be used just like predefined data types. Any place where the name of a data type is used, the keyword struct can be used followed by the name of a previously defined structure.

Unions

Unions are like structures except that unions do not lay items end to end as structures do; unions lay the items they contain on top of each other. So if you need a name for a piece of memory that could hold either of two or more structures, indeed any number of types of variables, you would declare a union containing members of all the types that could be put in that space. The syntax of union declarations is almost identical to that of structures:

```
union [identifier] { declaration; [declaration;...] }
     [identifier];
```

As with structures, the result of declaring a union is a cookie cutter that cuts out pieces of memory the size of the largest element in the union. If the union can hold the largest member of the union, it can hold any member of the union.

Defined Data Types

C has a means of defining new data types. This mechanism is very similar in syntax and in its use to Pascal's defined data types. The greatest difference is that defined data types are seldom used in C, although some books that teach C strongly advocate their use.

Defined data types are widely used in the Toolbox interface. Even if you have not used defined data types extensively in C programs you may have written, you will need to be familiar with them for programming the Macintosh.

This is the syntax of data-type definition:

```
typedef abstract-declaration identifier;
```

An abstract declaration is a declaration without the name of the variable. So instead of creating a variable of a given type and name, an abstract declaration simply provides information about size and type. Defined types use this information, because the newly defined type inherits the characteristics, such as size and structure element names, from the data types used in the abstract declaration. The name of the defined data type is given as an identifier, which can then be used like any other data type name (ie. anywhere that you can use int you can use a defined data type).

Enumerated Constants

Enumerated constants are the other way of creating symbolic constants in C. Enumerated constants are somewhat like Pascal sets. Not only do you create symbolic constants when you define enumerated constants, you can, at the same time, create a class of variables to hold those constants.

Creating enumeration data types provides a means of enforcing the correct use of enumerated constants only in situations where they ought to be used. They will not properly fit in variables of other types, and a good compiler will warn you of abuse of enumeration types and constants.

This is the syntax of enumerated constant declarations:

```
enum [identifier] { [identifier [= initializer]] [,
        [identifier [= initializer]]... };
```

The identifier that may appear just after the enum keyword names an enumeration type for variables that can hold only the constants named in the list between the braces. To declare a variable of a class defined in an enum declaration, use the following syntax:

```
enum identifier [= initializer];
```

Aggregate Declarations: An Example

The following declaration creates an array of structures. The structure is called "ball" and the array is called "in_play."

```
/* At most three balls can be in play */
struct ball
{    int x_position;
     int y_position;
     double x_velocity;
     double y_velocity;
     int mass;
} in_play[3];
```

Pointer Declarations

Pointers are variables that hold the addresses of other variables. In C, pointer declarations are syntactical variations of the declarations of the variables they can point to.

In pointer declarations, the identifier naming the pointer is preceded by an asterisk. Asterisk, used as a unary operator, is the dereferencing operator. (Dereferencing is the action that takes place when a pointer is followed to the object it points to; this is also called indirection.)

This is the syntax of pointer declarations:

```
data-type *identifier [= initializer];
```

This is the declaration for a pointer to an integer:

```
int *ptr_to_a_number;
```

Operators

The C language has a rich enough set of operators to perform almost any arithmetic or logical operation supported by hardware primitives in most computers. Operators are evaluated in a predetermined order. Several operators may be at the same level in this order, in which case they are evaluated from left to right. Unary operators are an exception, evaluating right to left.

The operators responsible for delivering values to operate have highest precedenceon. These include subscripting, the dot operator between a structure variable name and the name of an element in that kind of structure, the arrow between a pointer to a structure and the name of a structure element, the square braces around subscripts, the parentheses around parameter lists in procedure calls, and parentheses used to group other operators. In the case of parentheses and the square braces around subscripts, which can be nested, the order of evaluation is left to right and inside to outside.

The reason operators that yield structure elements and array subscripts are evaluated first is that they work on names. They turn combinations of structure variable names, array names, structure element names, and array subscripts into operands for other operators.

The following list summarizes the operators that form the primary expressions in C (expressions delivering values for other C operators to work on). The following operators have the highest evaluation priority. If they are not explicitly grouped using parentheses, they evaluate in left-to-right order.

()   Parentheses can be used to group operators and their operands so that the default order of evaluation is overridden. Parentheses also enclose the arguments of a procedure call.

The dot operator selects an element, named on the right of the dot, from a structure variable, named on the left of the dot.

-> The arrow operator selects an element, named on the right of the arrow, from the structure, the location of which is specified on the left of the arrow.

[] Square braces enclose expressions that yield array subscripts. Array subscripts are always integers.

The rest of the operators in C fall into several groups. Order of evaluation never crosses the borders of these groups. Therefore, knowing what these groups are makes it much easier to remember the order of evaluation of all the operators in C.

Just as there is a group of operators that yield operands for the rest of the operators in the language, there are groups of operators that have only one operand, perform multiplicative operations, perform additive operations, perform bit-shift operations, perform relational and equality comparison, perform bit-wise-and and bit-wise-or operations, perform logical-and and logical-or operations, perform the conditional operation, perform assignment, and concatenate expressions.

Unary operators in C are evaluated right after the above group of operators that operate on names to produce operands. Unary operators are the common sense next step in evaluating expressions. After an operand is arrived at, one or more unary operators may modify it before it is combined with other operands.

Unary operators differ from most other C operators (except for assignment operators) in that they are all evaluated from right to left if not explicitly grouped. Think of this as an order of evaluation where the operator closest to the operand operates first, and then the next closest, and so on. There are no other rules for grouping in the use of unary operators.

C has the following unary operators:

* Asterisk is the C indirection operator. Applied to a pointer, the result is the value stored in the location being pointed to.

& Ampersand is the C address operator. Any entity that has storage associated with it and is in the machine's address space (not, for instance, in the 68000's registers) can have the address operator applied to it, yielding a pointer to that entity.

sizeof "sizeof" yields the size of its operand. This is not to be confused with library functions that measure the length of null-terminated strings. "sizeof" gets its information from the data type of its operand.

(type-name) A type name enclosed in parentheses is the C cast operator. In C, casting not only changes the type of the entity being cast, it may also convert the entity. It is beyond the scope of this chapter to enumerate all the things that can happen when casting from any type to any other type.

– Unary minus yields the arithmetic negative of its operand.

! Exclamation point yields the logical negative of its operand. In C, logical true is any nonzero value, including negative values, and false is represented only by zero.

~ Tilde is the bit-wise negation operator. The result is a value in which every corresponding bit in the operand is inverted.

++ The increment operator can be placed before or after its operand. Placed before an operand it yields a value one unit greater than the operand. In addition to yielding this value, the operand is immediately updated to have this new value as well. Placed after an operand, the result is simply the value of the operand. After the value is copied from the operand, the operand itself gets a new value one unit greater than it had before.

-- The decrement operator operates similarly to the increment operator, except that it decrements where the increment operator would increment.

Using Unary Operators: An Example

The following code fragment assigns the complement of an array element to "test" and bumps the pointer to point to the next element:

```
test = ~*thing_ptr++;
```

Even though the ++ operator is the leftmost unary operator, and so evaluated first, it still *postincrements* the pointer. That is, it has no effect until after the expression is evaluated.

Binary Operators

Unlike unary operators, which are all evaluated in left-to-right order, binary operators have an inherent precedence in which some operators will be evaluated before others, no matter what order they appear in. Thus binary operators are not all part of the same group. This inherent order of evaluation is overridden, when necessary, by the use of parentheses.

The binary operators are presented here from highest to lowest precedence. The first operators presented are the first to be evaluated. When several binary operators have the same precedence, they are evaluated from left to right, just as they would be read aloud. Where it makes sense to do so, precedence rules follow those typically used in mathematics. The exception to left-to-right order is the order of evaluation for assignment operators, which are evaluated right to left. So, when two or more assignments take place in a single expression, the right side is evaluated before the left side, just as in the case of a statement with a single assignment operation.

The binary operators with the highest precedence are the multiplicative operators that multiply, divide, and yield remainders. These operators have the same precedence and are evaluated left to right:

* An asterisk used between two operands is the multiplication operator. This is the same symbol as the indirection operator, but the syntax of the language prevents confusion; there is no situation in which an asterisk meant to multiply two operands would be taken for an indirection operator.

/   Virgule (or slash) is the division operator. The result is the quotient, and, in the case of integer operands, the remainder is unavailable.

%   Percent sign is the modulus operator, yielding the remainder of a division operation rather than the quotient. The modulus operator cannot be applied to floating-point numbers.

Following the multiplicative operators, in precedence, are the additive operators:

+   Plus sign is the addition operator in C. It yields the sum of its two operands.

–   Minus sign is the subtraction operator. It yields the difference of its two operands.

C evaluates its arithmetic operators first among its binary operators. C has no more arithmetic operators. Transcendental functions are usully available in the library(s) of functions that comes with most C compilers. C does have a rich set of logical and bit-wise logical operators, so almost any operation a processor can perform with a single instruction, such as shifting, masking, and or-ing, can be specified directly in C.

The logical operators come after the arithmetic operators in precedence and are divided into several groups, some containing only one operator. The logical operators with the highest precedence are the shift operators. They are evaluated left to right:

\>\>   This is the shift-right operator. The right operand is converted, if need be, to an integer. The result is the value of the left operand shifted right as many bits as is specified by the right operand.

\<\<   This is the left-shift operator. It operates the same way as the right shift operand, but shifts the left operand left.

Following the shift operators in precedence are the relational operators. The relational (and equality) operators are all ahead of the logical operators because relational results are often combined by logic.

The relational operators are evaluated left to right. The result you get by concatenating relational operations is legal, but not very useful. The result of a relational operation is one if the relation is true and zero if it is not, not a useful result for use in other relational operations.

\>   This is the greater-than operator. It yields one if the left operand is greater than the right operand, and zero otherwise.

\<   This is the less-than operator. It yields one if the left operand is less than the right operand, and zero otherwise.

>=   This is the greater-than-or-equal-to operator. It yields one if the left operand is greater than or equal to the right operand, and zero otherwise.

<=   This is the less-than-or-equal-to operator. It yields one if the left operand is less than or equal to the right operand, and zero otherwise.

The equality operators follow the relational operators, in precedence, and they share the properties of the relational operators in the usefulness of cascading them:

==   This is the C equal-to operator. It yields one if the operands are equal and zero otherwise.

!=   This is the C not-equal-to operator. It yields one if the operands are not equal, and zero otherwise.

Following the equality operators are the bit-wise operators. These come one to a group. The highest bit-wise operator with the highest precedence is the bit-wise and operator:

&   When used as a binary operator, ampersand is the bit-wise and operator. If the corresponding bit of both operands is one, then the corresponding bit in the result is one; otherwise it is zero.

After the bit-wise and operator comes the bit-wise exclusive-or operator:

^   Caret is the bit-wise exclusive-or operator. If the corresponding bit of either operand, but not both, is one, then the corresponding bit in the result is one, otherwise it is zero.

And after the bit-wise exclusive-or operator comes the bit-wise inclusive-or operator:

| The vertical bar is the bit-wise exclusive-or operator. If the corresponding bit of either operand is one, then the corresponding bit in the result is one, otherwise it is zero.

The logical operators in C operate on values where nonzero values mean true and zero means false. The logical operators, like the bit-wise logic operators, come in groups of one. The and operator is evaluated before the or operator.

Unlike relational and equality operators, it does make sense to cascade logical operators. Cascaded or operators and cascaded and operators are both evaluated left to right.

&&   This is the logical and operator. If both operands are nonzero, the result is one, otherwise it is zero.

Following the logical and operator, in precedence, is the logical or operator:

| | This is the logical or operator. If either operand is nonzero or if both operands are nonzero, the result is one; otherwise it is zero.

After the logical operators comes the conditional operator. The conditional operator is C's only ternary operator. The conditional operator is documented here, among C's binary operators, because it takes precedence over some binary operators, the assignment operators and the comma operator. Cascaded conditional operators are

? : This is the conditional operator. The three operands of the conditional operator are located (1) before the question mark, (2) between the question mark and the colon, and (3) after the colon. If the value of the first operand is nonzero, the result is the value of the second operand, otherwise it is the value of the third operand.

The conditional operator may seem too much like an "if statement," but an if statement does not have a result value.

After the conditional operators come the assignment operators. In addition to an operator that assigns the value of the left operand to the right operand, C has assignment operators that perform the functions of most of the binary operators (except for the boolean logical operators). In the combination assignment operators, the value sof the left and right operandsare used as operands of the binary operator that the assignment is combined with. The result is then assigned to the left operand. Cascaded assignment operators are eveluted right to left.

= This is the assignment operator. The left operand gets the value of the right operand.

*= Multiplication and assignment.

/= Division and assignment.

%= Modulus and assignment.

+= Addition and assignment.

-= Subtraction and assignment.

<<= Shift left and assignment.

>>= Shift right and assignment.

&= Bit-wise and and assignment.

^= Bit-wise exclusive-or and assignment.

|= Bit-wise inclusive-or and assignment.

Strangely, perhaps, assignment operators do not have the lowest precedence in C. That honor belongs to the comma operator:

> The comma operator is a binary operator that yields the value of the second operand as a result. This is not the same as the comma that separates arguments in a procedure-call.

Control Flow Statements

Control flow statements determine where in a program control will flow. That is, they control the path of execution. C has five control flow statements and two keywords that modify the behavior of the control flow statements.

This is the syntax of C's control flow statements:

```
while ( expression ) statement

do statement while ( expression );

for ( [expression] ; [expression] ; [expression] )
    statement

switch ( expression ) statement
```

A statement may be an expression followed by a semicolon, a block enclosed in braces, or a control flow statement.

In switch statements, statements within the statement may be labeled with a case label:

```
case constant-expression:
```

The constant expression must have a unique value in the switch statement it is part of. If the constant expression's value matches that of the expression enclosed in parentheses at the top of the switch statement, control will pass to the expression immediately after the case label when the switch statement is entered.

While statements and do-while statements repeatedly return control flow to the statement that is the body of the loop, until the expression in parentheses has a value of zero.

For statements have three expressions, separated by semicolons, in parentheses. The first expression is evaluated only once, before the first time through the body of the loop. The second expression is evaluated before each time through the loop, just as the expressions in while and do-while statements are; if it has the value zero, the loop body is not executed and control is passed to the statement following the for statement. The last expression in parentheses is evaluated after each time through the body of the loop.

Two keywords are used to modify the behavior of control flow statements. The **continue** keyword modifies the behavior of the loop statement it is in. When a statement consisting of the **continue** keyword is evaluated, control passes to the point just before the end of the loop body, skipping over the rest of the statements in the loop body.

The **break** keyword modifies all the control flow statements. When a statement consisting of the **break** keyword is evaluted, control passes to the statement following the control flow statement where the **break** keyword is encountered.

Procedures

C programs consist of global declarations and procedure definitions. Procedures have a return type, local storage, and statements. Procedures that return a value have return statements that contain an expression that yields the return value.

This is the syntax of C procedure definitions:

```
[return-type] procedure-name
     ( [parameter-name] [, parameter-name]...) statement
```

Example Program 3-1

```
#include <quickdraw.h>          /* Include the macros and declarations
                                 * associated with quickdraw
                                 */
int a_global;                    /* A global variable */

/* With the following union, a 32 bit long can be treated as two 16 bit
 * ints. The long and the structure containing the two integers would
 * occupy the same storage in a variable of this type.
 */
typdef union                     /* Make a defined type out of this union... */
{
    struct                       /* One member is a structure... */
    {   int a;                   /* With integers a and b as elements */
        int b;
    } halves
    long longword;               /* The other union member is a long */

} split_long;                    /* call the type "split_long" */

/* The main routine */
main(argc, argv)
    char *argv[];                /* A vector of character pointers */
{
    int a_local;                 /* A local variable */

    switch (argc)
    {   case 1:                       /* In case argc is one... */
            p_to_c(argv[0]);     /* Pass the first pointer in argv */
            break;
        default:                      /* The default case */
            a_global = do_default(); /* Assign the return value to
                                      * a_global
                                      */
```

```
        }
}

/* Process an element of argv */
p_to_c(string)
        char *string;
{
        int i, length = string[0];

        if (string)               /* If this pointer is not null */
        {     /* In this example we convert a Pascal style string into a
               * C style string with no length byte at the beginning and a null
               * at the end.
               */
                for (i = 1, i <= length; i < length; i++)
                        string[i - 1] = string[i];
        }
}

/* Do a few things that illustrate some arithmetic operators in C. */
do_default()
{
        /* a local variable */
        long a_value = 0xd2d7;    /* initialize a_value to hex d2d7 */

        a_value *= 17; /* Multiply it by 17 */

        /* Here we cast a_value to the split_long type, take the high word
         * and assign the value to a_value. We parenthesize the cast operation
         * because unary operators have a lower precedence than the operations
         * that pick out structure and union members.
         */
        a_value = ((split_long)a_value).halves.b;
}
```

The Meaning and Use of Style

The style conventions used in this book are the generally accepted conventions used widely in Macintosh, Unix, and MS-DOS programming. No major changes in C style have to be made to accommodate the toolbox style system interface of the Macintosh.

In companies and schools that use and teach C you will find both stricter and more relaxed standards. In this book we strive for readability without sacrificing performance. If you are considering writing programs to sell to others, we encourage you to adhere to style conventions at least as strictly as we do. Software publishers often review the software offered to them to assess the cost of maintaining it and fixing any bugs that may turn up. The clarity of your code may make the difference between selling a useful program or not.

Points to Consider

1) Why do assignment operators have such low precedence? What would happen if they were evaluated *before* arithmetic operators?

2) What is wrong with the following "if" statement:

```
if (value = INVALID)
    report_error();
```

3) Most compilers come with example programs. Compile a short example and disassemble the program. Match up the lines of the source program to the instructions in the disassembled object.

Chapter Four

QuickDraw and Windows

In this chapter you will find out about:

- The system of graf ports used by QuickDraw to support drawing in windows.
- The coordinate system used by QuickDraw.
- Graf port regions, which are used to limit the area drawn in.
- How the Window Manager, in concert with QuickDraw, manages updating.
- How applications can use graf port regions to clip.

This chapter covers the two parts of the Toolbox ROM most responsible for giving the Macintosh its unique character. Windowing and event-driven programming are intertwined and form the foundation of all Macintosh applications. The theory behind windowed, event-driven applications presented here will prepare you to design and program your own applications.

This chapter is meant to bring together concepts from the Window Manager and QuickDraw so that you understand their relationship. Only aspects of QuickDraw and the Window Manager that support windowing will be discussed here. Both of these managers have features that are not part of the Macintosh's windowing support. *Inside Macintosh* gives a thorough explanation of *all* the features of both these Toolbox managers separately.

The Obvious and Subtle Parts of QuickDraw

QuickDraw is the basis of all activity on the Macintosh screen. The obvious part of this activity is QuickDraw painting bits on the screen in response to requests that characters, lines or patterns be drawn. QuickDraw also forms the basis of the Macintosh window system. The Window Manager is the ROM manager that applications call when they want to create windows, move windows around, and change which window is the active window. QuickDraw supports the Window Manager by helping it maintain the illusion that the application has several small screens that can be moved around the Macintosh screen.

QuickDraw provides numerous drawing routines that draw lines, fill areas, copy bits from one place to another (while stretching or shrinking the image painted in those bits), draw characters, scroll, and so on. QuickDraw also provides routines that perform calculations on points, lines, rectangles, areas, and so on. Using QuickDraw, an application can, for example, determine whether objects overlap, set up the grafport so that the overlapped region is clipped, and draw those objects so that one appears to be in front of the other. Another example of using QuickDraw calculations would be the use of the PtInRect call to determine whether the mouse was clicked in some particular part of the screen.

The Window Manager uses the calculation routines in QuickDraw to create the desktop. Without QuickDraw, the Window Manager would be a hopeless kludge, and without the Window Manager, QuickDraw could not provide enough support for windowing. Working together, these two Toolbox managers provide both high-level support for windows, such as the code that automatically draws the frames of windows as needed, and low-level support for drawing in windows. The low-level support that an application uses to draw what it wants displayed in its windows is the same as what the Window Manager uses to draw window frames.

Starting with QuickDraw coordinates, we will see how windows and the Window Manager are built on QuickDraw. Using this information, you will be better able to manage the contents of your applications' windows.

QuickDraw Coordinates

All the drawing and calculating on the Macintosh are done in a coordinate system that needs to be understood before QuickDraw can be used effectively. Many of the errors encountered during the development of a Macintosh program have to do with being one bit off of the desired place when drawing, erasing, or scrolling.

The QuickDraw coordinate system is the basis of the algorithms embodied in QuickDraw, and knowing the coordinate system and the conventions used in it lets you predict what QuickDraw will do. Otherwise you may waste a lot of time in trial and error.

Drawing is done at a location, or between two locations, or in the space enclosed by several locations connected together. Locations in QuickDraw are positions on a lattice that *runs between the pixels*. Two parts of a QuickDraw coordinate system are depicted in Figure 4-1.

Keeping this lattice in mind helps to avoid confusion: If you picture a lattice running between pixels, rather than pixels with row and column addresses, there is no confusion over whether a rectangle includes or excludes a pixel, because the rectangle runs between and not on top of the pixels. Because the points on the lattice are infinitely small, the size of a pixel and how much of its area is on one side or the other of a bounding line never enters into QuickDraw calculations.

A QuickDraw rectangle is shown in Figure 4-2. The coordinates of the rectangle are (0, 0) and (7, 10). One of the two black pixels is inside, and the other is outside. If the rectangle were filled with black, only the pixels inside the rectangle's boundary would be black. Since the rectangle itself is *not* a graphic and it has no visible boundaries that occupy pixels themselves, what is meant by "inside" is unambiguous.

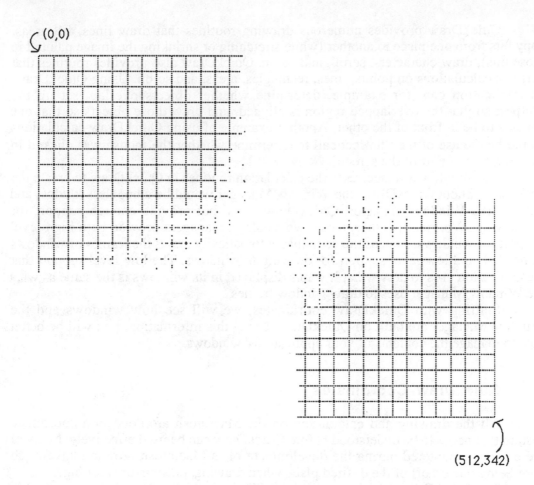

Figure 4-1 Two parts of a QuickDraw coordinate system.

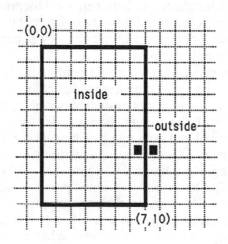

Figure 4-2 A QuickDraw rectangle.

The QuickDraw coordinate system is not just a mathematical basis for thinking about QuickDraw. The fact that QuickDraw coordinates are integers and the lines in the QuickDraw lattice are infinitely thin means that integer arithmetic yields the correct results. No rounding is required to decide whether a pixel falls on one side of a line or the other. This makes QuickDraw quick.

Graf Ports: Environments for Drawing

Macintosh windows are built on graf ports. Graf ports are a place to draw things. The Macintosh screen is where graf ports' bitmaps are almost always located, but graf ports may be associated with bitmaps anywhere in memory. The Macintosh screen is distinguished only by the fact that if drawing is done in a graf port that uses the Macintosh's screen memory for its bitmap, the drawing is rendered visible by the Macintosh's video hardware.

Apart from a bitmap, a graf port holds all the other information that pertains to painting bits in the graf port's bitmap. This information ranges from the current typeface for the graf port to the foreground and background colors for the graf port to a list of customized routines for drawing in the graf port.

This is the data structure that holds graf port information:

```
struct GrafPort
{    int device;
     BitMap portBits;
     Rect portRect;
     RgnHandle visRgn;
     RgnHandle clipRgn;
     Pattern bakPat;
     Pattern fillPat;
     Point pnLoc;
     Point pnSize;
     int pnMode;
     Pattern pnPat;
     int pnVis;
     int txFont;
     Style txFace;
     int txMode;
     int txSize;
     int spExtra;
     long fgColor;
     long bkColor;
     int colrBit;
     int patStretch;
     QDHandle picSave;
     QDHandle rgnSave;
     QDHandle polySave;
     QDProcsPtr grafProcs;
};
```

While the graf port hold's all the information associated with drawing in a bitmap, the memory associated with the bitmap is pointed to by the graf port and is not part of the structure. The graf port structure associated with the Macintosh screen could be anywhere in memory, but the memory of the graf port's bitmap has to be where the video hardware can access it.

Graf ports contain numerous fields for storing the state of the graf port. The field that determines where the graf port is is the portRect field. When a window is moved around the Macintosh screen, all that happens to the graf port structure is that the portRect field is changed. The portRect is defined in terms of the bitmap.

Bitmaps

Bitmaps are a way of describing a piece of memory used for drawing in. This is the bitmap data structure:

```
struct bitmap
{    QDPtr baseAddr;
     int rowBytes;
     Rect bounds;
}
```

The baseAddr field of a bitmap points to the first location of memory to be drawn in. The rowBytes field holds information about how many bytes wide the bitmap is. The width of the bitmap of the Macintosh screen is 64 bytes, a number constrained by the hardware that displays the bitmap on the video display. Memory set aside for a bitmap by an application can have any width that fits in the amount of memory set aside an integral number of times. The bounds rectangle is always anchored at the top left corner above the topmost, leftmost bit in the bitmap. The bottom right corner can be anywhere in the bitmap, but typically the bounds rectangle encloses all the bits in the bitmap.

Graf Port Regions: Support for Windows

Graf ports alone would let an application create rectangles on the screen that would act something like windows. Several graf ports often share the bitmap that is the Macintosh screen. By moving around the portRect of a graf port, the location where drawing takes place in that graf port changes. But there still is quite a bit missing: There is no notion of one graf port being in front of another, no way of telling the user which is the active graf port, and no facility for keeping track of which parts of the screen need updating. To provide complete windowing, the Window Manager uses regions to add the ability to hide parts of windows behind other windows. The Window Manager also provides indicators to the user of which window is active.

Regions are a kind of Quickdraw structure that describe arbitrarily shaped areas. You do not have to know how regions work in order to use them, but their underlying structure is interesting: The documented part of region structures consists of a word containing the size of the region data structure and a boundary rectangle. If the region is more complex than a rectangle, additional information following the first two fields of the region structure describes the region. This information consists of lists of coordinates of the apexes of the region: One vertical coordinate is followed by all the horizontal coordinates that share that vertical coordinate.

Since C does not check for accesses beyond the ends of data structures or arrays, variable-sized objects are easy to manipulate in C programs. Regions can describe areas that are convex, concave, areas that have holes in them, and even areas that are not contiguous. If you are interested in studying how Macintosh regions are used by Quickdraw routines that fill them in or perform calculations using them, the process underlying operations on regions is called *scan conversion*.

The Window Manager

The Window Manager builds on QuickDraw's graf ports. This is the window structure:

```
struct WindowRecord
{    GrafPort port;
     int WindowKind;
     BOOLEAN visible;
     BOOLEAN hilited;
     BOOLEAN goAwayFlag;
     BOOLEAN spareFlag;
     RgnHandle structRgn;
     RgnHandle contRgn;
     RgnHandle updateRgn;
     Handle windowDefProc;
     Handle dataHandle;
     StringHandle titleHandle;
     int titleWidth;
     ControlHandle controlList;
     WindowPeek nextWindow;
     PicHandle windowPic;
};
```

The Window Manager manipulates graf ports to create the impression of overlapping pieces of paper on a desktop. To do this the Window Manager manipulates the visRgn field of the graf port. Whenever the windows on the Macintosh screen are moved, grown or shuffled, the Window Manager makes sure the visRgn is the region of each of the windows that would be "visible" if windows are to behave like pieces of paper on a desktop. The visRgn is one of two regions associated with each graf port.

The other region associated with the graf port is the clip region (clipRgn). The purpose of the clip region is to limit the part of the graf port where drawing takes place. The clip region is used like masking tape when an application finds that it is more convenient to issue Quickdraw calls to draw an entire object and when it is appropraite for only part of that object to appear on the screen. This usually happens when objects are near the scroll bars of a window, as we will see in the example program.

The Window Manager maintains a region associated with each window that describes the part of the window that needs updating. Applications can use the Window Manager routines InvalRgn and InvalRect to add areas to the update region. In this way, the update region collects all the areas that need updating because of both Window Manager related activity and because of the application changing its display.

When the update region is not empty, an *update event* is posted. Handling an update event consists of three steps: (1) calling BeginUpdate; (2) drawing (at least) the objects that fall inside the area that needs updating; and (3) calling EndUpdate. Calling BeginUpdate causes the Window Manager to temporarily change the visRgn of the window being updated to consist of the intersection of the update region and the previous visRgn. This leaves the clipRgn free for the application to use. Calling

EndUpdate restores the visRgn to its previous value.

Update events are the most important part of creating interactive Macintosh applications. Few computer systems tell applications running on them which part of the screen needs updating. The Macintosh takes care of this for applications. This is convenient for the user, and it is also one important mechanism behind the uniformity of Macintosh user interfaces. Compare the the basic structure of a Unix program against that of a Macintosh program. The Unix program has an I/O driven main loop. A Macintosh application has an event-driven main loop. Both user interaction and housekeeping events such as update events are processed in this one loop. Figure 4-3 shows how regions are manipulated by the application and by the window system while updating a window.

Drawing from Applications

If the Macintosh's Window Manager only lets areas that need updating be drawn in, how does an application draw on the screen? Applications need to declare parts of the screen invalid before they can be drawn in. Regions can be declared valid as well. This gives applications two options for updating the screen: (1) An application can declare a region invalid, draw in it, and then declare it valid. (2) It can declare a region invalid, update its internal representation of what is on the screen, get an update event, and redraw the invalid region then. The second approach has the advantage that any other objects lying in the invalid region would be updated as well.

The Active Window

Another important type of event is the *activate event*. The activate event means that the window the event pertains to is now being activated or deactivated (these events come in pairs). Activate events tell an application absolutely nothing about updating. Although activation and updating often happen together, separate events are used to signal activation and updating. The active window is a way for the user to tell where he or she is. Since one keyboard is used to enter information in possibly a large number of windows, the active window, with the highlighted title-bar, is the one that is actually receiving information.

What Windows Are Not

By manipulating the visRgn and clipRgn fields of graf ports, the Window Manager gives life to the desktop metaphor. But it is also important to know what windows do not do, and why.

While QuickDraw and the Window Manager provide a lot of support for applications, they stop short of providing virtual devices. The virtual-device approach to window systems is another widely used approach. Virtual devices are pretty much

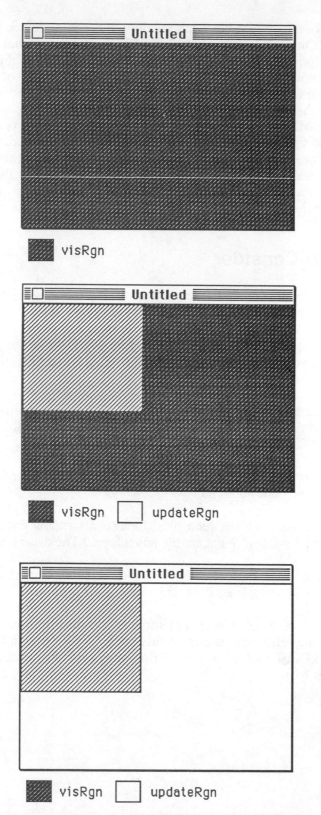

Figure 4-3 Regions manipulated by the application and window system

what they sound like they might be: Each window in a virtual device system behaves like a real device. One window might behave like a vt100 terminal, another might behave like a Tektronix graphics scope. Window systems that use the virtual-device approach are common among UNIX workstations. The purpose of those window systems is to provide a windowed environment for applications that were written with the assumption that they had the whole terminal to themselves.

Because the Macintosh does not provide virtual devices, it is difficult to port UNIX and MS-DOS application to the Macintosh. Such "quick and dirty" ports would look impoverished next to applications that take full advantage of the mouse, menus, windows, dialogs, and QuickDraw. Because it isn't expedient to do a poor job of porting a program to the Macintosh, Macintosh applications are among the most polished and easy to use.

Points to Consider

1) UNIX programs that read characters from an input and write characters to an output while performing some transform on them are called filters. Some kinds of programs, like compilers, sort programs and search programs, fit the filter model well. How would you port a typical UNIX filter to the Macintosh? What would you use the display for? How would you have the user specify input and output?

2) Some programs, like text processors, spreadsheets, and project management programs, do not fit the filter model well at all. Why is this so? What does this mean to UNIX? To the Macintosh?

3) What tasks is the Macintosh user-interface style ill suited for? What, if anything, can be done about it?

4) What is the difference between the Macintosh window environment and a virtual terminal system? What are the advantages? The disadvantages?

5) On paper, apply the FrameRect call to the rectangle depicted in Figure 4-2. Where are the framing lines drawn?

6) Take a piece of graph paper and look at the descriptions of QuickDraw routines in the reference section of this book. Walk through the operation of some QuickDraw toolbox traps by drawing what they would draw on the graph paper.

Chapter Five

Revolutionary Software, Classical Microcomputer Hardware

In this chapter you will find:

- The Macintosh runs some of the most advanced systems software in existence.
- Macintosh hardware is very simple.
- An overview of the 68000 instruction set to help you use a debugger or disassembler.
- The Macintosh software developer can count on a large base of installed machines that have capabilities that would cost hundreds of dollars to add to computers that lacked them.
- There are interesting off-the-shelf parts in the Macintosh. They were chosen because they provide a lot of features in a single part.
- The Macintosh hardware is always hidden behind at least one layer of Toolbox software.
- Although the Macintosh is a closed box, the Macintosh is an expandable system.
- How Macintosh hardware affects the applications writer (you).

The Macintosh's system software has its roots in the Xerox Alto and the Lisa computers' window-oriented user interfaces and simple, pared-down operating systems. Despite the fact that the Macintosh is a far less expensive machine than its workstation predecessors, it is in many ways more polished and sophisticated. The level of sophistication has to do with the fact that the Macintosh was designed by experienced designers working for a company that knew that to fall slightly short, as Apple did with the Lisa, would be disastrous. The low cost of the Macintosh is due to the simplicity of the Macintosh's hardware.

In this chapter we will look at the Macintosh's hardware. Although it is always hidden beneath a layer of software, the Macintosh's hardware has a strong influence on what a Macintosh is. It would be very difficult to move the Macintosh's software over to a machine that did not strongly resemble the Macintosh.

The Macintosh and the Apple II

There are few computers that are as different as the Macintosh and the Apple II. The Apple II is *the* traditional microcomputer. Inexpensive to build, and hence inexpensive to buy, the Apple II is the mainstay of educational computing in elementary schools, is a workhorse in homes and small businesses, and plays a key role in the hobbyist market – a market it helped establish.

When the Apple II was introduced, software had little to do with its attractiveness to hobbyists who bought it in order to write programs in the Apple II's easy-to-learn 6502 assembly language. At a time when disk controllers cost around a thousand dollars, condemning hobbyists to use cassette tapes to store their work, the Apple II was a real, disk-based computer that almost any hobbyist could afford. The Apple II was the first computer with affordable color graphics. Today, now that color and disk drives are commonplace, the Apple II's simplicity and low cost have made it the standard for elementary schools, home and small business accounting and word processing. The Apple II has *evolved* from a machine, bought largely owing to the value and merits of its hardware, to a machine that is bought mostly because of the power and simplicity of the huge library of educational and business software that runs on it.

In the case of the Macintosh, software has had everything to do with the machine's success. The Macintosh has attracted two groups of buyers. The biggest group is the first-time computer user who never liked obscure command languages and the lack of system-wide integration found in most microcomputers. The Macintosh has also attracted a loyal following among knowledgeable, experienced computer users and programmers because Macintosh software is as sophisticated and powerful as that found on workstation computers that cost many times more than the price of a Macintosh.

The Macintosh *had* to be much more sophisticated than the Apple II because hardware alone will no longer make a successful computer. Computer engineering has progressed, and more significantly, the potential computer buyer's expectations are much higher now than at the birth of the microcomputer industry. People rightly expect a complete computer system when they buy a microcomputer. The Apple II had many years to evolve into a comprehensive system, the Macintosh had to be born as a system.

Yet the Macintosh and Apple II have a common heritage and have similarities at the hardware level. Both machines are a carefully chosen collection of parts that delivers features and performance that cost a lot more in other computers. Just as the Apple II has the least expensive color graphics and disk interfaces available, the Macintosh is still the only microcomputer that has an inexpensive network interface built into every machine. At its introduction, the Macintosh was the only microcomputer to have wholly abandoned the character-only display in favor of a bitmap display. The Macintosh uses the same simple, inexpensive floppy-disk interface used in the Apple II. In the Macintosh, this interface is contained in two chips. Every Macintosh comes with a completely indispensable mouse. All the features of the

Macintosh, including the power supply and monitor electronics, are implemented entirely on two fairly small printed circuit cards. The simplicity of the Macintosh hardware means that it is unlikely that the Macintosh will be outmoded anytime soon. Apple has discovered that the Apple II is "forever," but the Macintosh was designed that way.

You Can Count on Macintosh Features

Software developers benefit from the Macintosh's large array of built-in features. Every music program for the Macintosh can count on the Macintosh's sound-generating hardware. Every multiuser data base can count on every Macintosh to have the same network hardware built in. Despite the fact that there are far fewer Macintoshes in the world than IBM-PC compatibles, the Macintosh software developer can count on every Macintosh having the same basic capabilities. For programs that require sound, or a network, or a mouse, or high-speed serial ports, there is a far greater base of Macintoshes capable of running those programs than any other computer. The lack of graphics, sound, and networking standards impede the development of networked applications for other computers. No such obstacles exist for the Macintosh.

The Major Players on the Macintosh Logic Board

The logic board of the Macintosh has remarkably few parts. Some of these parts perform numerous and/or powerful functions that make the Macintosh hardware what it is. Understanding what these parts do will enable you to know what the Macintosh is capable of.

The Motorola M68000

The Motorola 68000 processor is, of course, central to what a Macintosh is. Unlike microprocessors with smaller address spaces, Macintosh users almost never need to be aware of what kind of processor is executing instructions in their computers. Although you may never need to write any code in assembly language, chances are you will do a lot of debugging with only a disassembler available to tell you what code is being executed. Therefore an overview of the 68000 instruction set will arm you with the knowledge you need to keep track of where your program is when you trace its execution with a debugger. If you are completely unfamiliar with assembly-language conventions, you will want a copy of *M68000 16/32-bit Microprocessor Programmer's Reference Manual,* by Motorola, Inc. (Prentice-Hall, Inc., Englewood Cliffs, N.J.).

In the following lists, the details of the instructions' operations are left out. Most 68000 instructions do exactly what you would expect them to do from reading the mnemonics. Instructions peculiar to the 68000 are briefly explained. Only the basic operations are listed. Variations of these operations, like immediate, byte, and longword variations are not listed separately.

Move instructions

MOVE	Move.
EXG	Exchange the contents of two registers.
SWAP	Swap words in a register.
LEA	Load effective address (perform address arithmetic; load the address, not the data at the address).
PEA	Push effective address.

Logic instructions

AND	And.
OR	Or.
EOR	Exclusive or.
NOT	Not.
S*cc*	Set byte according to condition code.
CLR	Clear.

Bit manipulation instructions

BSET	Test, then set a bit.
BCLR	Test, then clear a bit.
BCHG	Test, then complement a bit.
BTST	Test a bit.
TAS	Test a bit, while setting high-order bit. Uninterruptible.

Shift instructions

LSL	Logical shift left.
LSR	Logical shift right.
ASR	Arithmetic shift right.
ROL	Rotate left.
ROR	Rotate right.

Comparison instructions

TST	Test.
CMP	Compare.
CHK	Bounds check. Causes a trap if it fails.

Arithmetic instructions

ADD   Add.
SUB   Subtract.
MUL   Multiply.
DIV   Divide.
NEG   Negate.
EXT   Sign extend.

BCD arithmetic

ABCD   Add BCD numbers.
SBCD   Subtract BCD numbers.
NBCD   Negate BCD numbers.

Control transfer instructions

BRA   Branch always (up to 64k displacement).
Bcc   Branch on condition code (up to 64k displacement).
BSR   Branch to subroutine (up to 64k displacement).
JMP   Jump.
JSR   Jump to subroutine.
RTE   Return from exception.
RTS   Return from subroutine.
TRAP   Initiate exception opportunity. Trap *macros* are not TRAP instructions; they are unimplemented instructions.

Stack frame maintenance

LINK   Push an address register on the stack; store the stack pointer's value in the saved register; bump the stack pointer to allocate space for local variables.
UNLK   Undo a LINK instruction.

Processor control

STOP   Load status register and stop until an interrupt, exception, or reset occurs.
RESET   Reset *external* devices.
NOP   Sit one out.

Most of the instructions that move information around and perform logic and arithmetic operations can operate on three different sizes of operands: 8-bit bytes, 16-bit words, and 32-bit *longwords*. To specify the size of the operands of an instruction, a suffix is appended to the instruction. ".b" means byte operands, ".w" means word operands, and ".l" means longwords. Word operands are the default, and the 68000 is at its most efficient when dealing with 16-bit words.

The 68000 was designed from a very pragmatic point of view. It provides 32-bit capabilities in a comparatively simple design. It does not provide the high degree of *orthogonality* found in the PDP-11 or the National Semiconductor 32016. The 68000 cannot apply the same addressing modes to every operand of every instruction. This means that to write 68000 code you will probably have to keep a reference manual handy; not all the instruction variations apply to all the instructions. If you are reading 68000 code, like the disassembled code of one of your C programs, you may never notice the restrictions placed on 68000 instructions, because most instructions and their permitted addressing modes do most of the things a C compiler or an assembly-langauge programmer would like done. In most practical situations, the 68000 performs at least as well as its more elegant competitors.

The other specialized parts in the Macintosh are less visible to the programmer than the microprocessor. But these parts, and the functions they perform may inspire you to develop unusual applications based on untapped abilities in the Macintosh.

The Synertek SY6522 Versatile Interface Adapter

The one small, inexpensive device performs an astounding range of functions with the Macintosh. The VIA is responsible, in whole or in part, for controlling sound generation and sound volume in two separate modes, controlling disk-drive motor speed, generating interrupts when keys are pressed or the mouse is moved, and providing an interface to the real-time clock. A shift register on the VIA is used to serialize output to the keyboard and optional keypad and to parallelize input from the keyboard and keypad.

The VIA is involved in so many functions because it can interrupt the processor when interesting events in other parts of the Macintosh have occurred. Interrupts are generated by the VIA when either of two timers on the VIA time out, when the one-second clock ticks, when the keyboard interface requires attention, or when the vertical blanking interval begins. The VIA also controls memory mapping in the Macintosh that temporarily maps the ROM into low memory on power-up so that the initialization code executes.

One Toolbox manager involved in the operation of the VIA is the Task Manager, also known as the Vertical Retrace Manager because it enables code to be run while the electron gun that paints bits on the video tube is returning to the top of the video tube. The vertical retrace interval of the Macintosh display is useful for applications, such as games, that move a lot of graphics around the screen and want that movement to appear as smooth as possible. By updating the display during the vertical retrace interval, half-updated objects will never be visible to the user.

The Zilog Z8530 Serial Communications Controller

The Zilog SCC controls the two serial ports on the Macintosh. Together with the 26LS30 differential driver and 26LS32 receiver, it implements RS422 serial ports and the AppleTalk network ports. The SCC connectors on the back of the Macintosh may be used as either serial ports or network ports. Interrupts that signal mouse movement are generated by the SCC, but the mouse and keyboard input is handled primarily though the VIA, leaving the SCC to deal with modem, printer, terminal line, and network connection options.

An interesting artifact in the SCC's control register addressing is that word accesses to any of the SCC's registers shift the system clock's phase by 128 nanoseconds. This *phase-space* access is used at system startup time to synchronize the RAM memory to the processor. Buggy programs that spuriously access phase space may cause the Macintosh's memory to be clocked out of phase with the processor, causing rain on the screen. *Rain* , random bits on the screen winking on and off, looks like a hardware problem and is in most instances the manifestation of a hardware bug. But on the Macintosh rain is almost always a symptom of buggy code.

The Macintosh Toolbox includes a serial driver, a Printing Manager that uses the serial driver to talk to serial printers, and an AppleTalk Manager. All these modules use the SCC.

The Integrated Woz Machine

The Integrated Woz Machine (IWM) is a single chip that inplements the same style of floppy disk interface found in the Apple II. Because of the simplicity of the IWM disk interface, the disk-drive port of the Macintosh can be used as a general-purpose high-speed serial port. The Apple Hard Disk 20 connects to the Macintosh through the floppy disk port and uses it simply as a another serial connection.

If you are interested in writing a program that uses the IWM port of the Macintosh, some information on the timing and protocols used in the IWM are contained in an Apple Technical Note about the Hard Disk 20. Apple technical notes are available from the Developer Relations Department of Apple and can also be found through users groups.

The NCR SCSI Host Adapter

Although it doesn't look like much (you can't open the Macintosh up and look at rows of connectors inside), the SCSI adapter found in the Macintosh Plus does provide true, general-purpose expandability for the Macintosh. The SCSI standard was designed to accommodate a wide variety of peripherals. SCSI addressing supports up to 2^{32} separate disk blocks or other addressable entities in peripherals. Integrated SCSI controllers in disks, tape drives, and other peripherals mean that the Macintosh does not need an expansion bus to talk to these peripherals. The SCSI interface allows up to eight peripherals to be connected externally to the Macintosh Plus model.

The Macintosh Plus is the first inexpensive computer to utilize the SCSI standard. As with the AppleTalk network, the wide availability of the SCSI interface will spur development of products that take advantage of it.

How Closed Is It?

The Macintosh comes in a sealed box. But Macintosh system software always allows for expansion. It is beyond the scope of this book to discuss writing Macintosh system software, but it is important to note that the Macintosh has software features, like loadable device drivers, that support expansion.

Points to Consider

1) What other computers have a user interface comparable to the Macintosh? How much do they cost in a usable configuration?

2) Because the Macintosh provides a "free" network, network applications are no longer limited to expensive workstation computers. What kind of business applications could make good use of a network? What kind of educational applications could use a network?

3) What kind of peripheral device would be uniquely suited to the Macintosh?

Chapter Six

The Resource Compiler

In this chapter you will find:

- What a resource compiler is.
- The reason for using resources.
- The extent to which resources permeate Macintosh toolbox software.
- A tutorial example of resource compiler use.
- A reference that covers the syntax of current resource compilers.
- When to use resource *editors* instead of the resource compiler.

Macintosh Resources: A Consistent Way of Initializing Macintosh Data Structures

Resources are part of every well-made Macintosh application. They make life easier for the program developer, the program publisher, and the user of the program. The user can change patterns, icons, and other parameters stored in the resource fork to suit his taste if the ones used by the developer do not suit him or her. The program publisher can translate a program's menu entries, window titles, and dialogs into foreign languages without touching the source code or troubling the developer. The messages a program displays on the screen are more closely related to documentation than to the code in a program, and the resource compiler lets non-programmers, such as technical writers, change these parts of a program and cooperate in the development of applications. The way resources benefit the developer is quite down to earth: A change in the resource fork of an application is much easier to make and takes much less time to compile than a change to the code itself. In many cases, the resource compiler does not need to be used to modify a resource fork: Small changes to a resource fork or changes that need to be made by nonprogrammers can be made through the use of a resource editor that interactively edits items in the resource fork of Macintosh files.

Resources are data: A pattern, like the gray pattern the desktop is usually covered by, is simply a data structure stuffed with the bits that determine a pattern. Somehow, the bits that spell out a particular pattern of bits on the screen must be put in the data structures that you have allocated space for in your program. A resource can be used to fill in that data structure. Resources are stored in the resource fork of a Macintosh file, read in by the Resource Manager, and used by many of the most important and visible parts of the Macintosh system.

Resources and Toolbox Managers

When a program creates a window on the screen, it passes the window manager a pointer to a structure that has been filled with data describing the new window. There are several ways for a program to fill in that structure: the structure could be initialized global data; the structure could be allocated at runtime and filled in, member by member, by a subroutine in the program; or it could be filled in by reading a resource from a file's resource fork into the space occupied by the data structure. This last approach is aided by Toolbox routines geared toward looking in the resource forks for resources to be used in initializing data structures.

The Window Manager contains the GetNewWindow function, which takes as arguments the resource ID (a 16-bit number used to identify resources) of a window resource and a WindowPtr, a pointer to a window data structure where the data from that window resource will be deposited. In a single step, using GetNewWindow, your program has filled in all the information about the window's size, location, type, and features, and has informed the Window manager that a new window, with these attributes, is to be created.

Nearly every Toolbox manager has one or more routines that use the Resource Manager to simplify initialization of data structures. Some do so overtly, like the Window Manager, and some, like the Font Manager, use the resource manager internally and have their own way of identifying their resources and retrieving them from resource forks. The Font Manager, for instance, imposes a special structure on the resource ID of a font, encoding both the font number and the point size of the font.

Your Own Resources

You aren't limited to using the resource fork to store information in formats that the various Toolbox managers already know about. You can create you own resource types and you can build up composites of existing resource types. The Macintosh system uses some resource types that cannot be defined by resource compiler input. Even 68000 instructions are a kind of resource. The output of any Macintosh compiler is a file with a resource fork full of compiled code. The type for this resource is "CODE."

Example: Designing a Dialog

The Dialog Manager makes the most use of resources. A dialog box, which is a kind of window and which may have controls, editable text, icons, static text, pictures, and so on, in it can be described in its entirety in the resource compiler input file. The following resource compiler input describes a dialog box:

```
* A resource compiler template for a dialog box:
Type DLOG
    ,256
    100 100 200 250
    Visible 1 NoGoAway 0
    270

Type DITL
    ,270
    2
    BtnItem Enabled
    60 10   80 70
    Resume

    StatText Disabled
    A sample dialog box
```

Starting at the top of this resource compiler input, there is a comment line preceded by an asterisk. Asterisk is the resource compiler's comment character. Then there is a "Type" keyword that begins the definition of a resource of type DLOG, a dialog box. The ID number of this dialog box is 256, it has the bounds 100 100 200 250, it is visible, its procID is 1, its refCon is 0, and it has an item list with an ID of 270. The item list describes two items that will appear inside this dialog box: A button labeled "Resume" and a static, uneditable string reading "A sample dialog box."

The ID numbers are the way your application accesses resources and the way resources are tied together in the resource compiler input file. Except for fonts, which have their own conventions for numbering, your own resources should have IDs that start somewhat above 0; in the examples here, we will generally start numbering our resources from 256. Resources of different types can reuse resource IDs. That is, the window resource numbered 256 is not going to be confused with the dialog numbered 256. Resource IDs are 16-bit numbers and so have to be less than 65535.

Resource Compiler Syntax

The resource compiler compiles a language, like any computer language. Like the best purpose-built languages, the resource compiler's syntax is very simple. The general form of a resource file is as follows:

Lines with asterisks at the right margin are comments:

```
*This is a resource file comment line
```

Comments on the same line as other resource compiler directives are preceded by two semicolons:

```
A resource compiler statement                    ;;another comment
```

Resource compiler lines that need to be folded in order to fit in your editor's windows can use the resource compiler continuation characters, which are two plus signs:

```
This is a very very long resource compiler input, perhaps a long ++
string that would not fit on one line and remain within your ++
editor's window
```

ASCII characters, particularly nonprinting control characters, may be entered as 8-bit hexadecimal numbers preceded by a backslash:

```
\0A          ;; This is control-J
```

The Header of a Resource Compiler Input File

Resource compiler input files start with two lines that tell the resource compiler what name and what file type it's output will have. The first line specifies the output file. If the first line begins with an exclamation point, the output of the resource compiler is added to an existing file. The second line specifies the type, typically APPL, for applications, and the creator of the file. The creator is not the resource compiler, but the application that the output file is associated with.

```
Sample
APPLMANX
```

These two lines begin a resource compiler input that would create a file called Sample that has the APPL type and is identified as having been created by MANX. The name of the compiler, in this case the Aztec C compiler by Manx Software, is used as the creator of this file because the primary use of the resource compiler is to add resources to a program emitted by a C compiler.

There are more than 35 different predefined types of resources, and future versions of the resource compiler may define more. Some 27 of these resources types are significant in that extant versions of the resource compiler provide a syntax for specifying the template information that goes into these resources. The rest of the resources are simply read from other files and included into the resource fork of the resource compiler's output. For example, the CODE resource type is used to include a compiler's output in the resource fork of your program. This is how the resources you specify in resource compiler format are combined with the 68000 instructions emitted by the compiler to form the complete resource fork of your program.

The General Format of Resource Specifications

Predefined resources that can be described through resource compiler input take on the following broad format:

```
TYPE [your-type =] type
[file-name!resource-name],ID [(attribute)]
data-for-this-resource
```

Characters in boldface ("**TYPE**," "**!**," "**(**," "**)**," "**=**," and "**,**") are literally part of a resource specification, brackets mean that the enclosed part of a resource specification is optional (brackets are not part of the resource compiler syntax), and words in plain typeface describe what goes in those positions in actual resource specifications. To see where these characters are used in a resource definition, match up this general description with the actual specification for a dialog given above.

Window Resources

The window manager is supported by a syntax that enables the creation of data to fill in window structures. The order of the items in a window resource specification roughly corresponds to the order of structure members in a window structure. The keywords used in the window manager specification and in other resource specifications roughly correspond to the names of the constants defined in the include files associated with the manager that the resource supports.

The following is a window definition commented to explain the resource compiler syntax specific to this type of resource:

```
Type WIND                  ;;WIND specifies a resource for windows
    ,256                   ;;no name, ID is 256
    A Good Window Title    ;;The title to appear in the title bar
    50 50 150 210          ;;top, left, bottom, right coordinates
    Visible NoGoAway       ;;Is visible, has no go away box
    0                      ;;ProcID (The funtion that draws it)
    0                      ;;RefCon (A slot for storing things)
```

Dialogs and Item Lists

Dialogs and alerts, being specialized types of windows, have resource compiler syntax similar to windows:

```
Type DLOG                  ;;A Dialog Box
    ,256                   ;;ID #256
    100 100 200 250        ;;The dialog's rectangle
    Visible 1 NoGoAway 0   ;;It's visible, has ProcId, no go away
    270                    ;;ID of its item list
```

Dialogs have an item list, identified by resource ID. The item list describes the features of the dialog box. Nine types of items can be included in dialogs, including a user-defined type of dialog item. One feature of all dialog item specifications is the ability to determine whether the item will be initially enabled or disabled. If an item is disabled, it will not respond to mouse clicks. This enabled or disabled state applies only to the Dialog Manager and determines whether the Dialog Manager notifies your application of mouse clicks in dialog items. It does not affect the way those items are displayed. For instance, to give a visual indication that a control is disabled, you would still have to call HiliteControl.

```
Type DITL                  ;;A dialog's item list
    ,270                   ;;ID #270
    5                      ;;Five items in the list

    StatText Disabled      ;;Uneditable text, not mouse sensitive
    20 40 35 180           ;;The text's rectangle
    A sample dialog box    ;;The text
```

```
BtnItem Enabled          ;;A button, mouse sensitive
50 10 70 70              ;;The button's rectangle
Resume                   ;;The button's label

ResCItem Enabled         ;;A control item, defined in a resource
70 10 120 26             ;;The rectangle for this control
257                      ;;The resource ID of the control

IconItem Disabled        ;;An icon
40 150 72 182            ;;A 32x32 rectangle
257                      ;;Resource ID of the icon

UserItem Disabled        ;;An application's own item
80 40 120 230            ;;The rectangle it will be displayed in
```

In addition to the StatText type of dialog item, there is a similar EditText item type that defines a possibly empty string of text that is edited with TextEdit. In addition to BtnItem, RadioItem and ChkItem types are available for defining check boxes and radio buttons. In addtion to the IconItem type, a PictItem can be specified for including pictures.

Icon Resources

Icons are 32- by 32-pixel entities supported by a couple of QuickDraw calls that look for items in resource forks and draw them. Icons are used where symbols in a typeface like the Cairo font are insufficient and where QuickDraw pictures are overkill. Icons are defined in the the resource compiler input file as 32 lines of two 4-digit hex numbers.

```
Type ICON          ;;An icon definition
 ,256              ;;Its resource ID
0F0F 0F0F          ;;32 lines like this one
0F0F 0F0F          ;;to enter each bit of the icon
0F0F 0F0F          ;;in a compact but still fairly
0F0F 0F0F          ;;readable form.
F0F0 F0F0          ;;
F0F0 F0F0          ;;This icon looks like a checkerboard
F0F0 F0F0          ;;with squares 4 pixels on a side.
F0F0 F0F0          ;;
0F0F 0F0F          ;;Since the Macintosh has a one-to-one
0F0F 0F0F          ;;aspect ratio, you can design your
0F0F 0F0F          ;;icon on graph paper before entering
0F0F 0F0F          ;;it in hexadecimal.
F0F0 F0F0
F0F0 F0F0
F0F0 F0F0
F0F0 F0F0
0F0F 0F0F
0F0F 0F0F
0F0F 0F0F
F0F0 F0F0
F0F0 F0F0
F0F0 F0F0
F0F0 F0F0
0F0F 0F0F
0F0F 0F0F
```

```
OFOF OFOF
OFOF OFOF
FOFO FOFO
FOFO FOFO
FOFO FOFO
```

Icons can also be defined in the resource compiler file in a list of icons. The resource type of an item list is ICN#. The format of an icon list is the same as that of an icon resource specification, except that a count of icons in the list precedes the rest of the data in the specification, and after that, instead of the data for one icon, are the data for however many there are in the list. Icon lists are used mostly to create desktop icons, which are actually icon lists of two icons.

Cursors

Cursors can be defined in the resource compiler file. A cursor consists of two 16- by 16-bit images and a hot spot. The hot spot is the point inside the cursor that is used in determining exactly where mouse-related events have occurred. Cursor resources consist of two lines of 64 hexadecimal digits that define the data and mask components of the cursor and one line that specifies the location of the hot spot in two 4-digit hexadecimal numbers.

The cursor data are a 16- by 16-bit image that defines the basic shape of the cursor. The mask is another such image that describes how that cursor gets displayed. Bits that are set to 1 in the cursor data will be displayed as black if the corresponding mask bit is 1, or as the inverse of the pixel under that bit if the mask bit is 0. For 0 bits in the cursor data, if the mask is 1, that bit will be displayed as white; if the mask bit is 0, that pixel will be transparent (it will always display the pixel under that part of the cursor unchanged).

The last part of the description of a cursor is the specification of its hot spot , the point relative to the upper-left corner of the cursor that is the actual pixel being pointed at by the cursor. For example, the default arrow cursor has a hot spot of (0,0). The crosshairs-style cursor that the control panel desk accessory uses has its hot spot at (8, 8), in the center of the crosshairs.

There is no more convenient way to specify a cursor than through resources. If you use more than just the standard arrow cursor in your applications, you will probably define the cursors in the resource fork. The following example shows a cursor somewhat like the I-beam cursor used in most text editing situations:

```
Type CURS
,256
0FF801C000800080008000800080008000800080008000800080008001C00FF8
008000800080008000800080008000800080008000800080008000800080080
0008 0002
```

Patterns

Not surprisingly, patterns are 8- by 8-bit patterns. Patterns are used to fill areas of the screen; they are backgrounds. The desktop is generally filled with a fine checkerboard pattern that looks gray. The patterns your application uses to fill in areas of the screen around controls, behind windows, and other areas on the screen are a large factor in determining the look of the application. If you use attractive, pleasing patterns, you can create the illusion of texture and depth. Patterns are specified in much the same way that icons and cursors are:

```
Type PAT
  ,256
  FF00FF00FF00FF00      ;; A pattern of horizontal lines
```

Patterns can also come in pattern lists, similar in form to icon lists. In addition to the components of a pattern specification, a pattern list has a length that is specified before the list of patterns:

```
Type PAT#
  ,256
  2                     ;; Two patterns in this list
  FF00FF00FF00FF00      ;; A pattern of horizontal lines
  AAAAAAAAAAAAAAAA      ;; A pattern of vertical lines
```

Pattern lists are useful when you are using so many patterns that you don't want to have to clutter the resource compiler file with lots of separate pattern specifications.

Strings

String resources are very important for two reasons: First, string resources allow Macintosh applications to be translated into foreign languages without recompiling the application's code. Thus people who are experts at translating documentation can translate the program itself. Also, since the program itself remains undisturbed, there is less likelihood that something might be broken by the translation process. This ease with which properly constructed Macintosh applications can be translated significantly reduces the barriers to entering foreign markets.

The use of string resources enables nonprogrammers, like technical writers, to compose the messages the user sees. It is easy to see why writers ought to be writing the English that goes into a product and programmers ought to be writing the code.

String resources give you for free a valuable tool for reducing the size of your programs. If you do not use all the strings in your program frequently, the seldom used ones can be brought in,if and when they are needed and purged from memory if they are no longer required. Many programmers have been forced to resort to this technique to fit a big powerful program in a microcomputer's memory. The Macintosh provides a uniform way of doing this, as well as all the routines that perform resource retrieval and memory management, giving every program writer a solution to the space crunch.

String resources have an added attraction for C programmers: One of the most common errors encountered by beginning Macintosh C programmers, even those who are highly experienced Unix or MS-DOS C programmers, is passing a null-terminated C-style string to a Toolbox routine that is expecting a Pascal string with a length byte at the beginning. By using string resources, you can keep your strings in a form that the Toolbox will accept, thereby avoiding string conversion errors.

String resources have a very simple format: The string corresponding to this resource is typed, on one line, right after the type and resource ID for the string. If you are using a large number of strings, a string list can lump a number of strings under the same resource ID.

```
Type STR                        ;; A string resource
 ,256
This is a string in a resource  ;; A string

Type STR#                       ;; A string list
 ,256
One string                      ;; A list of strings
Followed by another
Until you have run out
of things to\0Dsay.             ;; A carriage return: \0D
```

Menus

Menus are a close relation of string resources. Menus contain labels, in English, that correspond to commands. Many of the reasons you would want to change or translate string resources also apply to menus.

A menu specification consists of the type and resource ID followed by a list of menu items. If you want to specify several menus at once, you can omit the Type MENU line, skip a line between menu specifications and just give the resource ID of the next menu. Special characteristics of menu items, such as whether they are disabled and displayed dimmed, can be specified in the resource compiler file using special characters. They are the same special characters used in the AppendMenu routine:

! Makes the next character the mark character for the current item.

< Set character style in combination with the following:
B, bold
U, underline
I, italic
O, outline
S, shadow

/ Makes the next character a keyboard equivalent. It will be displayed with a cloverleaf symbol next to it.

(Disables the menu item.

The hyphen, when used in specifying a menu item, creates a horizontal line instead of a hyphen character. The hyphen, when used in combination with the open parenthesis, creates a horizontal line that is disabled, and so it is displayed dimmed. The effect is that a horizontal dotted line that does not respond to the mouse is displayed in place of a menu item. Such a line, which is usually left disabled throughout the running of an application, separates items on the same menu, the way the undo item is separated from the rest of the editing commands on MacWrite's edit menu.

```
Type MENU                    ;; A menu resource
 ,256
\14                          ;; The menu title: the apple symbol
About that example...        ;; Program information, usually

 ,257
File                         ;; The file menu
Quit                         ;; The label for the "quit" command

 ,258
Edit                         ;; The edit menu
Undo /Z                      ;; The label for the "undo" command
(-                           ;; The "dotted line"
Cut/X                        ;; The label for the "cut" command
Copy/C                       ;; The label for the "copy" command
Paste/V                      ;; The label for the "paste" command
```

Control Resources

Like menus, controls provide an obvious and rapid way for the user to issue commands to an application. Controls, unlike menus, provide visual and tactile feedback to the user. Macintosh controls are like physical controls in this respect. The steering wheel in your car is a control that you use to command the front wheels of your car to turn. When you look at the wheel or when you feel how far over your hands have moved with the wheel, you can tell how far the front wheels have turned. When a user moves the mouse over a control, he or she can see the control changing, and the act of moving the mouse gives physical feedback as well.

There are four kinds of predefined controls, each referred to by a different DefProc. The DefProc is a definition procedure that actually draws the control. The following table shows the contrants that refer to the definition procedures and the kinds of controls that each draws:

DefProc	Control type
0	Simple button with title in the button
1	Check box, with title next to it
2	Radio button, with title next to it
16	Scroll bar, same DefProc for vertical and horizontal

The most commonly used controls are scroll bars and buttons. Buttons are usually part of a dialog or alert, but scroll bars are frequently used in applications windows to enable users to move and scroll over a document and need to be defined separately from any dialog. Here is the syntax of the specification of control resources:

```
Type CNTL                    ;; A control resource
 ,256                        ;; Resource ID is 256
 vertical scroll bar ;; The title, invisible for scroll bars
 -1 241 157 257              ;; The bounds rectangle, window relative
 Visible                     ;; The scroll bar is initially visible
 16                          ;; The DefProc
 0                           ;; The RefCon
 0 50 0                      ;; initial value, minimum, maximum
```

Finder Resources

Finder resources are the way the Finder finds the icons that represent your application inside your application's resource fork. Three kinds of resources are involved in providing the finder with icons. The first of these is icon lists. Icon lists are used in place of simple icons, because the finder needs two icon resources to make one desktop icon. The first icon in the list describes the appearance of the icon, and the second icon describes the shadow of the icon, the filled in shape of the icon. These pairs of icons are grouped in icon lists. The second type of resource used to keep track of finder resources is the file reference. The file reference resource matches icons up with file types. The third kind of resource is the bundle resource. Bundle resources do two things: they list icon and file reference resources that make up the rest of the set of finder resources for an application, and they are used to assign local IDs to finder resources, so that the finder can change the resource IDs of the finder resource to keep them unique. The local IDs are used in the file reference resource to refer to the icon lists because the finder will not change these resource IDs.

Icon lists, which were covered under icon resources, are to icon resources what string lists are to strings and pattern lists to patterns. Here is the syntax of the file reference and bundle resources:

```
Type FREF ;; A file reference resource
 ,256     ;; The ID is 256
 APPL 0   ;; Application files get the icon with local ID 0

Type BNDL ;; A bundle resource
 ,256     ;; The ID is 256
 MYPG 0   ;; The owner is MYPG
 2        ;; There are two items in this bundle
 ICN# 1   ;; There is one icon list in this bundle
 0 256    ;; Its resource ID of 256 is given a local ID of 0
 FREF 1   ;; There is one file refernece in this bundle
 0 256    ;; Its resource ID of 256 is given a local ID of 0
```

The owner of a bundle is identified the same way an application is identified. If the output of this resource compiler file is an application, the owner of the bundle will be identified with the same four letters that are used in the heading of the resource compiler file to associate the output with a particular application.

Including Resources from Other Files

If you are using the resource compiler to create an application, you will need the output of your compiler, the code resource, included in the resource fork of the resource compiler's output. Fonts are typically imported from other resource files as well, because it would be more than tedious to type in a font in hexadecimal for the resource compiler. Fonts are typically careted with font editors that deposit a resource file full of the fonts as their output. Somehow you will need to merge these resource files together into a finished application.

The resource specifications for code, driver, and font resources do just that, they bring these resources in from other files. Their syntax consists soley of the resource type line followed by the resource ID line. But in addition to the resource ID, you will find on the same line the name of the file the data are to be found in and the name of the resource. In the case of fonts, a number of files can be specified for inclusion to make up a single font.

Here is the syntax of font, code, and driver resource specifications:

```
Type FONT
 !Cambridge,30@0        ;; Name only, no file, size is 0
 Cambridge9,30@9        ;; Cambridge 9 point from file "Cambridge9"
 Cambridge12,30@12      ;; 12 point from "Cambridge12"
 Cambrdige18,30@18      ;; 18 point from "Cambridge18"
 Cambridge24,30@24      ;; 24 point from "Cambridge24"

Type CODE               ;; A code resource
 MyProgram.code,0       ;; The code is in the file "MyProgram.code"

Type DRVR               ;; A driver resource
 MyDriver!MyDriver,256  ;; The driver is called Mydriver and
                        ;; is in the file "MyDriver"
```

The resource IDs for code resources are ignored, the resource compiler generates resource IDs beginning at 0 for each segment of code included. Font resource IDs have two parts. One is the font number, and it is put in the high byte of a font resource ID; the other part is the point size, which is put in the low byte of a font resource ID.

If That Is Not Enough: Defining New Kinds of Resources

Resources fill in data structures, and it would be nice to be able to fill in your own data structures with resources, as well as the data structures that are predefined by Toolbox software. The resource compiler provides three resource types that have no predefined use. They exist for you to use for your own purposes.

The most general of these free-form resource types is the general resource. The general resource type is formed from both the data that makes up the resource and information about the kind of data. Data-type information is specified by a period followed by a single letter. The following directives can be used to tell the resource compiler what kinds of data make up a general resource:

Directive	Data type
.P	Pascal string(s), one to a line
.S	Character string(s) without a length byte, one to a line
.I	Integers (C type "int")
.L	Long integers (C type "long")
.H	Any number of bytes of data entered in hexadecimal
.B	Bytes from another file

This is the syntax of general resources:

```
Type GNRL                      ;; A general resource
 ,256                          ;; The ID is 256
 .P                            ;; Pascal strings follow...
One Pascal style string        ;; The length byte gets added
```

```
Another one                          ;;    automatically
 .S                                  ;; Character strings follow...
A character string                   ;; A character string
One that is null terminated\00       ;; A C style string
 .I                                  ;; 16 bit integers follow...
17
256
77
.L                                   ;; 32 bit integers follow...
68000
6610777
.H                                   ;; Hex data follows...
FF00FF00FF00
AAAA
AA
.B                                   ;; Bytes form a file
ADataFile 128 1024                   ;; The file id called "ADataFile"
                                     ;; The byte count is 128
                                     ;; The length is 1k
```

Two less powerful free-form resources are also provided: the hexadecimal type and the any bytes type. These two types do what two parts of the general resource do. The hexadecimal type has a format identical to the part of a general resource specification following a ".H" and an any bytes resource is specified in the same way that the part of a general resource following a ".S" is specified. Here is the syntax of these two resource-type specifications:

```
Type HEXA        ;; A hexadecimal resource
 ,256            ;; The ID is 256
FF00FF00         ;; Some data in hexadecimal
AAAAAAAA

Type ANYB        ;; An any bytes resource
 WhereFrom,256   ;; The file is "WhereFrom," The ID is 256
256 512          ;; 256 bytes are extracted at an offset of 512
```

In addition to creating new resource formats and entering free-format resources, the resource compiler lets you define your own resource types. Take another look at the general format for resource specifications near the beginning of this chapter. On the first line of *any* resource specification you can specify a new resource type that inherits the properties of an existing resource type. This is most often used with the free format resource types. Creating new resource formats usually means you have a corresponding data structure to fill with resource data. Creating new resource types serves to associate a particular free-format resource with a particular type of data structure.

Resource Editors

Resource editors are programs that create resources, like fonts and icons, interactively. The most important resource editor is REdit, which can edit a wide variety of resources. Specialized resource editors that edit only fonts and icons also exist.

The most readily available example of resource editing is the desktop pattern editor in the control panel desk accessory. If you don't have a real resource editor handy, the control panel illustrates the general nature of resource editors: You manipulate a visual representation of a resource, such as an enlarged version of a pattern, by pointing and clicking with the mouse. When you are done, the resource fork of the file that you have applied the resource editor to is modified to reflect the editing you have done.

For some jobs, resource editors are the only reasonable tool to use: It would be painfully laborious to create a font resource with the resource compiler, but with a resource editor, the same task becomes much easier and much less prone to error. Complex dialogs are best composed with a resource editor so that you can see what the user will see without having to compile and run your application (which may not be completely written when you sit down to design the dialogs).

The disadvantage of resource editors is exactly their advantage. You have to interact with them. That is fine when you want instant feedback about the look of a font or icon, but it is an inconvenience if all you want to do is combine the code resources your compiler has created with a few string resources. Even in an application that requires very complex resources, you will not be changing them everytime you compile, so using the resource editor to create the finished application file is not nearly as convenient as letting the resource compiler create the application without your intervention. The solution to the dilemma of whether to use the powerful resource editors, or the convenient compiler is to use both: A resource editor can be used to modify resources when they need to change, and the resource compiler simply combines the code resources with the dialogs, fonts, patterns, and strings that you have composed interactively with a resource editor. Here is an example of that use of the resource compiler:

```
include foo.code
include foo.rsrc
```

Benefits

Using resources and the Resource Manager for initializing data structures is convenient both in terms of the number of steps required to program in that initialization and in terms of the time it takes to modify resources. No recompilation of the program is required; only the resource compiler needs to be run. Resources can reduce the cost of producing a foreign-language version of a program. Resources let advanced users modify your program without any added effort to provide such facilities on your part. Due to the convenience of resources and due to the program writer's responsibility to provide as much flexibility as possible, the program writer should use resources liberally.

Points to Consider

1) What resources are best described in resource compiler statements?

2) What resources are best created interactively?

3) There are two major types of font design tools. What are they, and what two purposes do they serve?

4) What kinds of user-configuration settings can you think of? What would be the best way to present them to the user? What would be the best way to store them for future use? What settings would go in the application's resource fork? What settings would go in the document's resource fork?

Chapter Seven

An Example: Internal Structure of a Macintosh Application

In this chapter you will learn:

- How to place a window on the screen with "Hello World" in the title bar.
- How to enable the user to move that window around the screen.
- How to enable the user to change the size of the window.
- How to create menus.
- How to respond to a user's menu selection.
- How to put scroll bars in a window.
- How your programs will interact with scroll bars and other controls.

The Evolution of an Example

This chapter presents an example of a Macintosh application. This application is evolved through four steps. By the end of this chapter, the example program has successfully used the Toolbox to meet the standards of the better commercial Macintosh programs.

Step 1: Getting Started

The following program puts a window on the Macintosh's screen, with "Hello World" in the title bar. When you click on the mouse, the program goes away and you are returned to the finder. Like a sumo wrestling match, there are a lot of preliminaries for a very short bit of action. In a UNIX environment, the program to display "Hello World" on your terminal's screen could be much shorter. It might consist only of the "main" procedure, with a call to printf, the UNIX standard formatted printing routine.

The concepts embodied in the UNIX system make it easy to construct simple programs, but difficult to construct visually powerful applications. In the Macintosh environment the opposite is true: Almost every Macintosh application has a powerful, easy to use, and pleasing to look at visual interface because the Macintosh has all the parts of such an interface built right in. This is great for professional software developers! They can spend their time on the guts of their programs and be sure that the appearance their program will have can be just as polished and professional as those from the biggest software companies. By contrast, UNIX lacks all but the most rudimentary tools for creating visually appealing programs.

The richness of the Macintosh user interface Toolkit is, at least at first glance, not so good for the person writing software for their own consumption. To get anything at all done, they have to achieve a fairly high degree of polish in their programs. Achieving that level of polish takes about two pages of code just to get things moving.

Here are those pages of code:

C Code for the Hello World Program

```
#include <QuickDraw.h>
#include <window.h>
#include <control.h>
#include <event.h>
#include <desk.h>
#include <menu.h>
#include <inits.h>

WindowRecord w_record; /* storage for a window's information */
WindowPtr hello_window;      /* a pointer to that storage */

main()
{
  init_process(); /* do all the initialization */
  make_window();
  event_loop();
}

/* Do all the random initialization things
 */
init_process()
{
  init_mgrs();
  FlushEvents(everyEvent, 0);
}

/* Do the right thing for most applications: Call the toolbox
 * initialization routines.
 */
init_mgrs()
{
  InitGraf(&thePort);
  InitFonts();
  InitWindows();
  InitCursor();
}
```

```
event_loop()
{
  EventRecord event;

  do /* Nothing */ ; while (!GetNextEvent(mDownMask,&event));
  exit(0);
}

/* Make a window */
make_window()
{
  hello_window = GetNewWindow(256, &w_record, (WindowPtr)-1L);
  ShowWindow(hello_window);
}
```

Resource Compiler File (RMaker) for the Hello World Program

```
helloworld
APPLMANX

Type WIND
  ,256
  Hello World!
  50 40 300 450
  Visible NoGoAway
  0
  0

INCLUDE helloworld.code
```

The Edit/Compile/Run Cycle

You can use this program to get used to your compiler's development cycle. All compilers come with example programs, and you might find this program or those examples useful if you want to jump right in and do some programming. The Macintosh is an immensely satisfying machine when you run a program you have just compiled, it looks just like a professionally written program you might buy!

If you have already done that or if you want to know about the mechanisms behind this program before you experiment, we will pick it apart and explain each piece in detail here. As you read the description of the sample program that follows, go back every now and then and reread the part of the example that is being described.

Initializing Toolbox Managers

First, there is a fairly long list of *include* files. These are needed even though we aren't using preprocessor macros or constants from these files. The locations of the Toolbox routines that we call are declared in these files (although some compilers use other methods, such as libraries of "glue" routines to link to the Toolbox). Since we call a number of initialization routines, each from a diffcrent part of the Toolbox, we need at least as many include files. We also use defined data types from these include files.

A look at each of these initialization routines yields a rough idea of what parts of the Toolbox are involved in putting a window on the screen:

First there is a call that goes InitGraf(&thePort). InitGraf is in the QuickDraw part of the toolbox. InitGraf initializes QuickDraw, and thePort is a toolbox global symbol that consists of enough storage to hold QuickDraw's global variables. InitGraf is called once and only once at the very beginning of every Macintosh application. Everything that touches the Macintosh screen, and that is just about everything, relies on QuickDraw to draw on the screen, so before anything else can be accomplished, QuickDraw has to be ready.

Next, there is a call to InitFonts, without any parameters. Apart from the lines and patterns that make up the desktop background of the Macintosh screen and the window we are putting on the screen, there will be the phrase "Hello World!" in the title bar of the window. Putting any characters on the screen involves the Font Manager part of the toolkit. Initializing the Font Manager by calling InitFonts means that the Font Manager will be ready to go find the system font for use in the title-bar of our window.

Next, the Window Manager itself is initialized with a call to InitWindows. This principally does two things: The port that the Window Manager works in is created and the desktop is drawn. A port, also called a grafPort in Apple's documentation, is the data structure that holds information such as the part of memory that is to be drawn in, the current font, information about the "pen," and the like. You can see just when in the course of an application this call is made: When you start a program, one of the first things that happens is the replacement of the desktop with the disk and file icons with an empty desktop with an empty menu bar over it. This is the result of calling InitWindows.

Finally InitCursor is called. This is a call to the QuickDraw part of the Toolbox. InitCursor makes sure that the cursor that appears on your screen is the arrow pointing up and to the left and that the cursor is visible.

The initialization part of this program is now complete. The number of initialization routines called in this minimal program is one of the effects of the flexibility of the Macintosh toolkit. Since we put text on the screen, but we don't change it once it gets there, we don't need to involve TextEdit, the part of the Toolbox that provides a means of entering and changing text on the screen. We also didn't use sound, memory management, dialog boxes or the printer, and so none of the parts of the system or Toolbox that manage these facilities needed to be initialized. If we didn't have such precise control over the parts of the toolbox we initialize to prepare to use, every program would have to wait for toolbox managers to prepare themselves for nothing. That would waste time, and on the 128k Macintosh it would also be a significant waste of space taken up by memory allocated to data structures that those unused Toolbox managers require.

Creating a Window

The first significant thing this sample program does is create a window. It does this by creating a data structure for the information about that window, with the initial information coming from the window resource we have defined. The program then draws the window. Because the Toolbox routines that manage windows are geared toward updating their contents during the course of the interactive use of a program, there is no "draw this window for the first time" routine. Instead we tell the Toolbox to set aside all the information that would cause that window to be drawn, and then we call the routines that update the screen on the basis of this set-aside information.

It takes two calls to the Window Manager part of the Toolbox to do this: First, GetNewWindow is called with three parameters: a *window ID*, a pointer to memory where the window structure will be stored, and a *behind* parameter that points to the window that we want to put our window behind. The window ID is the ID we gave to the window resource defined in the RMaker file above. The second parameter is a pointer to a window structure (of type WindowRecord). It points to the window structure declared at the top of the program source. This is the chunk of memory the window manager will use to store things about our "Hello World" window. The last parameter is also a pointer to a window structure. In this case, the value is -1L, which indicates that the window we are creating should be placed in front of all the other windows on the screen.

That -1L is used as an invalid pointer value probably rubs some experienced C programmers the wrong way. Using -1L this way relies on the binary representation of -1L being a 32-bit word with all the bits set to 1, and on that memory location lying outside the address space of the 68000 processor. On many machines that UNIX runs on -1 is a perfectly good address and it *is* bad practice to use anything other than 0 as an invalid pointer in the UNIX environment. But since the Macintosh environment is an indivisible whole that cannot be separated from the Macintosh hardware, it is permissible to take into account the characteristics of the 68000 processor and the Macintosh architecture in selecting special pointer values that have meanings other than being the addresses of memory locations.

The second call in the set of calls that draws the "Hello World" window is a call to the ShowWindow routine. This Window Manager routine takes as a parameter a pointer to the window that is to be drawn. The result of this call is that the frame of the window, the part the Window Manager itself knows how to draw, is drawn on the screen. An update event is also generated so that, if the program itself had anything to draw in the window, an event directing it to do so would be in the event queue.

The Event Loop

At this point in the execution of this program the "Hello World!" window has appeared on the screen. The program then waits for a mouse click and then exits. In a sense, the loop that waits for the mouse button to be pushed is the heart of the program: it is the event loop.

This program has a very simple event loop. All we are looking for is the event of the mouse button being pressed. We use the *event mask* to tell GetNextEvent that we are only interested in the mouse button being pressed. The event mask is a kind of bit mask, so called because it is figuratively placed over the bits that represent all of the various kinds of events that could occur, revealing only those that the mask will allow through. The predefined event mask called mDownMask reveals only mouse button presses. When GetNextEvent returns a value other than 0, an event has occurred. In this program the only event that can can be reported is a mouse button press, so when GetNextEvent returns something other than 0, we don't bother checking tha data structure that holds information about the event; we can be sure the mouse button was pressed and it is time to exit.

Your programs will call GetNextEvent frequently. To those of you familiar with C programming in the UNIX environment, all this *polling*, or waiting for something to happen, may seem like a waste of processor resources. On the Macintosh, polling for events serves an important purpose: before your program is informed of the presence or absence of events it is interested in, the Macintosh system software takes a look at the events, if any, that have occurred. If the system software wants to handle an event, it does so before control is returned to your program. Event polling serves to divide the processing resources of the Macintosh between your program and the Macintosh system sofware (such as desk accessories that need to be updated periodically).

Step 2: Building Up

Now we are ready to build on this first program. If you had trouble with your compiler's edit–compile–run cycle, you should review your compiler's documentation, we will be adding to this program and you might want to see what happens each step of the way.

The first thing we will add is a proper event loop. The event we will handle will be the mouse-down event. Now, instead of waiting for a mouse button press, the program will exit when the mouse button is pressed and then let go in the "go-away box" of the window. (We will modify the description of the window in the resource compiler file to give the window a go-away box).

C Code for the Second Version of Our Hello World Program

```
#include <quickdraw.h>
#include <window.h>
#include <control.h>
#include <event.h>
#include <desk.h>
#include <menu.h>
#include <inits.h>

WindowRecord w_record;
WindowPtr hello_window;

#define    mk_long(x)  (*((long *)&(x)))

main()
{
      init_process();   /* do all the initialization */
      make_window();
      event_loop();
}

/* Do all the random initialization things
 */
init_process()
{
      init_mgrs();
      FlushEvents(everyEvent, 0);
}
```

```
/* Do the right thing for most applications: Call the toolbox
 * initialization routines.
 */
init_mgrs()
{
    InitGraf(&thePort);
    InitFonts();
    InitWindows();
    InitCursor();
}

/* Read window information from the resource branch into a window
 * structure
 */
make_window()
{
    hello_window = GetNewWindow(256, &w_record, -1L);
    ShowWindow(hello_window);
}

/* Get an event, switch on its type, and perform the appropriate
 * action
 */
event_loop()
{
    EventRecord event;

    while (1)
    {   GetNextEvent(everyEvent, &event);
        switch(event.what)
        {       case nullEvent:
                    break;
                case mouseDown:
                    do_mouse_down(&event);
                case mouseUp:
                case keyDown:
                case keyUp:
                case autoKey:
                case updateEvt:
                case diskEvt:
                case activateEvt:
                case networkEvt:
                case driverEvt:
                case app1Evt:
                case app2Evt:
                case app3Evt:
                case app4Evt:
                default:
                    break;
        }
    }
}

/* Find out where a mouse-down event has occured and do what ought
 * to be done for that location on the desktop
 */
do_mouse_down(eventp)
    EventRecord *eventp;
{
    WindowPtr windowp;
```

```
        switch(FindWindow(mk_long(eventp->where), &windowp))
        {       case inDesk:
                case inMenuBar:
                case inSysWindow:
                case inContent:
                case inDrag:
                case inGrow:
                        break;
                case inGoAway:
                        if (TrackGoAway(windowp, mk_long(eventp->where)))
                                finish();
                        break;
                default:
                        break;
        }
}

/* Exit the program cleanly */
finish()
{
        exit(0);
}
```

Resource Compiler File for the Second Version of Our Hello World Program

```
* Helloworld: The canonical first program
helloworld
APPLMANX

Type WIND
  ,256
  Hello World!
  50 40 300 450
  Visible GoAway
  0
  0

INCLUDE helloworld.code
```

Beefing Up the Event Loop

The most important changes here are the addition of a switch statement in the event loop and another routine, consisting mostly of a switch statement, that distinguishes between and handles the various kinds of mouse-down events.

The switch statement in the event_loop routine has labels for all 15 different kinds of events, even though we are only handling the mouse-down event. The labels were included to elicit a feel for the number of different events that can take place. In the do_mouse_down routine, all the different kinds of mouse-down events also all have their labels included in the switch statement. This lets you see that ,while there are only 15 distinct event types (4 of which are reserved for your application to use) there is a rich set of mouse-down events, distinguished by where on the Macintosh screen they occurred. The event mask has also been changed to allow any event through. This is so the event queue does not fill up with events that we have no interest in, instead we let them fall though our switch statement.

It's Event Driven!

If you have compiled this program, you can see how control is passed back and forth between the Macintosh system and your program: When you press the mouse button while the mouse cursor is in the go-away box, your program gets the mouse-down event and finds out (through the use of a Window Manager routine) that the mouse button was pressed in the go-away box. Control is passed back to the Macintosh Toolbox when the program calls TrackGoAway and is retained by that routine until the mouse button is released. The window's go-away box reflects whether the cursor is still in the box through highlighting. If the cursor remains in the go-away box, the box is highlighted. If the cursor is moved out of the go-away box, the box is unhighlighted. The return value of TrackGoAway reflects the final state of the mouse cursor: If it was inside the go-away box when the button was lifted, a nonzero value is returned, indicating that the window should be disposed of. If the mouse button was lifted outside the go-away box, TrackGoAway returns 0, indicating that the user had second thoughts about extinguishing the window.

This give and take between your application and the Macintosh Toolbox software will be echoed throughout the evolution of this example program.

Step 3: Growth and Movement

The next step in the evolution of this example program will bring us two steps closer to presenting a complete set of controls over the size and placement of windows that the user can manipulate. We will allow the user to move the window and change its size.

```
#include <quickdraw.h>
#include <window.h>
#include <control.h>
#include <event.h>
#include <desk.h>
#include <menu.h>
#include <inits.h>
#include <toolutil.h>

GrafPtr w_port;
WindowRecord w_record;
WindowPtr hello_window;
Rect drag_rect, grow_bounds;

#define    mk_long(x)  (*((long *)&(x)))

main()
{
     init_process();    /* do all the initialization */
     makc_window();
     event_loop();
}
```

```
/* Do all the right initialization things
 */
init_process()
{
      init_mgrs();
      set_parameters();
}

/* Do the right thing for most applications: Call the toolbox
 * initialization routines.
 */
init_mgrs()
{
      InitGraf(&thePort);
      InitFonts();
      FlushEvents(everyEvent, 0);
      InitWindows();
      InitCursor();
}

/* Set parameters based on screen size, etc. */
set_parameters()
{
      drag_rect = thePort->portRect;
      SetRect(&grow_bounds, 64, 64, thePort->portRect.right,
            thePort->portRect.bottom);
}

/* Read window information from the resource branch into a window
 * structure
 */
make_window()
{
      hello_window = GetNewWindow(256, &w_record, -1L);
}

/* Get an event, switch on its type, and perform the appropriate
 * action
 */
event_loop()
{
      EventRecord my_event;
      Boolean valid;

      while (1)
      {     SystemTask();
            valid = GetNextEvent(everyEvent,&my_event);
            if (!valid) continue;
            switch(my_event.what)
            {     case nullEvent:
                        break;
                  case mouseDown:
                        do_mouse_down(&my_event);
                        break;
                  case mouseUp:
                  case keyDown:
                  case keyUp:
                  case autoKey:
                        break;
```

```
                        case updateEvt:
                                do_update(&my_event);
                                break;
                        case diskEvt:
                                break;
                        case activateEvt:
                                do_activate(&my_event);
                                break;
                        case networkEvt:
                        case driverEvt:
                        case app1Evt:
                        case app2Evt:
                        case app3Evt:
                        case app4Evt:
                        default:
                                break;
                }
        }
}

/* Find out where a mouse-down event has occured and do what ought
 * to be done for that location
 */
do_mouse_down(event)
        EventRecord *event;
{
        WindowPtr mouse_window;
        int place_type = FindWindow(mk_long(event->where),
                &mouse_window);

        switch(place_type)
        {       case inDesk:
                case inMenuBar:
                case inSysWindow:
                        break;
                case inContent:
                        if (mouse_window != FrontWindow())
                                SelectWindow(mouse_window);
                        break;
                case inDrag:
                        DragWindow(mouse_window, mk_long(event->where),
                                &drag_rect);
                        break;
                case inGrow:
                        grow_window(mouse_window, mk_long(event->where));
                        break;
                case inGoAway:
                        if (TrackGoAway(mouse_window,
                                        mk_long(event->where)))
                                finish();
                        break;
                default:
                        break;
        }
}

/* Handle and update event - first determine if the event is in one
 * of this application's windows, and if so, update that window.
 */
do_update(event)
        EventRecord *event;
{
```

```
      GrafPtr save_graf;
      WindowPtr update_window;

      if (FindWindow(mk_long(event->where), &update_window) !=
          inSysWindow)
      {     if (update_window = hello_window)
            {     GetPort(&save_graf);
                  SetPort(update_window);
                  BeginUpdate(update_window);
                  ClipRect(&update_window->portRect);
                  EraseRect(&update_window->portRect);
                  DrawGrowIcon(update_window);
                  draw_content(update_window);
                  EndUpdate(update_window);
                  SetPort(save_graf);
            }
      }
}


/* Draw the grow icon for the window to indicte whether or not
 * it is active
 */
do_activate(event)
      EventRecord *event;
{
      WindowPtr event_window = (WindowPtr)event->message;

      if(event_window == hello_window)
      {     DrawGrowIcon(event_window);
            if (event->modifiers & 1)
                  SetPort(event_window);
      }
}


/* Call the window manager routines that cause a window to grow */
grow_window(window, mouse_point)
      WindowPtr window;
      Point mouse_point;
{
      long new_bounds;

      inval_bars(window);
      new_bounds = GrowWindow(window, mk_long(mouse_point),
            &grow_bounds);
      if (new_bounds == 0)
            return;
      SizeWindow(window, LoWord(new_bounds),
            HiWord(new_bounds), TRUE);
      inval_bars(window);
}


/* Invalidate the scroll bar and grow icon area of a standard window
 */
inval_bars(window)
      WindowPtr window;
{
```

```
      Rect temp_rect, port_rect;

      port_rect = window->portRect;
      SetRect(&temp_rect, port_rect.left, port_rect.bottom - 16,
            port_rect.right, port_rect.bottom);
      InvalRect(&temp_rect);
      SetRect(&temp_rect, port_rect.right - 16, port_rect.top,
            port_rect.right, port_rect.bottom);
      InvalRect(&temp_rect);
}

draw_content(window)
      WindowPtr window;
{
}

/* Exit the program cleanly */
finish()
{
      exit(0);
}
```

Strengthening the Framework

Our program has grown considerably! To support the added features of moving and changing the size of our window, we have had to add to our framework. First, we added a routine called set_parameters. This new routine performs an important job: It ensures that this program will look nice and perform as the user expects even if the next-generation Macintosh has a much larger screen. set_parameters sets this program's parameters according to the values it finds in global variables or through calls to Toolbox routines. So, if the screen of some future Macintosh has a thousand pixels in each direction, this program will allow the window to be dragged all over that huge screen without recompilation or any other modification.

This version of our example program does only two things in the set_parameters routine: The rectangle in which the window can be dragged is set to be the entire screen, and the limits to that the window can grow or shrink are set to have a fairly arbitrary lower bound and an upper bound which allows our window to grow to the size of the screen. The second operation is done with the QuickDraw routine SetRect, simply because SetRect is more convenient than a series of C assignment statements. Using Toolbox routines for even minor jobs like assigning values to a Toolbox data structure's elements is a good idea because other Macintosh programmers will know immediatly that you are assigning, in this case, values to elements of a rectangle, where a series of assignment statements would be much more difficult to read and understand.

The event loop has also "grown up" a bit. While event polling provides a measure of resource division, to more completely cooperate with the Macintosh system the program needs to call SystemTask, a Desk Manager routine that allows desk accessories, such as the alarm clock, to get processor resources so that they can still operate even though their windows are not active. The next version of this program will further explore the use of the Desk Manager.

Drawing the Grow Icon

The following changes to the event loop and to other parts of our program are in large measure a consequence of drawing the grow icon. The grow icon isn't really an icon at all, as far as the routines that support Macintosh icons are concerned. The grow icon is part of the Window Manager. The grow icon is also not really part of the window frame; unlike the window frame, the window manager doesn't draw it for you automatically. Fortunately, there *is* a Toolbox routine that will draw the grow icon for a given window. But you have to know when to call this routine.

Knowing when to do this is not obvious, and when you find out, it is still a bit tedious. You can make the best of this situation by learning a bit about the wWndow Manager and how windows are *activated*. The active window is the one that interacts with the user. It ought to be obvious to the user which window is active, so visual indications, such as the presence of horizontal lines in the title bar and the presence of the overlapping squares in the grow icon, are provided to the user. Our example program has to cooperate with the Window Manager to produce the right effects in the grow icon. You will also learn a bit about graphics update, an important part of every Macintosh program.

Updating and Activating

To deal with activation and updating, our application needs to grab the events that tell it what to do and when. The event loop of the example now includes a call to do_update everytime an update event occurs and a call to do_activate every time an activate event occurs. These routines are defined in the example and contain code that cooperates with the Macintosh system to correctly update the contents of the window (in this case only the grow icon) and to correctly indicate that the window is active.

Responding to the Mouse

The switch statement in do_mouse_down has also been modified to include calls to Toolbox routines and routines within the example program to drag the window, to grow the window, and to "select" the window, causing it to be activated.

Toolbox Support for Activating, Updating, Growing, and Dragging

Let's take a close look at the routines that support the example program's new abilities. The simplest of these is the call to DragWindow, a Window Manager routine that moves the location of our window on the screen. The interesting thing about DragWindow is the simplicity of the operation of moving the window around: we don't need to know where it is, and we don't need to know where it winds up. This is due to the use of graf ports. All the drawing we do is within the graf port of our window. As long as we remember to set the current port for drawing to be the port associated with the window we want to draw in, our program will draw in the right place.

Do_activate is called in response to activate events. There are two kinds of activate events: ones that signify that a window has become inactive and others that signify that a window has become active. Activate events, therefore, usually happen in pairs, one for the window becoming active and another for the window becoming inactive. If the activate event has 1 in the zeroeth bit of the modifiers field, that is, if the modifiers field is odd, then it signals the activation of a window. Because the Window Manager itself relies on the current graf port being the graf port of the active window, when our window is activated, SetPort is called with the graf port of the newly active window.

The maintenance of the graf port is demonstrated in the do_update routine. First, the pointer to the current graf port is saved in save_graf; then the current graf port is set to be the graf port of the window the program is updating. Then the program calls the Window Manager routine BeginUpdate to inform the Window Manager that it is updating this window. The port rectangle of our window is then erased. Actually, only the invalid part of the window (the part of the window that has changed on the screen) will be erased on the screen, and the other bits remain untouched. Then, the example program has a call to a routine called draw_content. Right now this routine doesn't do anything, but it does mark the place where this example program will draw the contents of its windows.

What causes update events in this version of our example? Growing and shrinking the window. In the example program, the routine grow_window supports changing the size of the window by clicking in the grow icon and then dragging the mouse. Because the grow icon is in the content region of the window, our example program has to take care of making sure that the grow icon disappears from its previous location and is displayed in the new location. It does so through calls to InvalRect. InvalRect is a Window Manager routine that adds the rectangle that it takes as an argument to the invalid region associated with the window. Adding the present location of the grow icon to the invalid region will make sure the old grow icon is erased. After the window is resized, the new location of the grow icon is added to the invalid region, so the new grow icon will be drawn.

The grow_window routine is where our program grows its window. First, as was just explained, the present grow icon is added to the invalid part of the window. Then a call to the Window Manager routine GrowWindow is made. GrowWindow returns the new width and height as the low-and-high order words of a 32-bit long word. All GrowWindow does is show an outline of the window on the screen that tracks the user's mouse movements and, when the user releases the mouse button, informs the program where the window's bounds *ought* to be. The Toolbox Utility routines LoWord and HiWord extract the width and height for use in SizeWindow, which tells the Window Manager that the window has a new width and height. You, of course, have the option to ignore what the user did with the grow icon and size the window to some other dimensions. This might be done to prevent the window from covering up some other part of the screen. To use the Toolbox Utility routines, we had to add another include file at the top of the program (toolutil.h).

What to Do About Invalid Areas

What actually happens to invalid parts of our window? Take a look at do_update: Invalid regions are erased as a result of a call to EraseRect. Even if the program were to draw something in the invalid parts of the window, those parts should be erased first. Otherwise the program might be scribbling over leftover pieces of grow icon and other detritus.

An Invitation to Tinker

Now that our program has grown to a substantial size, it can be tinkered with to see why all the Toolbox calls are where they are. For example, you could take out one or the other, or both, of the calls to InvalRect in the grow_window routine and see how bits of the grow icon are left in their old position or how new grow icons sometimes fail to appear. Growing the window will still work, but if the invalid region is not kept up the user will not have a proper visual indication of the state of the window. The next version of the example program, and the last one presented in this chapter, will be much more complex, since it will unleash the desk accessories. So if you want to tinker around and willfully break this program, do so at this stage. And if you have the slightest inclination to tinker, do so! Playing with an example, commenting out Toolbox calls and seeing what effect that has, is the fastest way to connect in your mind parts of a program and their effect on interaction with the user.

Step 4: Menus and Scroll Bars

The following version of our example program is the last version for this chapter. While this framework will be used in the following two chapters, this will be the last version that maintains a pristine emptiness; it does nothing, but it does it with all the refinement a Macintosh application could ask for. If you need a break from all that nothing, start up a desk accessory! If you want to see some different nothing, use the scroll bars!

In this version of the example, the menu bar will have menus on it, and the scroll bars will be placed in the presently empty spaces above and to the left of the grow icon. This adds quite a bit of code, and the discussion of this version will be divided into a discussion of menus and a discussion of scroll bars and other controls.

Running this version of the program will provide the first example of the "Hello World" window being unactivated. By starting up some desk accessories you can see how the Window Manager brings windows to the foreground when they become active, and how the example program behaves in the background when another window is active.

Here is the final version of the "Hello World!" program:

```
#include <quickdraw.h>
#include <window.h>
#include <control.h>
#include <event.h>
#include <desk.h>
#include <menu.h>
#include <inits.h>
#include <toolutil.h>
```

```
GrafPtr w_port;
WindowRecord w_record;
WindowPtr hello_window;
Rect drag_rect, grow_bounds;

struct long_halves
{       int high;
        int low;
};

pascal void up_action(), down_action();

#define V_SCROLL 256    /* Resource ID of the vertical scroll bar */
#define H_SCROLL 257    /* Resource ID of the horizontal scroll bar */

#define UP 1
#define DOWN 2

#define APPLE_MENU 1
#define FILE_MENU 256
#define EDIT_MENU 257
#define DRVR 0x44525652L        /* The string "DRVR" as a long */

#define    mk_long(x)  (*((long *)&(x)))

main()
{
        init_process();   /* do all the initialization */
        make_window();
        event_loop();
}

/* Do all the right initialization things
 */
init_process()
{
        init_mgrs();
        set_parameters();
        fill_menus();
}

/* Do the right thing for most applications: Call the toolbox
 * initialization routines.
 */
init_mgrs()
{
        InitGraf(&thePort);
        InitFonts();
        FlushEvents(everyEvent, 0);
        InitWindows();
        InitCursor();
        InitMenus();
        TEInit();
}

/* Set parameters based on screen size, etc. */
set_parameters()
{
        drag_rect = thePort->portRect;
        SetRect(&grow_bounds, 64, 64, thePort->portRect.right,
                thePort->portRect.bottom);
}
```

```
fill_menus()
{
    MenuHandle menu;

    menu = GetMenu(APPLE_MENU);
    AddResMenu(menu, DRVR);
    InsertMenu(menu, 0);
    InsertMenu(GetMenu(FILE_MENU), 0);
    InsertMenu(GetMenu(EDIT_MENU), 0);
    DrawMenuBar();
}

/* Read window information from the resource branch into a window
 * structure. Get the scroll bars for this window and mark them to
 * distinguish them from any other controls that might be in this
 * window
 */
make_window()
{
    ControlHandle scroll_bar;

    hello_window = GetNewWindow(256, &w_record, -1L);
    scroll_bar = GetNewControl(V_SCROLL, hello_window);
    SetCRefCon(scroll_bar, (long)V_SCROLL);
    scroll_bar = GetNewControl(H_SCROLL, hello_window);
    SetCRefCon(scroll_bar, (long)H_SCROLL);
}

/* Get an event, switch on its type, and perform the appropriate
 * action
 */
event_loop()
{
    EventRecord my_event;
    Boolean valid;

    while (1)
    {   SystemTask();
        valid = GetNextEvent(everyEvent,&my_event);
        if (!valid) continue;
        switch(my_event.what)
        {   case nullEvent:
                break;
            case mouseDown:
                do_mouse_down(&my_event);
                break;
            case mouseUp:
            case keyDown:
            case keyUp:
            case autoKey:
                break;
            case updateEvt:
                do_update(&my_event);
                break;
            case diskEvt:
                break;
            case activateEvt:
                do_activate(&my_event);
                break;
```

```
                        case networkEvt:
                        case driverEvt:
                        case app1Evt:
                        case app2Evt:
                        case app3Evt:
                        case app4Evt:
                        default:
                                break;
                }
        }
}

/* Find out where a mouse-down event has occured and do what ought to
 * be done for that location
 */
do_mouse_down(event)
        EventRecord *event;
{
        WindowPtr mouse_window;
        int place_type = FindWindow(mk_long(event->where),
&mouse_window);

        switch(place_type)
        {       case inDesk:
                        break;
                case inMenuBar:
                        do_menu(MenuSelect(mk_long(event->where)));
                        break;
                case inSysWindow:
                        SystemClick(event, mouse_window);
                        break;
                case inContent:
                        if (mouse_window != FrontWindow())
                                SelectWindow(mouse_window);
                        else
                                do_controls(mouse_window,
                                        mk_long(event->where));
                        break;
                case inDrag:
                        DragWindow(mouse_window, mk_long(event->where),
                                                        &drag_rect);
                        break;
                case inGrow:
                        grow_window(mouse_window, mk_long(event->where));
                        break;
                case inGoAway:
                        if (TrackGoAway(mouse_window, mk_long(event->where)))
                                finish();
                        break;
                default:
                        break;
        }
}
```

```
/* Find which part of which control was used. Then find out how the
 * value of that control has changed. Then call one of this
 * applications routines that performs the action that reflects the
 * change in the control. In the case of the up and down buttons,
 * TrackControl calls an action routine that should show some
 * intermediate result, like srolling the screen
 * one line in an editor.
 */
do_controls(window, where)
      WindowPtr window;
      long where;
{
      int part_code, old_value, new_value;
      ControlHandle control;

      GlobalToLocal(&where);
      part_code = FindControl(where, window, &control);
      if (!part_code) return;
      switch(part_code)
      {     case inUpButton:
                  TrackControl(control, where, up_action);
                  break;
            case inDownButton:
                  TrackControl(control, where, down_action);
                  break;
            case inPageUp:
            case inPageDown:
                  page_movement(window, control, part_code);
                  break;
            case inThumb:
                  old_value = GetCtlValue(control);
                  TrackControl(control, where, 0L);
                  new_value = GetCtlValue(control);
                  thumb_movement(window, control, old_value, new_value);
            default:
                  break;
      }
}

 pascal void
up_action(control, part_code)
      ControlHandle control;
{
      WindowPtr window = (*control)->contrlOwner;
      int old_value = GetCtlValue(control);

      SetCtlValue(control, old_value - 1);
      scroll_window(window, control, UP, 1);
}

 pascal void
down_action(control, part_code)
      ControlHandle control;
{
      WindowPtr window = (*control)->contrlOwner;
      int old_value = GetCtlValue(control);

      SetCtlValue(control, old_value + 1);
      scroll_window(window, control, DOWN, 1);
}
```

```
page_movement(window, control, part_code)
      WindowPtr window;
      ControlHandle control;
{
      int units = get_page_units(window, control);
      int direction = part_code == inPageUp ? UP : DOWN;
      int old_value = GetCtlValue(control);

      if (direction == DOWN)
            SetCtlValue(control, old_value + units);
      else
            SetCtlValue(control, old_value - units);
      scroll_window(window, control, direction, units);
}

thumb_movement(window, control, old_value, new_value)
      WindowPtr window;
      ControlHandle control;
{
      int units = old_value - new_value;
      int direction = units < 0 ? DOWN : UP;

      if (units)
      {     units = units < 0 ? - units : units;
            scroll_window(window, control, direction, units);
      }
}

get_page_units(window, control)
      WindowPtr window;
      ControlHandle control;
{
      return 5;
}

scroll_window(window, control, direction, units)
      WindowPtr window;
      ControlHandle control;
{
}

/* Handle and update event - first determine if the event is in one of
 * this application's windows, and if so, update that window.
 */
do_update(event)
      EventRecord *event;
{
      GrafPtr save_graf;
      WindowPtr update_window;

      if (FindWindow(mk_long(event->where), &update_window) !=
                                                inSysWindow)
      {     if (update_window = hello_window)
            {     GetPort(&save_graf);
                  SetPort(update_window);
                  BeginUpdate(update_window);
                  EraseRect(&update_window->portRect);
                  DrawGrowIcon(update_window);
```

```
                    DrawControls(update_window);
                    draw_content(update_window);
                    EndUpdate(update_window);
                    SetPort(save_graf);
            }
        }
}

/* If the modifiers are odd, then this is an activate event for the
 * window pointed to in the message field of the event. If that is
 * the case then the graf port is set to that window's graf port
 */
do_activate(event)
        EventRecord *event;
{

        WindowPtr event_window = (WindowPtr)event->message;
        WindowPeek peek = (WindowPeek)event_window;
        ControlHandle control = (ControlHandle)peek->controlList;
        long label;

        if(event_window == hello_window)
        {       if (event->modifiers & 1)
                {       SetPort(event_window);
                        DisableItem(GetMHandle(EDIT_MENU), 0);
                        while (control)
                        {       label = GetCRefCon(control);
                                if (label == V_SCROLL || label == H_SCROLL)
                                        ShowControl(control);
                                control = (*control)->nextControl;

                        }
                }
                else
                {       EnableItem(GetMHandle(EDIT_MENU), 0);
                        while (control)
                        {       label = GetCRefCon(control);
                                if (label == V_SCROLL || label == H_SCROLL)
                                        HideControl(control);
                                control = (*control)->nextControl;
                        }
                }
                DrawGrowIcon(event_window);
        }
}

/* Call the window manager routines that cause a window to grow */
grow_window(window, mouse_point)
        WindowPtr window;
        Point mouse_point;
{

        long new_bounds;

        inval_grow(window);
        new_bounds = GrowWindow(window, mk_long(mouse_point),
                                        &grow_bounds);
        if (new_bounds == 0)
                return;
        SizeWindow(window, LoWord(new_bounds), HiWord(new_bounds), TRUE);
        move_bars(window);
        inval_grow(window);
}
```

```
/* Invalidate the grow icon area of a standard window */
inval_grow(window)
      WindowPtr window;
{
      Rect temp_rect, port_rect;

      port_rect = window->portRect;
      SetRect(&temp_rect, port_rect.right - 16, port_rect.bottom - 16,
            port_rect.right, port_rect.bottom);
      InvalRect(&temp_rect);
}

/* Go through the list of controls for this window, identify the
 * scroll bars, and change their position and size to conform to the
 * window's new size
 */
move_bars(window)
      WindowPtr window;
{
      WindowPeek peek = (WindowPeek)window;

      ControlHandle control = peek->controlList;
      int new_top = window->portRect.top;
      int new_left = window->portRect.left;
      int new_bottom = window->portRect.bottom;
      int new_right = window->portRect.right;
      long label;

      while (control)
      {     label = GetCRefCon(control);
            if (label == V_SCROLL)
            {     HideControl(control);
                  MoveControl(control, new_right - 15, new_top - 1);
                  SizeControl(control, 16, new_bottom - new_top - 13);
                  ShowControl(control);
            }
            else if (label == H_SCROLL)
            {     HideControl(control);
                  MoveControl(control, new_left - 1, new_bottom - 15);
                  SizeControl(control, new_right - new_left - 13, 16);
                  ShowControl(control);
            }
            control = (*control)->nextControl;
      }
}

do_menu(command)
      long command;
{
      int menu_id = HiWord(command);
      int item = LoWord(command);
      char item_name[32];

      switch(menu_id)
      {     case APPLE_MENU:
                  GetItem(GetMHandle(menu_id), item, item_name);
                  OpenDeskAcc(item_name);
                  break;
```

```
        case FILE_MENU:
                finish();
                break;
        case EDIT_MENU:
                SystemEdit(item - 1);
                break;
}

        HiliteMenu(0);
}

draw_content(window)
        WindowPtr window;
{
}

/* Exit the program cleanly */
finish()
{
        exit(0);
}
```

Resource Compiler File for the Fourth Version of Hello World

```
* Helloworld: The canonical first program
helloworld
APPLMANX

Type WIND
  ,256(36)
  Hello World!
  85 128 256 384
  Visible GoAway
  0
  0


* Scroll bars have rectanges chosen to fit properly in the above
* window
Type CNTL
  ,256
  vertical scroll bar
  -1 241 157 257
  Visible
  16
  0
  0 50 0

  ,257
  horizontal scroll bar
  156 -1 172 242
  Visible
  16
  0
  0 50 0

Type MENU
  ,1
  \14

  ,256
  File
    Quit
```

```
,257
Edit
  Undo
  (-
  Cut
  Copy
  Paste
  Clear
```

```
INCLUDE helloworld.code
```

Setting Up Menus and Scroll Bars

In the first three versions of this example program, the framework of this program was built. Here that framework is relied on to support more or the same sort of meshing with Toolbox routines. The first framework that we go back to and add more to is the resource compiler input file. In addition to the decription of the window record of the "Hello World" window, it now includes descriptions of three menus and two controls. If you are unfamiliar with the syntax for specifying controls and menus, go back to the previous chapter, which describes resource compiler input, to find descriptions of the syntax.

An interesting aspect of menu resources definitions is that items that are disabled by preceding them with a (are disabled forever. So even though, in the course of running the example program, all of the items in the edit menu are enabled and disabled en masse, the horizontal line is always a disabled menu item because it was disabled in the resource.

The two scroll bars are also described with the aid of the resource compiler. The boundaries of the scroll bars are carefully chosen to conform to the areas above and to the left of the grow icon that were blank in the previous version of the example. The range of values (0 to 50) that the scroll bars display is arbitrarily chosen, and since our window doesn't display anything, manipulating the scroll bars has no effect other than to move the "thumb" in the scroll bar being used.

To initialize the menus, the routine fill_menus has been added to the program and is called from init_process. fill_menus gets menus that have been filled with the templates from the resource fork by calling GetMenu and inserts the menus into the menu bar by calling InsertMenu.

The Apple menu is treated specially: Instead of consisting of names of commands, the Apple menu cosists of the names of desk accessories. These are loaded into the menu by calling AddResMenu, a Menu Manager routine that hunts down all the resources of a given type (in this case DRVR) and adds them to the specified menu.

The scroll bars are initialized when the "Hello World" window is created. Controls have a close relationship with windows: Windows have a list of controls that are associated with that window, and controls each have a pointer that points to the window that owns that control. The scroll bar controls are created – and initialized with the data in the resource fork by a call to GetNewControl. Because controls cannot be easily identified by looking at their control records, the scroll bars in the example program have their resource IDs stashed away in the RefCon field of their control records.

Interacting with Menus

The use of menus introduces yet another major catogory of interaction between Macintosh applications and the Toolbox. Like the switch statement in the event loop and in do_mouse_down, do_menu has a switch statement that switches on the result of a call to a Toolbox routine.

In the case of menus, the Toolbox routine MenuSelect is used to track the user's mouse after a mouse-down event has occurred in the menu bar. If a menu item was selected by the user having released the mouse button over that menu item, then MenuSelect returns a menu ID and item number encoded in a longword. This result is passed to our example's routine do_menu, where a switch statement is used to dispatch according to the menu where the selection occurred. If no menu item was selected or if an item from a desk accesory's menu was selected, do_menu will do nothing.

The action associated with the apple menu is launching desk accessories. This takes two steps: In the first step the name of the desk accessory is found through calls to the Menu Manager routines GetMHandle and GetItem. The return value of GetMHandle is passed to GetItem, which deposits the name of the menu item (in this case the name of the desk accessory we want to start) in a buffer. The second step is the actual launch of the desk accessory through a call to OpenDeskAcc.

The file menu consists of only one item: Quit. So the program does no checking to see which item from the file menu was picked; it knows right away that it is time to quit.

Our program does no editing, so the items on the Edit menu are all disabled if the "Hello World" window is the active window. When our window in inactive (when a desk accessory's window is the active window) the edit menu is enabled. This is done in do_activate.

Interacting with Controls

Controls are the most direct way to translate the user's desires into actions. In combination with the mouse, the scroll bars solve one of the thorniest problems facing user-interface designers: How will the user scroll and move the cursor? On the Macintosh the design issues are clear-cut, but your programs still have to interface to the scroll bars to benefit from them. Using scroll bars is fairly complex because scroll bars have three major components: The arrows at the end that are used for scrolling up one "line", whatever a line may mean to your program; The areas above and below the thumb which are used for paging up and down in screen-sized units; and the thumb itself, which is used to move the window over large expanses of the document being viewed.

Each of these components interacts with the application in a somewhat different way. Because the up and down buttons (the arrows) need to show intermediate results, the application passes a function pointer to TrackControl, the Control Manager routine that is called when a mouse down is detected in the up or down buttons. The page up and down areas are easier: all we need to show are the results, which in the case of our example is only the new location of the thumb. The thumb is moved by the control manager, and the new value of the control is set for us, so to interact with the thumb the program needs to store the value of the control before the thumb is moved so that the difference between its old and new location can be reflected in the contents of the window.

Because our sample program has no content to display in the window, the range of values that the scroll bar controls display and the number of units in a page are choosen arbitrarily to demonstrate the use of these controls. When there is something to display, a program will have to set the range of control values and calculate the page size based on the size of the window and the size of the document being viewed. In the example program, we have put in a dummy scrolling routine to show what information is available for determining how much to scroll and in which direction and a dummy get_page_units routine that returns a value.

Controls and Activation

When a window is inactive, its title bar is plain white, its grow icon is gone, and its scroll bars are hidden. To achieve this effect, the program has to call HideControl when the window is deactivated and ShowControl when it is activated. Because you may want to treat some controls differently than others, the example program uses the RefCon field of the control to label the scroll bars as such, and only the scroll bars are hidden on deactivation.

Use Them!

Although controls are complex and require a fair bit of cooperation from your application to make them work, you should use them liberally. They are the most intuitive form of user interface available. Nobody needs a manual to operate a stereo; if the volume is set to 11, it is obviously louder than 10. So it is with controls.

Chapter Eight

An Example: Exploring the Mandelbrot Set

In this chapter you will find:

- What the Mandelbrot set is.
- How to find the complex numbers that form this set.
- How to design a Macintosh application that explores the Mandelbrot set.
- How to write such an application in C, using the framework created in the previous chapter.
- How to use menus and controls to enable the user to manipulate an application
- What graphics update is and how to do it.
- How to have a meaningful dialog with a user.
- The source code for a program that maps the Mandelbrot set.

Figure 8-1 shows a portion of the border of the Mandelbrot set. The border of the Mandelbrot set is a fractal. No matter how closely you look at the border of a fractal, there is still more detail to be seen. The border of the Mandelbrot set, and any fractal, is infinitely long. So if you think fractals are interesting and beautiful, there is an infinite amount of interest and beauty to be found along the edge of the Mandelbrot set.

The example application presented in this chapter, built on the foundation laid in the previous chapter, is a tool for exploring the neighborhood of the Mandelbrot set.

Calculating and plotting the Mandelbrot set is an attractive target for an example Macintosh application. The math behind the Mandelbrot set is easy and the code that does the calculations will not overshadow the purpose of the example program. But the huge number of calculations involved in computing the boundaries of the Mandelbrot set ensure that this example will not be a "toy" program that tackles a problem too small to be worth automating in the first place. Instead, a simple, repetitive task is being performed by the Macintosh to yield a visually interesting result. It would not be practical to explore the Mandelbrot set without a computer.

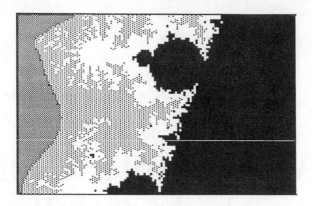

Figure 8-1 A portion of the border of the Mandlebrot set.

In fact, the scale of the problem affects the implementation: On a minicomputer, you might just let a long calculation run its course, even if it takes days to complete. But the Macintosh is an interactive personal computer. You don't want it to sit there, silent and unresponsive, while it is grinding through a lengthy calculation. At the very least, the desk accessories ought to remain available. This means that long calculations, like spreadsheet updates, document re-pagination in word processors, or long scientific or engineering calculations, ought to be done piecemeal. In this chapter we will examine this issue and the other issues involved in designing a worthwhile, easy-to-use, and powerful Macintosh application.

A Shift in Presentation

In the previous chapter the example program was presented in stages. In this chapter and in the next, the example program will be presented as a *fait accompli* because it would be too large to include program listings and commentary for each stage in the development of our Mandelbrot set exploration program. Instead, the program listing is presented at the end of the chapter and it shows only the final version (for this chapter) of the example program. The stages of development that went into this example, and would go into programs you write, are discussed in each of the sections in the rest of this chapter. In part, this chapter is organized in the same order that the example program took shape: The section on computing the results comes before the section on creating the user interface because that is the way most programs are developed.

Each section will present excerpts from the code. These excerpts will be discussed in detail, but will be presented only once – in their final form. The stages of development each part of the program went through will be part of the subject of the commentary for those excerpts.

Stating the Problem

The Mandelbrot set is a set of complex numbers. Since complex numbers have two components, the most obvious way of plotting a set of complex numbers is a two-dimensional map. In this case, the numbers inside the Mandelbrot set will be mapped in black, and those outside the set, in white or some other pattern.

Numbers that lie inside the Mandlebrot set can be found by dropping them into the following equation in place of c:

$$z = z^2 + c$$

The variable z starts at zero. The value of the expression $z^2 + c$ yields a new value for z. By repeating the process of determining the value of the expression and using the value as the value of z for the next calculation, two classes of numbers emerge: numbers that cause the calculation to run off to infinity, and those that cause the result of the calculation to perpetually have a magnitude less than two. In practice it takes about 700 iterations of this calculation to decide that the calculation will not run away to infinity and that the initial value of c is therefore in the Mandelbrot set.

In the case of the Mandelbrot set, more information than the in-the-set-or-out, black-or-white information about complex numbers can be presented. Numbers that lie outside the Mandlebrot set can be assigned a distance from the set. Distance, in this case, is determined by the number of calculations required to decide that a number is outside the Mandlebrot set. If it takes a large number of calculations to make this determination, a number is near the set, if it takes one or a only a few calculations, the number is far away.

Goals and Desired Results

Simply stated, the results we want are interesting pictures. Exploring the Mandelbrot set is like looking through a telescope at the stars or through a microscope at things that are normally invisible. Because there is little value in the naked data about which complex numbers are in or out of the Mandelbrot set, the way the data are presented is very important. In addition to providing a solution to the stated problem, *the goal of this program is to turn the Macintosh into an instrument for exploring the Mandelbrot set.*

The notion behind this goal is that people do not use very many general-purpose devices in day-to-day life. They use scissors to cut paper and cloth, knives to cut food, and saws to cut wood. They use telescopes to look at stars and microscopes to look at bugs. They do not expect to turn their telescopes around and use them as microscopes. They do not even expect their dishwashers to be their clothes washers, even though both slosh hot water around in a big white box.

The universal problem faced by software designers is the problem of transforming, temporarily, a general-purpose computer into an instrument specific to an application. How can the Macintosh, which sloshes code around in a small beige box, be transformed into a sketch-pad, a printed page, a drafting board, a ledger, or, in this case, a tool for looking at a mathematical object?

Visual Goals: Presentation

A broad hint at the solution is in the picture at the beginning of this chapter. In that picture, numbers in the Mandelbrot set are plotted as little black squares, numbers just outside the set are plotted as little white squares, and numbers that are increasingly distant from the set are plotted in increasingly *darker* patterns. By juxtaposing white and black, the border of the Mandelbrot set is highlighted. The black regions that form the body of the set itself are surrounded by a halo of white, which then fades to a dark gray as points grow more distant from the set. Our choice of visual representation was made in a way that combines accuracy (the border of the set is sharply defined) with esthetics.

By creating a program that maps parts of the Mandlebrot set in an accurate and pleasing format and that allows the user to steer around the map in an intuitive manner we are temporarily transforming the Macintosh into an instrument for inspecting the neighborhood of the Mandelbrot set. The example program presented in this chapter is an example of an implementation of a software instrument. Software instruments like this one have an advantage over physical instruments in that they can be used to look at things like the Mandelbrot set that don't exist in the physical world.

Enumerating the Parameters

Exploring the Mandelbrot set means changing parameters: The point in the upper-left hand corner of the map could be moved to a new location; the distance between points could be changed; the size of the map could be changed; the portion of the map being viewed could be changed.

The following paramters are used in the example program:

- The starting point. This is the point in the complex plane mapped in the upper-right corner of the screen.
- The granularity. This is the distance, in both the real and imaginary axes, between points being mapped.
- The scale factor for calculating the data. If we do not want to calculate a result for every pixel, the scale factor specifies how many pixels to skip in each direction.
- The scale factor for viewing the data. This allows map plotting to occur at a larger scale factor than the calculations.
- The X dimension. The number of colums in the map.
- The Y dimension. The number of slots for results in each column of the map.
- The offset we begin drawing at. In case the user has shrunk a map window and then used the scoll bars to move around the map, the point at which drawing begins is specified by an X and Y offset.

It is impossible to know all the parameters of a problem when you sit down to devise a solution. For example, our Mandelbrot Set exploration program started out with only one scale factor, used in both viewing and in calculating. It was later split in two because changing the scale factor for calculations means changing the size of the vectors holding the results of the calculations, which makes it hard to go back to a larger scale factor for viewing without throwing away hard won results.

Designing the Data Structures

On the screen, the Mandelbrot set is represented by squares filled with patterns. Because the window containing the plot of the Mandelbrot set will have to be redrawn after, for instance, a desk accessory is closed, a representation of the plot must be kept in memory so that the plot can be re-created.

The on-screen map reflects the parameters the user has selected and the results of the calculations that have been performed. The data structure used to represent a map in the sample application has a *header* portion used to hold the parameters of the map, and a *data* portion used to hold the results of calculations. The size of the header is fixed, and the size of the data can be inferred from the parameters in the header.

Here is the *map* data structure from the example program:

```
struct map                       /* A map structure */
{ struct cx_num start_at;        /* Complex number at top left corner */
  double step;                   /* The granularity from point to point */
  int scale;                     /* Scale at which we calculate the map */
  int view_scale;                /* Scale at which we draw the map */
  int x_offset, y_offset;        /* The offset we begin drawing at */
  int x_dim, y_dim;              /* The dimensions of the map */
  int last_x, last_y;            /* Where we left off */
  Handle map_values[1];          /* An array  of column handles, allocated
                                            to the correct size */

};
```

The data portion of the structure is not laid out in the structure definition. The structure member map_handles (Figure 8-2) just holds the first pointer in the data section of a map. The storage needed to hold all the data for a map is allocated when the dimensions of the map are changed and when the map is first created. The data portion of a map is a vector of pointers, x_dim long, that points to vectors y_dim long that store the results of the computations.

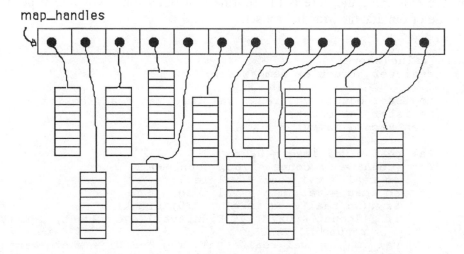

Figure 8-2 The structure member map_handles

Solving the Problem: Computing the Results

The guts of the Mandelbrot Set exploration program are the routines that fill in the map. The primary goal of these routines is efficiency (although utmost efficiency has been sacrificed for clarity in the example sources and flexibility in the program).

The example program spends more than 90 percent of its time in the loop that determines whether a point lies in the Mandlebrot set. This loop evaluates the expression z^2+c up to several hundred times. z and c are both complex numbers with real and imaginary parts. The result of the expression is the new value of z, so the result has two parts as well.

There are at least two alternative strategies for coding this computation in C:

1) Write subroutines that do complex-number multiplication, addition, and magnitude comparison. The structure of the computation is then very clean and easy to read:

```
struct cx_num z, c;
struct cx_num *cx_add(), *cx_square();
int cx_magnitude();

...
do
{    z = *cx_add(cx_square(&z), c);
}    while (cx_magnitude(z) < 2);
```

2) Code the complex number arithmetic in-line, right in the loop. This approach has two advantages: First, there is no procedure call overhead. Instead of three procedure calls per pass through the loop, there are none. Second, intermediate results can be used. For instance, finding the magnitude of a complex number involves a square-root operation that need not be performed for this application. Instead, the intermediate result before the square-root operation can be used in the comparison in the while statement. This is the approach taken in the example, and here is the routine that determines whether a point lies inside or outside the Mandlebrot set:

```
 char
calc_value(where)
    register struct cx_num *where;
{
    register double val_real, val_imag, sq_real, sq_imag;
    register int count;
    EventRecord dummy;

    val_real = val_imag = 0.0;
    for (count = 0; count < 700; count++)
    {    sq_real = val_real * val_real;
        sq_imag = val_imag * val_imag;
        if ((sq_real + sq_imag) > 4.0) break;
        if (!(count & 0x7F) && EventAvail(everyEvent, &dummy))
            return NO_VALUE;
        val_imag = (val_real * val_imag * 2.0) + where->imag;
        val_real = sq_real - sq_imag + where->real;
    }
    return which_pattern(count);
}
```

The solution used in our example program is really a compromise between efficiency, readability, and flexibility. Including the complex number calculations in-line makes the program acceptably efficient, but greater efficiency could have been attained. Instead of using C's built-in floating-point numbers, we could have used fixed-point numbers and done our own fixed-point multiplication in-line (as well as the complex number arithmetic).

Graphic Display and Graphics Update

Visual applications all have to update the screen. On a character-only display, like a terminal, screen update involves figuring out which character positions need to be changed after the user has done something (like deleting a word in a paragraph). On the Macintosh, information on the screen or in the windows on the screen is not locked into a grid of character positions as it is on a terminal. Therefore, on the Macintosh the pixels on the screen that need to be changed have to be kept track of. Keeping track of pixels as opposed to character positions is part of *graphics update* – something that every Macintosh application must do.

To support graphics update the Window Manager keeps track of the parts of the screen that need to be updated. Dragging and changing the size of windows can cause parts of windows to require redrawing. The Window Manager draws what it knows how to draw – window frames and the desktop. The rest of the screen has to be updated by the application. To make this easier for the application, the Window Manager has collected all of the "dirty" areas of the screen into the invalid region. Window Manager routines allow the application to use the invalid region to draw only the parts of its windows that need updating. Calling these routines causes a *clip region* to be set up. Clipping is like masking off the parts of a car that don't need painting. In this case, the parts of the screen that don't need updating are masked off and the application can "paint" the entire window without causing any unnecessary drawing on the screen to occur.

Our example program contains two sets of routines for plotting the map of the Mandelbrot set. One that plots the map in response to update events and one that displays the results of the calculations for a point immediately after they are completed. The following routines from the example program update a window in response to update events:

```
draw_content(window)
  WindowPtr window;
{
  Rect clip_rect;
  RgnHandle old_clip = NewRgn();

  clip_rect = window->portRect;
  clip_rect.right -= BAR_WIDTH;
  clip_rect.bottom -= BAR_WIDTH;
  GetClip(old_clip);
  ClipRect(&clip_rect);
  plot_map(window);
  SetClip(old_clip);
  DisposeRgn(old_clip);
}
```

```
plot_map(window)
  WindowPtr window;
{
  register map_handle map = (map_handle)((WindowPeek)window)->refCon;
  register int scale_ratio = (*map)->view_scale / (*map)->scale;
  register int x, y;
  for (x = 0; x < (*map)->x_dim; x += scale_ratio)
  {     for (y = 0; y < (*map)->y_dim; y += scale_ratio)
            plot_one(map, x, y);
  }
}

/* Plot one point in the map. If clipping has not be set up for the
 * map window, a rectangle may be provided to clip an individual point
 * to.
 */
plot_one(map, x, y)
  map_handle map;
  register int x, y;
{
  register int fill_with = VALUE(map, x, y);
  register int scale = (*map)->scale;
  register int view_scale = (*map)->view_scale;
  Rect to_fill;

  x -= (*map)->x_offset; y -= (*map)->y_offset;
  x *= scale; y *= scale;
  SetRect(&to_fill, x, y, x + view_scale, y + view_scale);
  switch(fill_with)
  {     case BLACK: FillRect(&to_fill, &black); break;
        case WHITE: FillRect(&to_fill, &white); break;
        case LIGHT_GRAY: FillRect(&to_fill, &ltGray); break;
        case GRAY: FillRect(&to_fill, &gray); break;
        case DARK_GRAY: FillRect(&to_fill, &dkGray); break;
        case NO_VALUE:
            break;
  }
}
```

draw_content is called by do_update while handling an update event. Prior to calling draw_content, BeginUpdate is called to set up the *vis-region* of the graf port to contain the intersection of the update region and the exposed part of the window. draw_content further restricts the part of the screen to be drawn on by setting the clip region.

The vis-region and the clip region are parts of the graf port. The Window Manager uses the vis-region to make sure that drawing is confined to the visible parts of a window that need updating, preventing applications from overwriting other windows and the borders of their own windows. Applications use the clip region to make sure that their own drawing is confined to the intersection of the vis-region and the clip region. In the case of our example program, the clip region is used to prevent plot_map from overwriting the scroll bars.

The preceding routines illustrate what happens when the section of a map window in the vis-region must be redrawn in response to an update event caused by, for instance, a desk accessory being closed. The vis-region consists of the space on the screen that had been occupied by some other object the Window Manager knows of. If an application wishes to draw in a window, it has to be sure that the place it wants to draw in is in the vis-region, otherwise the drawing will not appear on the screen. To support application-driven drawing, the Window Manager provides routines to place parts of the screen in the update region.

The following routine interacts with the Window Manager and QuickDraw to display the results of a calculation immediately after it is completed:

```
paint_point(window, x, y)
  WindowPtr window;
{
  GrafPtr save_graf;
  register map_handle map = (map_handle)GetWRefCon(window);
  register int scale = (*map)->view_scale;
  register int scale_ratio = scale / (*map)->scale;
  register int inval_x = (x - (*map)->x_offset) / scale_ratio,
        inval_y = (y - (*map)->y_offset) / scale_ratio;
  Rect rect, content;

  content = window->portRect;
  content.bottom -= BAR_WIDTH; content.right -= BAR_WIDTH;
  inval_x *= scale; inval_y *= scale;
  SetRect(&rect, inval_x, inval_y, inval_x + scale, inval_y + scale);
  if (SectRect(&rect, &content, &rect))
  {       GetPort(&save_graf);
          SetPort(window);
          InvalRect(&rect);
          plot_one(map, x, y);
          ValidRect(&rect);
          SetPort(save_graf);
  }
}
```

paint_point is called right after the pattern for a point has been determined. paint_point calls the Window Manager routine InvalRect to put the rectangle that it wants to fill in in the update region. Then the point is plotted. Then the call to ValidRect cancels the update event caused by the call to InvalRect, so the plotting done by paint_point does not cause the whole window to be replotted.

Creating a User Interface

Now that we have designed the data structures, coded the calculations that fill in those structures, and mapped the results, we need to provide a set of controls to enable the user to operate the Mandelbrot set mapping instrument we have created.

Macintosh user interfaces are usually made up of menus and dialogs. Simple operations are accessible from menus and take effect right away: The quit menu item usually returns the user to the finder without further prompting (unless a file may need to be saved). Other commands require a dialog with the new to get information or at least confirm that previously obtained information is still current.

Designing with Dialogs

In our example program we provide the user with the ability to move around the complex plane and change the granularity of the map. Position on the complex plane and granularity are changed through *modal* dialogs. Modal dialogs are the most common form of dialog and are so called because program is in a mode in which the user can do nothing but interact with the dialog.

The Macintosh user interface is for the most part modeless; the user can do anything at any time. This is in contrast with menu-driven software that insists on leading the user through a hierarchy of choices that can very quickly become tiresome. Because modes are undesirable when overused, modal dialogs should be used carefully. They should not, in general, be nested as menus are in menu-driven programs. The user should not need to use modal dialogs often, because even selecting the menu item that causes the dialog to appear can become tedious if that operation needs to be performed very often. In the case of the example program, the modal dialog that changes position would be used only infrequently after enough of a map has been calculated and displayed for the user to decide if the current place being mapped is interesting.

Modal dialogs are particularly easy on the implementor. One routine, ModalDialog, conducts the dialog with the user and returns when a potentially interesting result has been obtained. Modal dialogs "know" how to operate buttons and editable text boxes, so no interaction with the application is required while the dialog is under way. ModalDialog is called repeatedly until the dialog is either canceled or completed.

The following routine gets a new granularity for the map from the user through a modal dialog box that looks something like the control panel of a coffee grinder, with buttons for the various granularities:

```
/* Ask the user for a new scale for the map */
get_new_resolution(map)
  map_handle map;
{
  DialogPtr dialog;
  int scale = (*map)->view_scale;
  int item;

  dialog = GetNewDialog(RES_DIALOG, 0L, -1L);
  dialog_radio(dialog, scale_to_button(scale));
  while (1)
  {     ModalDialog(0L, &item);
        switch (item)
        {    case RES_D_CANCEL:
                  scale = (*map)->view_scale;       /* Fall through... */
             case RES_D_OK:
                  DisposDialog(dialog);
                  return scale;
             case RES_D_COARSE:
                  scale = COARSE;
                  dialog_radio(dialog, item);
                  continue;
             case RES_D_MEDIUM:
                  scale = MEDIUM;
                  dialog_radio(dialog, item);
                  continue;
             case RES_D_FINE:
                  scale = FINE;
                  dialog_radio(dialog, item);
                  continue;
```

```
                case RES_D_EXTRA_FINE:
                        scale = EXTRA_FILE;
                        dialog_radio(dialog, item);
                        continue;
                default:
                        continue;
            }
        }
        return (*map)->view_scale;
    }
```

The default action (the one that is taken when the user presses Return on the keyboard) is to cancel the dialog. In some cases the default action might be to complete the dialog. Typically, if the dialog changes a parameter or performs some action that is difficult or very inconvenient to undo, the default action should be to cancel the dialog. In this case, changing the granularity of the map can cause much more memory to be used up, so we make sure the user wants to do this.

Dialogs are described in resource compiler format. The description of dialogs is similar to that of windows. The resource compiler source for all the dialogs in our example is at the end of this chapter.

Source Listing

Here is the complete source listing for our example program, the Mandelbrot set mapper:

```
#include <quickdraw.h>
#include <window.h>
#include <control.h>
#include <event.h>
#include <desk.h>
#include <menu.h>
#include <inits.h>
#include <toolutil.h>
#include <types.h>
#include <memory.h>
#include <dialog.h>

GrafPtr w_port;
WindowRecord w_record;
WindowPtr hello_window;
Rect drag_rect, grow_bounds;

struct cx_num          /* A complex number */
{ double real;         /* The real part */
  double imag;         /* The imaginary part */
};

struct map                         /* A map structure */
{ struct cx_num start_at;          /* Complex number at top left corner */
  double step;                     /* The granularity from point to point */
  int scale;                       /* Scale at which we calculate the map */
  int view_scale;                  /* Scale at which we draw the map */
  int x_offset, y_offset;          /* The offset we begin drawing at */
  int x_dim, y_dim;                /* The dimensions of the map */
```

```c
    int last_x, last_y;                 /* Where we left off */
    Handle map_values[1];               /* An array  of column handles, allocated
                                                      to the correct size */
};

/* Find the X'th handle, and the Y'th byte in the array refered to by
 * that handle
 */
#define VALUE(MAP, X, Y) (*(*MAP)->map_values[X])[Y]

typedef struct map **map_handle;

pascal void SysBeep() = 0xA9C8;

pascal void up_action(), down_action();
char calc_value(), which_pattern();
Size calc_map_size();
map_handle make_map();
Handle new_column();
WindowPtr make_window();
ControlHandle lookup_control();

#define V_SCROLL 256        /* Resource ID of the vertical scroll bar */
#define H_SCROLL 257        /* Resource ID of the horizontal scroll bar */

#define BAR_WIDTH 15        /* The width of a scroll bar */

#define NO_VALUE 0          /* Haven't calculated the value */
#define BLACK 1             /* Corresponds to the pattern black */
#define WHITE 2             /* Corresponds to the pattern white */
#define LIGHT_GRAY 3        /* Corresponds to the pattern ltGray */
#define GRAY 4              /* Corresponds to the pattern gray */
#define DARK_GRAY 5         /* Corresponds to the pattern dkGray */

#define UP 1                /* Scrolling up? */
#define DOWN 2              /* Or down? */

#define APPLE_MENU 1        /* The menu marked by the Apple symbol */
#define FILE_MENU 256       /* The "File" menu */
#define EDIT_MENU 257       /* the "Edit" menu */
#define MAP_MENU 258        /* Controls map paramters */

/* Items on the map menu */
#define RESOLUTION 1
#define MAGNIFICATION 2
#define POSITIONING 3

#define RES_DIALOG 256      /* Get a new resolution for the map */

/* Buttons in the new-resolution dialog */
#define RES_D_CANCEL 1
#define RES_D_OK 2

#define RES_D_COARSE 3
#define RES_D_MEDIUM 4
#define RES_D_FINE 5
#define RES_D_EXTRA_FINE 6

#define POS_DIALOG 257      /* Start a map at a new position */
```

```
/* Items in the positioning dialog */
#define POS_D_CANCEL 1
#define POS_D_OK 2
#define POS_D_BOX 3

/* Scale values stored in maps */
#define EXTRA_FINE 1
#define FINE 2
#define MEDIUM 4
#define COARSE 8

/* Initial values */
#define INIT_REAL -0.745          /* The initial starting point */
#define INIT_IMAG 0.260           /* The initial starting point */
#define INIT_STEP 0.00025         /* The initial step value */
#define INIT_SCALE MEDIUM         /* The initial scale factor */

/* Operations the count routine supports */
#define SET 1
#define GET 2
#define ADD 3

#define DRVR 0x44525652L    /* The string "DRVR" as a long */

#define mk_long(x)          (*((long *)&(x)))

main()
{
  init_process();    /* do all the initialization */
  make_window(hello_window = &w_record);
  event_loop();
}

/* Do all the right initialization things
 */
init_process()
{
  init_mgrs();
  set_parameters();
  fill_menus();
}

/* Do the right thing for most applications: Call the toolbox
 * initialization routines.
 */
init_mgrs()
{
  InitGraf(&thePort);
  InitFonts();
  InitWindows();
  FlushEvents(everyEvent, 0);
  InitCursor();
  InitMenus();
  TEInit();
  InitDialogs(0L);
  MaxApplZone();
}
```

```
/* Set parameters based on screen size, etc. */
set_parameters()
{
  drag_rect = thePort->portRect;
  SetRect(&grow_bounds, 64, 64, thePort->portRect.right,
        thePort->portRect.bottom);
}


fill_menus()
{
  MenuHandle menu;

  menu = GetMenu(APPLE_MENU);
  AddResMenu(menu, DRVR);
  InsertMenu(menu, 0);
  InsertMenu(GetMenu(FILE_MENU), 0);
  InsertMenu(GetMenu(EDIT_MENU), 0);
  InsertMenu(GetMenu(MAP_MENU), 0);
  DrawMenuBar();
}


/* Read window information from the resource branch into a window
 * structure. Get the scroll bars for this window and mark them to
 * distinguish them from any other controls that might be in this window.
 * The parameter points to an uninitialized window record
 */
 WindowPtr
make_window(new_window)
  WindowPtr new_window;
{
  ControlHandle scroll_bar;
  struct cx_num start_at;
  map_handle new_map;

  new_window = GetNewWindow(256, new_window, -1L);
  scroll_bar = GetNewControl(V_SCROLL, new_window);
  SetCRefCon(scroll_bar, (long)V_SCROLL);
  scroll_bar = GetNewControl(H_SCROLL, new_window);
  SetCRefCon(scroll_bar, (long)H_SCROLL);
  move_bars(new_window);
  start_at.real = INIT_REAL; start_at.imag = INIT_IMAG;
  new_map = make_map(new_window, &start_at, INIT_STEP, INIT_SCALE);
  SetWRefCon(new_window, (long)new_map);
  init_bar(new_window, H_SCROLL, 0, 0);
  init_bar(new_window, V_SCROLL, 0, 0);
  fill_in_map(new_window);
}


/* Get an event, switch on its type, and perform the appropriate
 * action
 */
event_loop()
{
  EventRecord my_event;
  Boolean valid;

  while (1)
  {     SystemTask();
        valid = GetNextEvent(everyEvent,&my_event);
```

```
          if (!valid)
          {     fill_in_map(hello_window);
                continue;
          }
          switch(my_event.what)
          {     case nullEvent:
                      break;
                case mouseDown:
                      do_mouse_down(&my_event);
                      break;
                case mouseUp:
                case keyDown:
                case keyUp:
                case autoKey:
                      break;
                case updateEvt:
                      do_update(&my_event);
                      break;
                case diskEvt:
                      break;
                case activateEvt:
                      do_activate(&my_event);
                      break;
                case networkEvt:
                case driverEvt:
                case app1Evt:
                case app2Evt:
                case app3Evt:
                case app4Evt:
                      break;
                default:
                      break;
          }
     }
}

/* Find out where a mouse-down event has occured and do what ought to
 * be done for that location
 */
do_mouse_down(event)
  EventRecord *event;
{
  WindowPtr mouse_window;
  int place_type = FindWindow(mk_long(event->where), &mouse_window);

  switch(place_type)
  {     case inDesk:
              break;
        case inMenuBar:
              do_menu(MenuSelect(mk_long(event->where)));
              break;
        case inSysWindow:
              SystemClick(event, mouse_window);
              break;
        case inContent:
              if (mouse_window != FrontWindow())
                      SelectWindow(mouse_window);
              else
                      do_controls(mouse_window, mk_long(event->where));
```

```
                    break;
            case inDrag:
                    DragWindow(mouse_window, mk_long(event->where), &drag_rect);
                    break;
            case inGrow:
                    grow_window(mouse_window, mk_long(event->where));
                    break;
            case inGoAway:
                    if (TrackGoAway(mouse_window, mk_long(event->where)))
                            finish();
                    break;
            default:
                    break;
    }
}


/* Find which part of which control was used. Then find out how the value
 * of that control has changed. Then call one of this applications routines
 * that performs the action that reflects the change in the control. In the
 * case of the up and down buttons, TrackControl calls an action routine
 * that should show some intermediate result, like srolling the screen
 * one line in an editor.
 */
do_controls(window, where)
 WindowPtr window;
 long where;
{
  int part_code, old_value, new_value;
  ControlHandle control;

  GlobalToLocal(&where);
  part_code = FindControl(where, window, &control);
  if (!part_code) return;
  (void)count(SET, 0);
  switch(part_code)
  {     case inUpButton:
                TrackControl(control, where, up_action);
                break;
        case inDownButton:
                TrackControl(control, where, down_action);
                break;
        case inPageUp:
        case inPageDown:
                page_movement(window, control, part_code);
                break;
        case inThumb:
                old_value = GetCtlValue(control);
                TrackControl(control, where, 0L);
                new_value = GetCtlValue(control);
                thumb_movement(window, control, old_value, new_value);
        default:
                break;
  }
}

 pascal void
up_action(control, part_code)
  ControlHandle control;
{
```

```
    WindowPtr window = (*control)->contrlOwner;
    int old_value = GetCtlValue(control);

    SetCtlValue(control, old_value - 1);
    scroll_window(window, control, UP, 1);
    (void)count(ADD, 1);
 }

  pascal void
 down_action(control, part_code)
   ControlHandle control;
 {
   WindowPtr window = (*control)->contrlOwner;
   int old_value = GetCtlValue(control);

   SetCtlValue(control, old_value + 1);
   scroll_window(window, control, DOWN, 1);
   (void)count(ADD, 1);
 }
page_movement(window, control, part_code)
   WindowPtr window;
   ControlHandle control;
 {
   int units = get_page_units(window, control);
   int direction = part_code == inPageUp ? UP : DOWN;
   int old_value = GetCtlValue(control);

   if (direction == DOWN)
        SetCtlValue(control, old_value + units);
   else
        SetCtlValue(control, old_value - units);
   scroll_window(window, control, direction, units);
 }

thumb_movement(window, control, old_value, new_value)
   WindowPtr window;
   ControlHandle control;
 {
   int units = old_value - new_value;
   int direction = units < 0 ? DOWN : UP;

   if (units)
   {     units = units < 0 ? -units : units;
         scroll_window(window, control, direction, units);
   }
 }

get_page_units(window, control)
   WindowPtr window;
   ControlHandle control;
 {
   return 5;
 }

/* Set up the port rectangle and clipping for the window */
scroll_window(window, control, direction, units)
   WindowPtr window;
   ControlHandle control;
```

```
{
  Rect content;
  static RgnHandle save_clip = (RgnHandle)0;

  content = window->portRect;
  if (!save_clip) save_clip = NewRgn();
  else SetEmptyRgn(save_clip);
  content = window->portRect;
  content.right -= BAR_WIDTH;
  content.bottom -= BAR_WIDTH;
  GetClip(save_clip);
  ClipRect(&content);
  scroll_map(window, control, direction, units, &content);
  SetClip(save_clip);
}

/* Scroll the contents of the window and keep track of the offset in
 * the map structure
 */
scroll_map(window, control, direction, units, content)
  WindowPtr window;
  ControlHandle control;
  Rect *content;.
{
  map_handle map = (map_handle)GetWRefCon(window);
  int max = GetCtlMax(control);
  long bar_id = GetCRefCon(control);
  int sign = direction == UP ? 1 : -1;
  int current, n_to_scroll;
  int scale = (*map)->view_scale;
  static RgnHandle to_update = (RgnHandle)0;

  if (!to_update) to_update = NewRgn();
  else SetEmptyRgn(to_update);
  current = bar_id == V_SCROLL ? (*map)->y_offset : (*map)->x_offset;
  units *= sign;
  units = (current - units) < 0 ? -current : units;
  units = (current - units) > max ? max - current : units;
  n_to_scroll = units * scale;
  if (bar_id == V_SCROLL)
  {     ScrollRect(content, 0, n_to_scroll, to_update);
        OffsetRgn(to_update, 0, scale * count(GET, 0) * sign);
        (*map)->y_offset -= units;
  }
  else
  {     ScrollRect(content, n_to_scroll, 0, to_update);
        OffsetRgn(to_update, scale * count(GET, 0) * sign, 0);
        (*map)->x_offset -= units;
  }
  InvalRgn(to_update);
}

count(op, arg)
{
  static int counter;

  switch (op)
  {     case SET: counter = arg; break;
```

```
          case ADD: counter += arg; break;
          case GET: break;
     }
     return counter;
}


/* Handle and update event - first determine if the event is in one of
 * this application's windows, and if so, update that window.
 */
do_update(event)
  EventRecord *event;
{
  GrafPtr save_graf;
  WindowPtr update_window;

  update_window = (WindowPtr)event->message;
    {    if (update_window == hello_window)
         {    GetPort(&save_graf);
              SetPort(update_window);
              BeginUpdate(update_window);
              EraseRect(&update_window->portRect);
              DrawGrowIcon(update_window);
              DrawControls(update_window);
              draw_content(update_window);
              EndUpdate(update_window);
              SetPort(save_graf);
         }
    }
}


/* If the modifiers are odd, then this is an activate event for the
 * window pointed to in the message field of the event. If that is the case
 * then the graf port is set to that window's graf port
 */
do_activate(event)
  EventRecord *event;
{
  WindowPtr event_window = (WindowPtr)event->message;
  WindowPeek peek = (WindowPeek)event_window;
  ControlHandle control = (ControlHandle)peek->controlList;
  long label;

  if(event_window == hello_window)
    {    if (event->modifiers & 1)
         {    SetPort(event_window);
              DisableItem(GetMHandle(EDIT_MENU), 0);
              while (control)
              {    label = GetCRefCon(control);
                   if (label == V_SCROLL || label == H_SCROLL)
                        ShowControl(control);
                   control = (*control)->nextControl;
              }
         }
         else
         {    EnableItem(GetMHandle(EDIT_MENU), 0);
              while (control)
              {    label = GetCRefCon(control);
                   if (label == V_SCROLL || label == H_SCROLL)
                        HideControl(control);
```

```
                    control = (*control)->nextControl;
              }
         }
       DrawGrowIcon(event_window);
   }
}

/* Call the window manager routines that cause a window to grow */
grow_window(window, mouse_point)
  WindowPtr window;
  Point mouse_point;
{
  long new_bounds;

  inval_grow(window);
  new_bounds = GrowWindow(window, mk_long(mouse_point), &grow_bounds);
  if (new_bounds == 0)
        return;
  SizeWindow(window, LoWord(new_bounds), HiWord(new_bounds), TRUE);
  move_bars(window);
  inval_grow(window);
  size_map(window);
}

/* Invalidate the grow icon area of a standard window */
inval_grow(window)
  WindowPtr window;
{
  Rect temp_rect, port_rect;

  port_rect = window->portRect;
  SetRect(&temp_rect, port_rect.right - 16, port_rect.bottom - 16,
        port_rect.right, port_rect.bottom);
  InvalRect(&temp_rect);
}

/* Go through the list of controls for this window, identify the
 * scroll bars, and change their position and size to conform to the
 * window's new size
 */
move_bars(window)
  WindowPtr window;
{
  WindowPeek peek = (WindowPeek)window;

  ControlHandle control = peek->controlList;
  int new_top = window->portRect.top;
  int new_left = window->portRect.left;
  int new_bottom = window->portRect.bottom;
  int new_right = window->portRect.right;
  long label;

  while (control)
    {     label = GetCRefCon(control);
          if (label == V_SCROLL)
          {     HideControl(control);
                MoveControl(control, new_right - BAR_WIDTH, new_top - 1);
                SizeControl(control, 16, new_bottom - new_top - 13);
```

```
                ShowControl(control);
        }
        else if (label == H_SCROLL)
        {       HideControl(control);
                MoveControl(control, new_left - 1, new_bottom - BAR_WIDTH);
        SizeControl(control, new_right - new_left - 13, 16);
                ShowControl(control);
        }
        control = (*control)->nextControl;
    }
}

do_menu(command)
  long command;
{
  int menu_id = HiWord(command);
  int item = LoWord(command);
  char item_name[32];

  switch(menu_id)
  {     case APPLE_MENU:
                GetItem(GetMHandle(menu_id), item, item_name);
                OpenDeskAcc(item_name);
                break;
        case FILE_MENU:
                finish();
                break;
        case EDIT_MENU:
                SystemEdit(item - 1);
                break;
        case MAP_MENU:
                switch(item)
                {       case RESOLUTION:    do_resolution(); break;
                        case MAGNIFICATION: do_magnification(); break;
                        case POSITIONING:   do_positioning(); break;
                }
  }
  HiliteMenu(0);
}

/* Is this window one of my windows? */
my_window(window)
  WindowPtr window;
{
  if (window == hello_window)
        return TRUE;
  else
        return FALSE;
}

/* Find my front-most window */
 WindowPtr
foremost_window()
{
  WindowPeek window = (WindowPeek)FrontWindow();

  while (window)
  {     if (my_window(window)) return (WindowPtr)window;
        else window = window->nextWindow;
```

```
  }
  finish();
}

draw_content(window)
  WindowPtr window;
{
  Rect clip_rect;
  RgnHandle old_clip = NewRgn();

  clip_rect = window->portRect;
  clip_rect.right -= BAR_WIDTH;
  clip_rect.bottom -= BAR_WIDTH;
  GetClip(old_clip);
  ClipRect(&clip_rect);
  plot_map(window);
  SetClip(old_clip);
  DisposeRgn(old_clip);
}

/* Make a map and return a handle to it. It is sized to fit the values for
 * enought points in the complex plane to fill the specified window at the
 * specified scale
 */
 map_handle
make_map(window, start_at, step, scale)
  WindowPtr window;
  struct cx_num *start_at;
  double step;
{
  Size size = calc_map_size(window, scale);
  map_handle new_map = (map_handle)NewHandle(size);

  (*new_map)->start_at = *start_at;
  (*new_map)->step = step;
  (*new_map)->scale = (*new_map)->view_scale = scale;
  (*new_map)->last_x = (*new_map)->last_y = 0;
  (*new_map)->x_offset = (*new_map)->y_offset = 0;
  set_dimensions(window, new_map);
  make_columns(new_map);
  return new_map;
}

 Size
calc_map_size(window, scale)
  WindowPtr window;
{
  Size size = sizeof(struct map);
  long x_size = window->portRect.right - window->portRect.left;

  size += (((x_size - BAR_WIDTH) / scale) + 1) * sizeof(Handle);
  return size;
}

/* Set the dimensions of an existing map. The scale of the map must be set
 * before calling set_dimensions.
 */
set_dimensions(window, map)
```

```
  WindowPtr window;
  map_handle map;
{
  int x_size = window->portRect.right - window->portRect.left;
  int y_size = window->portRect.bottom - window->portRect.top;

  (*map)->x_dim = ((x_size - BAR_WIDTH) / (*map)->scale) + 1;
  (*map)->y_dim = ((y_size - BAR_WIDTH) / (*map)->scale) + 1;
}

make_columns(map)
  register map_handle map;
{
  register Size column_size = (*map)->y_dim;
  register int i;

  for (i = 0; i < (*map)->x_dim; i++)
        (*map)->map_values[i] = new_column(column_size);
}

 Handle
do_new_column(column_size, tries)
  register Size column_size;
{
  register Handle new = NewHandle(column_size);
  register int i;

  if (!new)
  {     if (tries > 5) finish();
        MoreMasters();
        return new_column(column_size, tries + 1);
  }
  for (i = 0; i < column_size; i++)
        (*new)[i] = NO_VALUE;
  return new;
}

 Handle
new_column(column_size)
  register Size column_size;
{
  return do_new_column(column_size, 0);
}

size_map(window)
  WindowPtr window;
{
  map_handle map = (map_handle)GetWRefCon(window);
  int x_size = window->portRect.right - window->portRect.left;
  int y_size = window->portRect.bottom - window->portRect.top;
  int new_x_dim, new_y_dim;

  new_x_dim = ((x_size - BAR_WIDTH) / (*map)->scale) + 1 +
                              (*map)->x_offset;
  new_y_dim = ((y_size - BAR_WIDTH) / (*map)->scale) + 1 +
                              (*map)->y_offset;
  if (new_x_dim > (*map)->x_dim || new_y_dim > (*map)->y_dim)
  {     grow_map(map, new_x_dim, new_y_dim);
        (*map)->last_x = (*map)->last_y = 0;
```

```
    }
  adjust_bars(window);
}


/* Grow the map, if needed */
grow_map(map, new_x_dim, new_y_dim)
  register map_handle map;
  register int new_x_dim, new_y_dim;
{
  int x_diff = new_x_dim - (*map)->x_dim;
  int y_diff = new_y_dim - (*map)->y_dim;
  register Size old_size, new_size;
  register int x, y, new_dim;

  /* Add new columns, if needed */
  if (x_diff > 0)
  {     old_size = GetHandleSize((Handle)map);
        new_size = old_size + (x_diff * sizeof(Handle));
        SetHandleSize((Handle)map, new_size);
        new_size = y_diff > 0 ? new_y_dim : (*map)->y_dim;
        for (x = (*map)->x_dim; x < new_x_dim; x++)
        {     (*map)->map_values[x] = new_column(new_size);
              if (MemError()) finish();
        }
  }
  /* Extend existing columns, if needed */
  if (y_diff > 0)
  {     new_size = new_y_dim;
        for (x = 0; x < (*map)->x_dim; x++)
        {     SetHandleSize((*map)->map_values[x], new_size);
              if (MemError()) finish();
              for (y = (*map)->y_dim; y < new_y_dim; y++)
                   VALUE(map, x, y) = NO_VALUE;
        }
  }
  /* Store the new dimensions in the map */
  if (x_diff > 0) (*map)->x_dim = new_x_dim;
  if (y_diff > 0) (*map)->y_dim = new_y_dim;
}


/* After a window has been re-sized, some parts of the map may no longer
 * be visible. If so, the scroll bars should be enabled and set to the
 * correct range and starting value for the new window size.
 */
adjust_bars(window)
  WindowPtr window;
{
  map_handle map = (map_handle)GetWRefCon(window);
  int scale = (*map)->scale;
  int x_max = (*map)->x_dim - 1;
  int y_max = (*map)->y_dim - 1;
  int x_max_in_view = (window->portRect.right - BAR_WIDTH) / scale;
  int y_max_in_view = (window->portRect.bottom - BAR_WIDTH) / scale;
  int diff;

  if (!(*map)->x_offset && (diff = x_max - x_max_in_view) <= 0)
        turn_off_control(window, V_SCROLL);
  else init_bar(window, V_SCROLL, (*map)->x_offset, diff);
```

```c
    if (!(*map)->y_offset && (diff = y_max - y_max_in_view) <= 0)
        turn_off_control(window, H_SCROLL);
    else init_bar(window, H_SCROLL, (*map)->y_offset, diff);
}


/* Initialize the range and value of a scroll bar */
init_bar(window, id, value, range)
  WindowPtr window;
{
  ControlHandle control = lookup_control(window, id);
  map_handle map  = (map_handle)GetWRefCon(window);

  if (!range) switch_control(window, id, 255);
  else
  {     SetCtlMin(control, 0);
        SetCtlMax(control, range);
        SetCtlValue(control, value);
        switch_control(window, id, 0);
        InvalRect(&(*control)->contrlRect);
  }
}


/* Hilite a control in such a way as to show that it is inactive. Here
 * we use "255" hiliting assuming we do not want to know about mouse
 * clicks in the control.
 */
turn_off_control(window, id)
  WindowPtr window;
{
  switch_control(window, id, 255);
}


/* Find a control and hilite it - if 254 or 255 are used as values
 * of hiliting, the control is turned off.
 */
switch_control(window, id, hilite)
  WindowPtr window;
{
  ControlHandle control = lookup_control(window, id);

  HiliteControl(control, hilite);
}

 ControlHandle
lookup_control(window, id)
  WindowPtr window;
{
  ControlHandle control = ((WindowPeek)window)->controlList;
  long label;

  while (control)
  {     label = GetCRefCon(control);
        if (LoWord(label) == id) break;
        control = (*control)->nextControl;
  }
  return control;
}
```

```
/* make the assumption that resolution changes by multiples of two */
do_resolution()
{
 WindowPtr window = foremost_window();
 map_handle map = (map_handle)GetWRefCon(window);
 int new_scale = get_new_resolution(map);
 int old_scale = (*map)->scale;
 int scale_factor = old_scale / new_scale;
 int new_x_dim, new_y_dim;

 if (new_scale < old_scale)
 {      new_x_dim = (*map)->x_dim * scale_factor;
        new_y_dim = (*map)->y_dim * scale_factor;
        grow_map(map, new_x_dim, new_y_dim);
        (*map)->scale = new_scale;
        spread_data(map, scale_factor);
 }
 if (((*map)->view_scale = new_scale) != old_scale);
 {      InvalRect(&window->portRect);
        (*map)->last_x = (*map)->last_y = 0;
        (*map)->x_offset *= scale_factor;
        (*map)->y_offset *= scale_factor;
        adjust_bars(window);
 }
}


/* Ask the user for a new scale for the map. */
get_new_resolution(map)
 map_handle map;
{
 DialogPtr dialog;
 int scale = (*map)->view_scale;
 int item;

 dialog = GetNewDialog(RES_DIALOG, 0L, -1L);
 dialog_radio(dialog, scale_to_button(scale));
 while (1)
 {      ModalDialog(0L, &item);
        switch (item)
        {       case RES_D_CANCEL:
                        scale = (*map)->view_scale;         /* Fall through... */
                case RES_D_OK:
                        DisposDialog(dialog);
                        return scale;
                case RES_D_COARSE:
                        scale = COARSE;
                        dialog_radio(dialog, item);
                        continue;
                case RES_D_MEDIUM:
                        scale = MEDIUM;
                        dialog_radio(dialog, item);
                        continue;
                case RES_D_FINE:
                        scale = FINE;
                        dialog_radio(dialog, item);
                        continue;
                case RES_D_EXTRA_FINE:
                        scale = EXTRA_FILE;
```

```
                        dialog_radio(dialog, item);
                        continue;
                default:
                        continue;
        }
  }
  return (*map)->view_scale;
}


scale_to_button(scale)
{
  switch(scale)
  {     case COARSE: return RES_D_COARSE;
        case MEDIUM: return RES_D_MEDIUM;
        case FINE: return RES_D_FINE;
        case EXTRA_FINE: return RES_D_EXTRA_FINE;
  }
}


/* Given an item number for a radio button, turn that button on
 * and the other buttons off. This assumes that all the radio buttons
 * in the dialog are related.
 */
dialog_radio(dialog, item)
  DialogPtr dialog;
{
  int type, i;
  ControlHandle button;
  Rect box;
  int n_items = **(int **)((DialogPeek)dialog)->items + 2;

  for(i = 1; i < n_items; i++)
  {     GetDItem(dialog, i, &type, (Handle *)&button, &box);
        if (type == (ctrlItem | radCtrl))
                SetCtlValue(button, i == item ? 1 : 0);
  }
}


/* Take a map that has been increased in size by the specified scale
 * factor and spread the existing data out over the map
 */
spread_data(map, scale_factor)
  register map_handle map;
  register int scale_factor;
{
  register int x, y, x1, y1;
  register Handle swap_temp;
  int old_x_dim = (*map)->x_dim / scale_factor;
  int old_y_dim = (*map)->y_dim / scale_factor;

  /* First spread the data in the columns */
  for (x = 0; x < old_x_dim; x++)
  {     for (y = old_y_dim - 1, y1 = (*map)->y_dim - scale_factor; y > 0;
                        y--, y1 -= scale_factor)
        {     VALUE(map, x, y1) = VALUE(map, x, y);
              VALUE(map, x, y) = NO_VALUE;
        }
```

```
    }
    /* Then spread the columns by switching them with the new columns */
    for (x = old_x_dim - 1, x1 = (*map)->x_dim - scale_factor; x > 0;
                x--, x1 -= scale_factor)
    {     swap_temp = (*map)->map_values[x];
          (*map)->map_values[x] = (*map)->map_values[x1];
          (*map)->map_values[x1] = swap_temp;
    }

}

do_magnification()
{
}

do_positioning()
{
  DialogPtr pos_dialog;
  int item, type, got_mouse = 0;
  Rect box;
  GrafPtr save_graf;
  Point mouse_point, new_mouse_point;

  pos_dialog = GetNewDialog(POS_DIALOG, 0L, -1L);
  if (!pos_dialog) return;
  GetDItem(pos_dialog, POS_D_BOX, &type, &item, &box);
  GetPort(&save_graf);
  SetPort(pos_dialog);
  draw_pos_box(&box);
  while (1)
  {     ModalDialog((ProcPtr)0L, &item);
        switch (item)
        {     case POS_D_BOX:
                    GetMouse(&mouse_point);
                    new_position(mk_long(mouse_point), 0);
                    while(StillDown())
                    {     GetMouse(&new_mouse_point);
                          if (mk_long(mouse_point) != mk_long(new_mouse_point))
                          {     mouse_point = new_mouse_point;
                                new_position(mk_long(mouse_point), 0);
                          }
                    }
                    got_mouse = 1;
                    continue;
              case POS_D_OK:
                    if (got_mouse)
                    {     new_position(0L, 1);
                          break;
                    }
                    else continue;
              case POS_D_CANCEL:
                    SetPort(save_graf);
                    DisposDialog(pos_dialog);
                    return;
              default:
                    continue;
        }
        break;
```

```
        }
    SetPort(save_graf);
    DisposDialog(pos_dialog);
    move_map(&box, mk_long(mouse_point));
}

/* Calculate the new origin of the map from the position of a point
 * withing the box, and initialize the map.
 */
move_map(box, place)
    Rect *box;
    long place;
{
    Point point;
    int side = box->right - box->left;              /* Assume it is square */
    WindowPtr map_window = hello_window;   /* For now only one window */
    register map_handle map = (map_handle)GetWRefCon(map_window);
    struct cx_num new_origin;
    register int x, y;
    Rect content;

    point = *(Point *)&place;
    point.h = (point.h - box->left) - side / 2;
    point.v = side / 2 - (point.v - box->top);
    new_origin.real = (double)point.h / (double)50;
    new_origin.imag = (double)point.v / (double)50;
    (*map)->start_at = new_origin;
    (*map)->last_x = (*map)->last_y = 0;
    for (x = 0; x < (*map)->x_dim; x++)
    {       for (y = 0; y < (*map)->y_dim; y++)
                VALUE(map, x, y) = NO_VALUE;
    }
    content = map_window->portRect;
    content.bottom -= BAR_WIDTH;
    content.right -= BAR_WIDTH;
    InvalRect(&content);
    EraseRect(&content);
    ValidRect(&content);
}

draw_pos_box(box)
    Rect *box;
{
    int side = box->right - box->left;      /* Assume it is square */

    FrameRect(box);
    MoveTo(box->left + side / 2, box->top);
    Line(0, side - 1);
    MoveTo(box->left, box->top + side / 2);
    Line(side - 1, 0);
    MoveTo(box->left + side / 2 + 3, box->top + side / 2 + 12);
    DrawText("(0,0)", 0, 5);
    draw_map_rects(box);
}

draw_map_rects(box)
    Rect *box;
{
```

```
  Rect rect;
  double x, y;
  int side = box->right - box->left;      /* Assume it is square */
  WindowPtr window = FrontWindow();
  map_handle map;

  for(; window; window = ((WindowPeek)window)->nextWindow)
  {     if (my_window(window))
        {       map = (map_handle)GetWRefCon(window);
                x = (*map)->start_at.real;
                y = (*map)->start_at.imag;
                rect.top = (side / 2) - (int)(y * 50) + box->top;
                rect.left = (side / 2) + (int)(x * 50) + box->left;
                rect.bottom = rect.top +
                        (int)((*map)->step * (*map)->scale * (*map)->y_dim * 50);
                rect.right = rect.left +
                        (int)((*map)->step * (*map)->scale * (*map)->x_dim * 50);
                FillRect(&rect, &gray);
                FrameRect(&rect);
        }
  }
}


/* Mark the new position. The pen mode is patCopy after this routine
 * is called. If "final" is non-zero, cur_position is used as a new
 * origin for the map.
 */
new_position(where, final)
  long where;
{
  static int position_valid = 0;
  static long cur_position;

  PenMode(patXor);
  if (position_valid)
        x_marks_new_spot(cur_position);
  x_marks_new_spot(where);
  cur_position = where;
  position_valid = 1;
  PenMode(patCopy);
  if (final)
        position_valid = 0;
}

/* Draws an "+" at the specified spot in the current pen mode. So if the
 * mode is patXor, this routine can be used to erase old spots.
 */
x_marks_new_spot(spot)
  long spot;
{
  Point point;

  point = *(Point *)&spot;
  MoveTo(point.h - 2, point.v);
  Line(4, 0);
  MoveTo(point.h, point.v - 2);
  Line(0, 4);
}
```

```
/* Fill in the map. Real numbers go left to right, increasing.
 * Imaginary numbers go top to bottom, decreasing. We calculate a value
 * for a point if: 1) It has no value; 2) It would be visible at the
 * current resolution OR we have already finished calculating all the
 * visible points.
 */
fill_in_map(window)
  WindowPtr window;
{
  register map_handle map = (map_handle)GetWRefCon(window);
  register double step = (*map)->step;
  register int x = (*map)->last_x;
  register int y = (*map)->last_y;
  register int scale = (*map)->scale;
  register int scale_ratio = (*map)->view_scale / scale;
  PicHandle pict;
  struct cx_num where;

  for (; x < (*map)->x_dim; x++)
    {      for (; y < (*map)->y_dim; y++)
        {      if (VALUE(map, x, y) == NO_VALUE &&
                        (scale_ratio == 1 ||
                            !(x % scale_ratio || y % scale_ratio)))
            {       where.real = (*map)->start_at.real + (x * step * scale);
                    where.imag = (*map)->start_at.imag - (y * step * scale);
                    ((VALUE(map, x, y) = calc_value(&where)) != NO_VALUE);
                        paint_point(window, x, y);
                    (*map)->last_x = x;  (*map)->last_y = y;
                    return;

            }
        }
        y = 0;        /* Start another column */

    }
}


/* Check if a point is inside the Mandelbrot Set. If the magnitude
 * of the complex number has not exceeded 2 in 700 iterations, it is
 * most likely IN the mandelbrot set. Otherwise it lies outside and
 * the the number of iterations it took to determine this is used to
 * select a pattern for that point. We check for pending events every
 * 128 iterations.
 */
 char
calc_value(where)
  register struct cx_num *where;
{
  register double val_real, val_imag, sq_real, sq_imag;
  register int count;
  EventRecord dummy;

  val_real = val_imag = 0.0;
  for (count = 0; count < 700; count++)
    {      sq_real = val_real * val_real;
        sq_imag = val_imag * val_imag;
        if ((sq_real + sq_imag) > 4.0) break;
        if (!(count & 0x7F) && EventAvail(everyEvent, &dummy))
            return NO_VALUE;
        val_imag = (val_real * val_imag * 2.0) + where->imag;
```

```
            val_real = sq_real - sq_imag + where->real;
    }
    return which_pattern(count);
}

/* Select a pattern based on whether a point is in the Mandlebrot Set, or
 * if it lies outside, how soon was it determined to lie outside.
 */
 char
which_pattern(count)
{
    if (count >= 700) return BLACK;
    else if (count > 60) return WHITE;
    else if (count > 24) return LIGHT_GRAY;
    else if (count > 15) return GRAY;
    else return DARK_GRAY;
}

paint_point(window, x, y)
    WindowPtr window;
{
    GrafPtr save_graf;
    register map_handle map = (map_handle)GetWRefCon(window);
    register int scale = (*map)->view_scale;
    register int scale_ratio = scale / (*map)->scale;
    register int inval_x = (x - (*map)->x_offset) / scale_ratio,
            inval_y = (y - (*map)->y_offset) / scale_ratio;
    Rect rect, content;

    content = window->portRect;
    content.bottom -= BAR_WIDTH; content.right -= BAR_WIDTH;
    inval_x *= scale; inval_y *= scale;
    SetRect(&rect, inval_x, inval_y, inval_x + scale, inval_y + scale);
    if (SectRect(&rect, &content, &rect))
    {       GetPort(&save_graf);
            SetPort(window);
            InvalRect(&rect);
            plot_one(map, x, y);
            ValidRect(&rect);
            SetPort(save_graf);
    }
}


plot_map(window)
    WindowPtr window;
{
    register map_handle map = (map_handle)((WindowPeek)window)->refCon;
    register int scale_ratio = (*map)->view_scale / (*map)->scale;
    register int x, y;
    for (x = 0; x < (*map)->x_dim; x += scale_ratio)
    {       for (y = 0; y < (*map)->y_dim; y += scale_ratio)
                plot_one(map, x, y);
    }
}

/* Plot one point in the map. If clipping has not be set up for the
 * map window, a rectangle may be provided to clip an individual point
 * to.
```

```
*/
plot_one(map, x, y)
  map_handle map;
  register int x, y;
{
  register int fill_with = VALUE(map, x, y);
  register int scale = (*map)->scale;
  register int view_scale = (*map)->view_scale;
  Rect to_fill;

  x -= (*map)->x_offset; y -= (*map)->y_offset;
  x *= scale; y *= scale;
  SetRect(&to_fill, x, y, x + view_scale, y + view_scale);
  switch(fill_with)
  {     case BLACK: FillRect(&to_fill, &black); break;
        case WHITE: FillRect(&to_fill, &white); break;
        case LIGHT_GRAY: FillRect(&to_fill, &ltGray); break;
        case GRAY: FillRect(&to_fill, &gray); break;
        case DARK_GRAY: FillRect(&to_fill, &dkGray); break;
        case NO_VALUE:
            break;
  }
}

/* Exit the program cleanly */
finish()
{
  exit(0);
}
```

Extracting Information from this Listing

Example program 8-3 above is hundreds of lines long. It would be impractical to try to comprehend every corner of it without a machine-readable copy and the time to modify and play with it. The information you can extract from this listing and the one in the next chapter, which lists the final form of the example program, is code that is *analogous* to code that you are trying to write. Not every type of graphics update situation is covered here, but a representative one is. Similarly, you may find solutions to other problems in the example program's code that handles scroll bars, mouse tracking, user items in dialogs, and so on. Just as examples cannot be comprehensive, you will need to refer to examples to give substance to reference information and to fill in the spaces between available reference information.

Example code is, in general, the fastest way to learn how to work within the framework of an unfamiliar system. But to keep from picking up other people's bad habits, you should accompany your study of examples with thorough familiarity with the reference material available to Macintosh programmers.

Chapter Nine

Extending Our Grasp

In this chapter, the example program is extended to interact with external software and devices. In this chapter you will find:

- How to create files and how to write into them and read from them.
- Why the Macintosh has two file systems.
- How to print out plots on any printer attached to the Macintosh.

Completing the Application

With the ability to file, and print, the Mandelbrot mapping program becomes a complete Macintosh application. By using the framework of this example program, you can conveniently create your own applications.

The source code of our Mandelbrot set explorer has become large compared to most example programs presented in books that describe programming techniques. It is that size because it illustrates how a whole program is put together, rather than disconnected pieces that might or might not be useful together. Often it is not possible to describe programming for a machine or system with a monolithic example. Unix programs have a much more varied structure than Macintosh programs: Graphics programs have fundamentally different structure than interactive editors, which are in turn very different from simple filter programs. MS-DOS applications are even more widely varied. The user-interface standards and programming techniques are extremely diverse, and this diversity is reflected in the complete lack of user-interface standards among MS-DOS programs.

We have already discussed the impact of the lack of a standard application structure on the user, but there is an effect on programmers as well: On systems other than the Macintosh, there is no comprehensive framework in which to present programming techniques. The example program presented here can be the foundation of almost any Macintosh application. The structure is equally applicable to business applications, games, and scientific programming.

Choices for Filing

The Macintosh has two file systems: the Macintosh File System (MFS) and the Hierarchical File System (HFS). This is deplorable, but not a disaster. If your application is written correctly, it does not need to know which kind of file system it is dealing with and it can even use both at the same time.

Another source of confusion in dealing with the Macintosh file system is the two sets of file system traps. There is one set of higher-level traps that perform simple file system operations like read, write, and seek. Another set of lower-level functions replicates capabilities of the higher-level functions but with a different interface. The lower level functions accept their arguments in parameter blocks, which are data structures that contain all the items that are used as parameters and return values in all the file system (and device manager) calls. The advantage, if any, of using parameter block calls is that one parameter block can be used in many calls and that the parameter block interface is more efficient than the high-level interface because the high level interface is translated into the parameter block interface.

In extending our application to save and restore Mandelbrot set plots in disk files, we keep the filing operations as simple as possible. We use only the higher-level file system interactions supplied by Toolbox routines, and we do not implement any filing operations that have to be aware of directories.

Filing in the Example Program

This prescription for file system independence may seem simple, but many existing programs do not work correctly on HFS volumes. They may fail to find their documents, or they may fail to find system resources. All in all, there is no excuse!

Why Two File Systems?

The newer Hierarchical File System is an improvement on the original Macintosh File System in several ways. In MFS, each volume could hold only a small number of files, and the organization of the volume into folders was maintained and displayed by the Finder. So although folders could be inside folders, and the Finder diplayed a desktop organized hierarchically, the hierarchy was visible only to the Finder. From an application's point of view, there was no hierarchy at all.

When a user opens a file on an MFS volume, he or she is presented with all the files (or a selection of up to four file types) on that volume. Now that hard disks are a common Macintosh accessory, the number of files displayed in a standard file dialog could become unwieldy. Even on disk systems like the Hyperdrive that can divide a physical disk into several volumes, the number of files in a volume could become unmanageable.

Choices for Printing

There are three primary choices for printing in Macintosh applications:

1) Draft printing. Draft printing uses a "native" printing style available on the printer being used. In MacWrite, draft printing provides a quick way to print out drafts of a document without much regard for the final appearance.

2) "Spool" printing. This kind of printing is not to be confused with the usual meaning of spooling. Spool printing is not deferred, and your application cannot, in general, do anything else but print while spool printing. This kind of printing is called spool printing because infomation may be buffered on disk in the course of printing a document. Spool printing is the most complicated form of printing. It involves creating bit images in graf ports that reflect the native resolution of the printer being used. It may take several passes to fill a page.

3) Bitmap printing. Bitmap printing is a simplified version of spool printing. Bitmap printing lets an application copy a bitmap onto a printer. This kind of printing is well suited to printing Mandelbrot set plots.

Printing in Our Application

In our application we will implement bitmap printing. Bitmap printing is the quickest and easiest printing method for graphics-oriented applications. Bitmap printing would have been a bad choice for an application that uses text heavily because many printer drivers handle text specially. Spool printing would be the best choice for text.

The Last Listing

Example program 9-1 shows a complete Macintosh applivation capable of all the operations any commercial application can perform.

mandelbrot.h

```
define LIGHTSPEED
#ifdef LIGHTSPEED
#include <Quickdraw.h>
#include <WindowMgr.h>
#include <ControlMgr.h>
#include <EventMgr.h>
#include <DeskMgr.h>
#include <MenuMgr.h>
#include <ToolboxUtil.h>
```

```
#include <MemoryMgr.h>
#include <DialogMgr.h>
#include <FileMgr.h>
#include <StdFilePkg.h>
#include <PrintMgr.h>
#endif
#ifdef AZTEC
#include <quickdraw.h>
#include <window.h>
#include <control.h>
#include <event.h>
#include <desk.h>
#include <menu.h>
#include <inits.h>
#include <toolutil.h>
#include <types.h>
#include <memory.h>
#include <dialog.h>
#endif

struct cx_num          /* A complex number */
{   double real;       /* The real part */
    double imag;       /* The imaginary part */
};

struct map                          /* A map structure */
{   int modified;                   /* Is this map modified */
    char save_file[32];             /* The file to save this map in */
    int save_volume;                /* The volume refnum of the save file */
    struct cx_num start_at;         /* Complex number at top left corner */
    double step;                    /* The granularity from point to point */
    int scale;                      /* Scale at which we calculate the map */
    int view_scale;                 /* Scale at which we draw the map */
    int x_offset, y_offset;         /* The offset we begin drawing at */
    int x_dim, y_dim;               /* The dimensions of the map */
    int last_x, last_y;             /* Where we left off */
    Handle map_values[1];           /* An array  of column handles, allocated
                                       to the correct size */
};

/* Find the X'th handle, and the Y'th byte in the array referred to by
 * that handle
 */
#define VALUE(MAP, X, Y) (*(*MAP)->map_values[X])[Y]

typedef struct map **map_handle;

pascal void SysBeep() = 0xA9C8;   /* The beep trap */

pascal void up_action(), down_action();
char calc_value(), which_pattern();
Size calc_map_size();
map_handle make_map(), read_in_map();
Handle new_column();
WindowPtr make_window(), foremost_window();
ControlHandle lookup_control();

#define V_SCROLL 256    /* Resource ID of the vertical scroll bar */
#define H_SCROLL 257    /* Resource ID of the horizontal scroll bar */

#define BAR_WIDTH 15    /* The width of a scroll bar */
```

```
#define NO_VALUE 0          /* Haven't calculated the value */
#define BLACK 1             /* Corresponds to the pattern black */
#define WHITE 2             /* Corresponds to the pattern white */
#define LIGHT_GRAY 3        /* Corresponds to the pattern ltGray */
#define GRAY 4              /* Corresponds to the pattern gray */
#define DARK_GRAY 5         /* Corresponds to the pattern dkGray */

#define UP 1                /* Scrolling up? */
#define DOWN 2              /* Or down? */

#define APPLE_MENU 1        /* The menu marked by the Apple symbol */
#define FILE_MENU 256       /* The "File" menu */
#define EDIT_MENU 257       /* the "Edit" menu */
#define MAP_MENU 258        /* Controls map paramters */

/* Items on the file menu */
#define NEW 1
#define OPEN 2
#define CLOSE 3
#define SAVE 4
#define SAVE_AS 5
#define REVERT 6
#define FILE_LINE_1 7
#define PRINT 8
#define FILE_LINE_2 9
#define QUIT 10

/* Items on the map menu */
#define RESOLUTION 1
#define MAGNIFICATION 2
#define POSITIONING 3

#define RES_DIALOG 256    /* Get a new resolution for the map */

/* Buttons in the new-resolution dialog */
#define RES_D_CANCEL 1
#define RES_D_OK 2

#define RES_D_COARSE 3
#define RES_D_MEDIUM 4
#define RES_D_FINE 5
#define RES_D_EXTRA_FINE 6

#define POS_DIALOG 257    /* Start a map at a new position */

/* Items in the positioning dialog */
#define POS_D_CANCEL 1
#define POS_D_OK 2
#define POS_D_BOX 3

/* Scale values stored in maps */
#define EXTRA_FINE 1
#define FINE 2
#define MEDIUM 4
#define COARSE 8

/* Initial values */
#define INIT_REAL -0.775          /* The initial starting point */
#define INIT_IMAG 0.260           /* The initial starting point */
#define INIT_STEP 0.001           /* The initial step value */
#define INIT_SCALE MEDIUM         /* The initial scale factor */
```

```
/* Operations the count routine supports */
#define SET 1
#define GET 2
#define ADD 3

#define DRVR 0x44525652L          /* The string "DRVR" as a long */
#define STR_ 0x53545220L          /* The string "STR " as a long */
#define MNAP 0x4d4e4150L
#define MANM 0x4d4e4150L

#define SAVE_AS_PROMPT   256      /* String resource for the prompt in the
                                   * SFPutFile dialog
                                   */

#define SAVE_CANCEL      -1       /* Returned if save operation is cancelled */

#define SC_CANCEL        1
#define SC_YES           2
#define SC_NO            3

#define mk_long(x)       (*((long *)&(x)))
```

Mandelbrot.c

```
#include "mandelbrot.h"

GrafPtr w_port;
WindowRecord w_record;
WindowPtr hello_window;
Rect drag_rect, grow_bounds;
Point get_put = { 100, 100 };

int white_max = 700;    /* Above this value, assign black */
int lt_gray_max = 60;   /* Above this value, assign white */
int gray_max = 24;              /* Above this value, assign light gray */
int dk_gray_max = 15;   /* Above this value, assign gray */
                                        /* Below dk_gray_max, assign
dark gray */

main()
{
        init_process();  /* do all the initialization */
        make_window(hello_window = (WindowPtr)&w_record);
        event_loop();
}

/* Do all the right initialization things
 */
init_process()
{
        init_mgrs();
        set_parameters();
        fill_menus();
}

/* Do the right thing for most applications: Call the toolbox
 * initialization routines.
 */
init_mgrs()
{
```

```
        InitGraf(&thePort);
        InitFonts();
        InitWindows();
        FlushEvents(everyEvent, 0);
        InitCursor();
        InitMenus();
        TEInit();
        InitDialogs(0L);
        MaxApplZone();
}


/* Set parameters based on screen size, etc. */
set_parameters()
{
        drag_rect = thePort->portRect;
        SetRect(&grow_bounds, 64, 64, thePort->portRect.right,
                thePort->portRect.bottom);
}


fill_menus()
{
        MenuHandle menu;

        menu = GetMenu(APPLE_MENU);
        AddResMenu(menu, DRVR);
        InsertMenu(menu, 0);
        InsertMenu(GetMenu(FILE_MENU), 0);
        InsertMenu(GetMenu(EDIT_MENU), 0);
        InsertMenu(GetMenu(MAP_MENU), 0);
        DrawMenuBar();
}


/* Read window information from the resource branch into a window
 * structure. Get the scroll bars for this window and mark them to
 * distinguish them from any other controls that might be in this window.
 * The parameter points to an uninitialized window record
 */
 WindowPtr
make_window(new_window)
        WindowPtr new_window;
{
        ControlHandle scroll_bar;
        struct cx_num start_at;
        map_handle new_map;

        new_window = GetNewWindow(256, new_window, -1L);
        scroll_bar = GetNewControl(V_SCROLL, new_window);
        SetCRefCon(scroll_bar, (long)V_SCROLL);
        scroll_bar = GetNewControl(H_SCROLL, new_window);
        SetCRefCon(scroll_bar, (long)H_SCROLL);
        move_bars(new_window);
        start_at.real = INIT_REAL; start_at.imag = INIT_IMAG;
        new_map = make_map(new_window, &start_at, INIT_STEP, INIT_SCALE);
        SetWRefCon(new_window, (long)new_map);
        init_bar(new_window, H_SCROLL, 0, 0);
        init_bar(new_window, V_SCROLL, 0, 0);
        fill_in_map(new_window);
}


/* Get an event, switch on its type, and perform the appropriate
 * action
 */
```

```
event_loop()
{
        EventRecord my_event;
        Boolean valid;

        while (1)
        {       SystemTask();
                valid = GetNextEvent(everyEvent,&my_event);
                if (!valid)
                {       fill_in_map(hello_window);
                        continue;
                }
                switch(my_event.what)
                {       case nullEvent:
                                break;
                        case mouseDown:
                                do_mouse_down(&my_event);
                                break;
                        case mouseUp:
                        case keyDown:
                        case keyUp:
                        case autoKey:
                                break;
                        case updateEvt:
                                do_update(&my_event);
                                break;
                        case diskEvt:
                                break;
                        case activateEvt:
                                do_activate(&my_event);
                                break;
                        case networkEvt:
                        case driverEvt:
                        case app1Evt:
                        case app2Evt:
                        case app3Evt:
                        case app4Evt:
                                break;
                        default:
                                break;
                }
        }
}

/* Find out where a mouse-down event has occurred and do what ought to
 * be done for that location
 */
do_mouse_down(event)
        EventRecord *event;
{
        WindowPtr mouse_window;
        int place_type = FindWindow(mk_long(event->where), &mouse_window);

        switch(place_type)
        {       case inDesk:
                        break;
                case inMenuBar:
                        do_menu(MenuSelect(mk_long(event->where)));
                        break;
                case inSysWindow:
                        SystemClick(event, mouse_window);
                        break;
```

```
                        case inContent:
                                if (mouse_window != FrontWindow())
                                        SelectWindow(mouse_window);
                                else
                                        do_controls(mouse_window,
mk_long(event->where));
                                break;
                        case inDrag:
                                DragWindow(mouse_window, mk_long(event->where),
&drag_rect);
                                break;
                        case inGrow:
                                grow_window(mouse_window, mk_long(event->where));
                                break;
                        case inGoAway:
                                if (TrackGoAway(mouse_window, mk_long(event->where)))
                                        do_close();
                                break;
                        default:
                                break;
                }
}


/* Find which part of which control was used. Then find out how the value
 * of that control has changed. Then call one of this applications routines
 * that performs the action that reflects the change in the control. In the
 * case of the up and down buttons, TrackControl calls an action routine
 * that should show some intermediate result, like scrolling the screen
 * one line in an editor.
 */
do_controls(window, where)
        WindowPtr window;
        long where;
{
        int part_code, old_value, new_value;
        ControlHandle control;

        GlobalToLocal(&where);
        part_code = FindControl(where, window, &control);
        if (!part_code) return;
        (void)count(SET, 0);
        switch(part_code)
        {       case inUpButton:
                        TrackControl(control, where, up_action);
                        break;
                case inDownButton:
                        TrackControl(control, where, down_action);
                        break;
                case inPageUp:
                case inPageDown:
                        page_movement(window, control, part_code);
                        break;
                case inThumb:
                        old_value = GetCtlValue(control);
                        TrackControl(control, where, 0L);
                        new_value = GetCtlValue(control);
                        thumb_movement(window, control, old_value, new_value);
                default:
                        break;

        }
}
```

```
  pascal void
up_action(control, part_code)
        ControlHandle control;
{
        WindowPtr window = (*control)->controlOwner;
        int old_value = GetCtlValue(control);

        SetCtlValue(control, old_value - 1);
        if (GetCtlValue(control) == old_value) return;
        scroll_window(window, control, UP, 1);
        (void)count(ADD, 1);
}


  pascal void
down_action(control, part_code)
        ControlHandle control;
{
        WindowPtr window = (*control)->controlOwner;
        int old_value = GetCtlValue(control);

        SetCtlValue(control, old_value + 1);
        if (GetCtlValue(control) == old_value) return;
        scroll_window(window, control, DOWN, 1);
        (void)count(ADD, 1);
}

page_movement(window, control, part_code)
        WindowPtr window;
        ControlHandle control;
{
        int units = get_page_units(window, control);
        int direction = part_code == inPageUp ? UP : DOWN;
        int old_value = GetCtlValue(control);

        if (direction == DOWN)
        {       SetCtlValue(control, old_value + units);
                units = GetCtlValue(control) - old_value;
        }
        else
        {       SetCtlValue(control, old_value - units);
                units = old_value - GetCtlValue(control);
        }
        if (units) scroll_window(window, control, direction, units);
}

thumb_movement(window, control, old_value, new_value)
        WindowPtr window;
        ControlHandle control;
{
        int units = old_value - new_value;
        int direction = units < 0 ? DOWN : UP;

        if (units)
        {       units = units < 0 ? -units : units;
                scroll_window(window, control, direction, units);
        }
}

get_page_units(window, control)
        WindowPtr window;
        ControlHandle control;
{
```

```
                return 5;
        }

        /* Set up the port rectangle and clipping for the window */
        scroll_window(window, control, direction, units)
                WindowPtr window;
                ControlHandle control;
        {
                Rect content;
                static RgnHandle save_clip = (RgnHandle)0;

                content = window->portRect;
                if (!save_clip) save_clip = NewRgn();
                else SetEmptyRgn(save_clip);
                content = window->portRect;
                content.right -= BAR_WIDTH;
                content.bottom -= BAR_WIDTH;
                GetClip(save_clip);
                ClipRect(&content);
                scroll_map(window, control, direction, units, &content);
                SetClip(save_clip);
        }

        /* Scroll the contents of the window and keep track of the offset in
         * the map structure. Units are visual units.
         */
        scroll_map(window, control, direction, units, content)
                WindowPtr window;
                ControlHandle control;
                Rect *content;
        {
                map_handle map = (map_handle)GetWRefCon(window);
                int max = GetCtlMax(control);
                long bar_id = GetCRefCon(control);
                int sign = direction == UP ? 1 : -1;
                int current, n_to_scroll;
                int scale = (*map)->view_scale;
                int scale_ratio = (*map)->view_scale / (*map)->scale;
                static RgnHandle to_update = (RgnHandle)0;
                if (!to_update) to_update = NewRgn();
                else SetEmptyRgn(to_update);
                current = bar_id == V_SCROLL ? (*map)->y_offset : (*map)->x_offset;
                units *= sign;
                n_to_scroll = units * scale * scale_ratio;
                if (bar_id == V_SCROLL)
                {    ScrollRect(content, 0, n_to_scroll, to_update);
                     OffsetRgn(to_update, 0, scale * scale_ratio * count(GET, 0) * sign);
                          (*map)->y_offset -= units * scale_ratio;
                }
                else
                {    ScrollRect(content, n_to_scroll, 0, to_update);
                     OffsetRgn(to_update, scale * scale_ratio * count(GET, 0) * sign, 0);
                          (*map)->x_offset -= units * scale_ratio;
                }
                InvalRgn(to_update);
        }

        count(op, arg)
        {
                static int counter;

                switch (op)
```

```
        {   case SET: counter = arg; break;
            case ADD: counter += arg; break;
            case GET: break;
        }
        return counter;
}


/* Handle and update event - first determine if the event is in one of
 * this application's windows, and if so, update that window.
 */
do_update(event)
    EventRecord *event;
{
    GrafPtr save_graf;
    WindowPtr update_window;
    update_window = (WindowPtr)event->message;
    {   if (update_window == hello_window)
        {       GetPort(&save_graf);
                SetPort(update_window);
                BeginUpdate(update_window);
                EraseRect(&update_window->portRect);
                DrawGrowIcon(update_window);
                DrawControls(update_window);
                draw_content(update_window);
                EndUpdate(update_window);
                SetPort(save_graf);
        }
    }
}


/* If the modifiers are odd, then this is an activate event for the
 * window pointed to in the message field of the event. If that is the case
 * then the graf port is set to that window's graf port
 */
do_activate(event)
    EventRecord *event;
{
    WindowPtr event_window = (WindowPtr)event->message;
    WindowPeek peek = (WindowPeek)event_window;
    ControlHandle control = (ControlHandle)peek->controlList;
    long label;

    if(event_window == hello_window)
    {   if (event->modifiers & 1)
        {   SetPort(event_window);
            DisableItem(GetMHandle(EDIT_MENU), 0);
            while (control)
            {   label = GetCRefCon(control);
                if (label == V_SCROLL || label == H_SCROLL)
                    ShowControl(control);
                control = (*control)->nextControl;
            }
        }
        else
        {   EnableItem(GetMHandle(EDIT_MENU), 0);
            while (control)
            {   label = GetCRefCon(control);
                if (label == V_SCROLL || label == H_SCROLL)
                        HideControl(control);
                control = (*control)->nextControl;
            }
        }
```

```
                DrawGrowIcon(event_window);
        }
}

/* Call the window manager routines that cause a window to grow */
grow_window(window, mouse_point)
    WindowPtr window;
    Point mouse_point;
{
    long new_bounds;

    inval_grow(window);
    new_bounds = GrowWindow(window, mk_long(mouse_point), &grow_bounds);
    if (new_bounds == 0)
        return;
    SizeWindow(window, LoWord(new_bounds), HiWord(new_bounds), TRUE);
    move_bars(window);
    inval_grow(window);
    size_map(window);
}

/* Invalidate the grow icon area of a standard window */
inval_grow(window)
    WindowPtr window;
{
    Rect temp_rect, port_rect;

    port_rect = window->portRect;
    SetRect(&temp_rect, port_rect.right - 16, port_rect.bottom - 16,
        port_rect.right, port_rect.bottom);
    InvalRect(&temp_rect);
}

/* Go through the list of controls for this window, identify the
 * scroll bars, and change their position and size to conform to the
 * window's new size
 */
move_bars(window)
    WindowPtr window;
{
    WindowPeek peek = (WindowPeek)window;

    ControlHandle control = peek->controlList;
    int new_top = window->portRect.top;
    int new_left = window->portRect.left;
    int new_bottom = window->portRect.bottom;
    int new_right = window->portRect.right;
    long label;

    while (control)
    {   label = GetCRefCon(control);
        if (label == V_SCROLL)
        {   HideControl(control);
            MoveControl(control, new_right - BAR_WIDTH, new_top - 1);
            SizeControl(control, 16, new_bottom - new_top - 13);
            ShowControl(control);
        }
        else if (label == H_SCROLL)
        {   HideControl(control);
            MoveControl(control, new_left - 1, new_bottom - BAR_WIDTH);
            SizeControl(control, new_right - new_left - 13, 16);
            ShowControl(control);
```

```
            }
            control = (*control)->nextControl;
        }
}


do_menu(command)
    long command;
{
    int menu_id = HiWord(command);
    int item = LoWord(command);
    char item_name[32];

switch (menu_id)
{   case APPLE_MENU:
        GetItem(GetMHandle(menu_id), item, item_name);
        OpenDeskAcc(item_name);
        break;
    case FILE_MENU:
        switch (item)
        {   case NEW:              do_new(); break;
            case OPEN:             do_open(); break;
            case CLOSE:            do_close(); break;
            case SAVE:             (void)do_save(SAVE); break;
            case SAVE_AS:          (void)do_save(SAVE_AS); break;
            case REVERT:           do_revert(); break;
            case PRINT:            do_print(); break;
            case QUIT:             do_quit(); break;
        }
        break;
    case EDIT_MENU:
        SystemEdit(item - 1);
        break;
    case MAP_MENU:
        switch (item)
        {   case RESOLUTION:       do_resolution(); break;
            case MAGNIFICATION:    do_magnification(); break;
            case POSITIONING:      do_positioning(); break;

        }
    }
    HiliteMenu(0);
}


/* Is this window one of my windows? */
my_window(window)
    WindowPtr window;
{
    if (window == hello_window)
        return TRUE;
    else
        return FALSE;
}


/* Find my front-most window */
 WindowPtr
foremost_window()
{
    WindowPeek window = (WindowPeek)FrontWindow();

    while (window)
    {   if (my_window(window)) return (WindowPtr)window;
        else window = window->nextWindow;
```

```
    }
    return (WindowPtr) window;
}

draw_content(window)
    WindowPtr window;
{
    Rect clip_rect;
    RgnHandle old_clip = NewRgn();

    clip_rect = window->portRect;
    clip_rect.right -= BAR_WIDTH;
    clip_rect.bottom -= BAR_WIDTH;
    GetClip(old_clip);
    ClipRect(&clip_rect);
    plot_map(window);
    SetClip(old_clip);
    DisposeRgn(old_clip);
}

/* Make a map and return a handle to it. It is sized to fit the values for
 * enough  points in the complex plane to fill the specified window at the
 * specified scale
 */
 map_handle
make_map(window, start_at, step, scale)
    WindowPtr window;
    struct cx_num *start_at;
    double step;
{
    Size size = calc_map_size(window, scale);
    map_handle new_map = (map_handle)NewHandle(size);

    (*new_map)->start_at = *start_at;
    (*new_map)->step = step;
    (*new_map)->scale = (*new_map)->view_scale = scale;
    (*new_map)->last_x = (*new_map)->last_y = 0;
    (*new_map)->x_offset = (*new_map)->y_offset = 0;
    (*new_map)->save_file[0] = 0;
    set_dimensions(window, new_map);
    make_columns(new_map);
    return new_map;
}

 Size
calc_map_size(window, scale)
    WindowPtr window;
{
    Size size = sizeof(struct map);
    long x_size = window->portRect.right - window->portRect.left;

    size += (((x_size - BAR_WIDTH) / scale) + 1) * sizeof(Handle);
    return size;
}

/* Set the dimensions of an existing map. The scale of the map must be set
 * before calling set_dimensions.
 */
set_dimensions(window, map)
    WindowPtr window;
    map_handle map;
{
```

```
        int x_size = window->portRect.right - window->portRect.left;
        int y_size = window->portRect.bottom - window->portRect.top;

        (*map)->x_dim = ((x_size - BAR_WIDTH) / (*map)->scale) + 1;
        (*map)->y_dim = ((y_size - BAR_WIDTH) / (*map)->scale) + 1;
}

make_columns(map)
        register map_handle map;
{
        register Size column_size = (*map)->y_dim;
        register int i;

        for (i = 0; i < (*map)->x_dim; i++)
                (*map)->map_values[i] = new_column(column_size);
}

 Handle
do_new_column(column_size, tries)
        register Size column_size;
{
        register Handle new = NewHandle(column_size);
        register int i;

        if (!new)
        {    if (tries > 5) finish();
             MoreMasters();
             return new_column(column_size, tries + 1);
        }
        for (i = 0; i < column_size; i++)
                (*new)[i] = NO_VALUE;
        return new;
}

 Handle
new_column(column_size)
        register Size column_size;
{
        return do_new_column(column_size, 0);
}

size_map(window)
        WindowPtr window;
{
        map_handle map = (map_handle)GetWRefCon(window);
        int x_size = window->portRect.right - window->portRect.left;
        int y_size = window->portRect.bottom - window->portRect.top;
        int new_x_dim, new_y_dim;

        new_x_dim = ((x_size - BAR_WIDTH) / (*map)->scale) + 1 +
                        (*map)->x_offset;
        new_y_dim = ((y_size - BAR_WIDTH) / (*map)->scale) + 1 +
                        (*map)->y_offset;
            if (new_x_dim > (*map)->x_dim || new_y_dim > (*map)->y_dim)
            {   grow_map(map, new_x_dim, new_y_dim);
                (*map)->last_x = (*map)->last_y = 0;
            }
            adjust_bars(window);
}

/* Grow the map, if needed */
grow_map(map, new_x_dim, new_y_dim)
```

```
        register map_handle map;
        register int new_x_dim, new_y_dim;
{
        int x_diff = new_x_dim - (*map)->x_dim;
        int y_diff = new_y_dim - (*map)->y_dim;
        register Size old_size, new_size;
        register int x, y, new_dim;

        /* Add new columns, if needed */
        if (x_diff > 0)
        {   old_size = GetHandleSize((Handle)map);
            new_size = old_size + (x_diff * sizeof(Handle));
            SetHandleSize((Handle)map, new_size);
            new_size = y_diff > 0 ? new_y_dim : (*map)->y_dim;
            for (x = (*map)->x_dim; x < new_x_dim; x++)
            {       (*map)->map_values[x] = new_column(new_size);
                    if (MemError()) finish();
            }
        }
        /* Extend existing columns, if needed */
        if (y_diff > 0)
        {   new_size = new_y_dim;
            for (x = 0; x < (*map)->x_dim; x++)
            {   SetHandleSize((*map)->map_values[x], new_size);
                if (MemError()) finish();
                for (y = (*map)->y_dim; y < new_y_dim; y++)
                    VALUE(map, x, y) = NO_VALUE;
            }
        }
        /* Store the new dimensions in the map */
        if (x_diff > 0) (*map)->x_dim = new_x_dim;
        if (y_diff > 0) (*map)->y_dim = new_y_dim;
}


/* After a window has been re-sized, some parts of the map may no longer
 * be visible. If so, the scroll bars should be enabled and set to the
 * correct range and starting value for the new window size.
 */
adjust_bars(window)
        WindowPtr window;
{
        map_handle map = (map_handle)GetWRefCon(window);
        int scale_ratio = (*map)->view_scale / (*map)->scale;
        int x_max = (*map)->x_dim - 1, y_max = (*map)->y_dim - 1;
        int x_max_in_view = (window->portRect.right - BAR_WIDTH) /
            (*map)->scale;
        int y_max_in_view = (window->portRect.bottom - BAR_WIDTH) /
            (*map)->scale;
        int diff;

        /* If the scale has changed, the offset is bumped down to the next
         * lower multiple of the new scale ratio.
         */
        (*map)->x_offset -= (*map)->x_offset % scale_ratio;
        (*map)->y_offset -= (*map)->y_offset % scale_ratio;
        if (!(*map)->x_offset &&
                (diff = ((*map)->x_dim - x_max_in_view) / scale_ratio) - 1
                    <= 0)
            turn_off_control(window, H_SCROLL);
        else init_bar(window, H_SCROLL, (*map)->x_offset / scale_ratio, diff);
        if (!(*map)->y_offset &&
                (diff = ((*map)->y_dim - y_max_in_view) / scale_ratio) - 1
```

```
                      <= 0)
          turn_off_control(window, V_SCROLL);
     else init_bar(window, V_SCROLL, (*map)->y_offset / scale_ratio, diff);
}


/* Initialize the range and value of a scroll bar */
init_bar(window, id, value, range)
     WindowPtr window;
{
     ControlHandle control = lookup_control(window, id);
     map_handle map  = (map_handle)GetWRefCon(window);

     if (!range) switch_control(window, id, 255);
     else
     {   SetCtlMin(control, 0);
         SetCtlMax(control, range);
         SetCtlValue(control, value);
         switch_control(window, id, 0);
         InvalRect(&(*control)->contrlRect);
     }
}


/* Hilite a control in such a way as to show that it is inactive. Here
 * we use "255" hiliting assuming we do not want to know about mouse
 * clicks in the control.
 */
turn_off_control(window, id)
     WindowPtr window;
{
     switch_control(window, id, 255);
}


/* Find a control and hilite it - if 254 or 255 are used as values
 * of hiliting, the control is turned off.
 */
switch_control(window, id, hilite)
     WindowPtr window;
{
     ControlHandle control = lookup_control(window, id);

     HiliteControl(control, hilite);
}


 ControlHandle
lookup_control(window, id)
     WindowPtr window;
{
     ControlHandle control = ((WindowPeek)window)->controlList;
     long label;

     while (control)
     {   label = GetCRefCon(control);
         if (LoWord(label) == id) break;
         control = (*control)->nextControl;
     }
     return control;
}


/* Make the assumption that resolution changes by multiples of two */
do_resolution()
{
```

```
    WindowPtr window = foremost_window();
    map_handle map = (map_handle)GetWRefCon(window);
    int new_scale = get_new_resolution(map);
    int old_scale = (*map)->scale;
    int scale_factor = old_scale / new_scale;
    int new_x_dim, new_y_dim;

    if (new_scale < old_scale)
    {   new_x_dim = (*map)->x_dim * scale_factor;
        new_y_dim = (*map)->y_dim * scale_factor;
        grow_map(map, new_x_dim, new_y_dim);
        (*map)->scale = new_scale;
        spread_data(map, scale_factor);
    }
    if (((*map)->view_scale = new_scale) != old_scale);
    {   InvalRect(&window->portRect);
        (*map)->last_x = (*map)->last_y = 0;
        (*map)->x_offset *= scale_factor;
        (*map)->y_offset *= scale_factor;
        adjust_bars(window);
    }
}


/* Ask the user for a new scale for the map */
get_new_resolution(map)
        map_handle map;
{
        DialogPtr dialog;
        int scale = (*map)->view_scale;
        int item;

        dialog = GetNewDialog(RES_DIALOG, 0L, -1L);
        dialog_radio(dialog, scale_to_button(scale));
        while (1)
        {   ModalDialog(0L, &item);
            switch (item)
            {   case RES_D_CANCEL:
                    scale = (*map)->view_scale;   /* Fall through... */
                case RES_D_OK:
                    DisposDialog(dialog);
                    return scale;
                case RES_D_COARSE:
                    scale = COARSE;
                    dialog_radio(dialog, item);
                    continue;
                case RES_D_MEDIUM:
                    scale = MEDIUM;
                    dialog_radio(dialog, item);
                    continue;
                case RES_D_FINE:
                    scale = FINE;
                    dialog_radio(dialog, item);
                    continue;
                case RES_D_EXTRA_FINE:
                    scale = EXTRA_FINE;
                    dialog_radio(dialog, item);
                    continue;
                default:
                    continue;
            }
        }
        (*map)->modified = 1;
```

```
        return (*map)->view_scale;
}


scale_to_button(scale)
{
    switch(scale)
    {   case COARSE: return RES_D_COARSE;
        case MEDIUM: return RES_D_MEDIUM;
        case FINE: return RES_D_FINE;
        case EXTRA_FINE: return RES_D_EXTRA_FINE;
    }
}


/* Given an item number for a radio button, turn that button on
 * and the other buttons off. This assumes that all the radio buttons
 * in the dialog are related.
 */
dialog_radio(dialog, item)
    DialogPtr dialog;
{
    int type, i;
    ControlHandle button;
    Rect box;
    int n_items = **(int **)((DialogPeek)dialog)->items + 2;

    for(i = 1; i < n_items; i++)
    {   GetDItem(dialog, i, &type, (Handle *)&button, &box);
        if (type == (ctrlItem | radCtrl))
            SetCtlValue(button, i == item ? 1 : 0);
    }
}


/* Take a map that has been increased in size by the specified scale
 * factor and spread the existing data out over the map
 */
spread_data(map, scale_factor)
    register map_handle map;
    register int scale_factor;
{
    register int x, y, x1, y1;
    register Handle swap_temp;
    int old_x_dim = (*map)->x_dim / scale_factor;
    int old_y_dim = (*map)->y_dim / scale_factor;

    /* First spread the data in the columns */
    for (x = 0; x < old_x_dim; x++)
    {   for (y = old_y_dim - 1, y1 = (*map)->y_dim - scale_factor; y > 0;
                 y--, y1 -= scale_factor)
        {   VALUE(map, x, y1) = VALUE(map, x, y);
            VALUE(map, x, y) = NO_VALUE;
        }
    }
    /* Then spread the columns by switching them with the new columns */
    for (x = old_x_dim - 1, x1 = (*map)->x_dim - scale_factor; x > 0;
            x--, x1 -= scale_factor)
    {   swap_temp = (*map)->map_values[x];
        (*map)->map_values[x] = (*map)->map_values[x1];
        (*map)->map_values[x1] = swap_temp;
    }

}
```

```
/* How do you think magnification should be controlled?
 * Put your code here:
 */
do_magnification()
{
        return;
}


/* This routine gets a new starting position for the map. */
do_positioning()
{
    DialogPtr pos_dialog;
    int item, type, got_mouse = 0;
    Handle box_item;
    Rect box;
    GrafPtr save_graf;
    Point mouse_point, new_mouse_point;

    pos_dialog = GetNewDialog(POS_DIALOG, 0L, -1L);
    if (!pos_dialog) return;
    GetDItem(pos_dialog, POS_D_BOX, &type, &box_item, &box);
    GetPort(&save_graf);
    SetPort(pos_dialog);
    draw_pos_box(&box);
    while (1)
    {   ModalDialog((ProcPtr)0L, &item);
        switch (item)
        {   case POS_D_BOX:
                GetMouse(&mouse_point);
                new_position(mk_long(mouse_point), 0);
                while(StillDown())
                {   GetMouse(&new_mouse_point);
                    if (mk_long(mouse_point) != mk_long(new_mouse_point))
                    {   mouse_point = new_mouse_point;
                        new_position(mk_long(mouse_point), 0);
                    }
                }
                got_mouse = 1;
                continue;
            case POS_D_OK:
                if (got_mouse)
                {   new_position(0L, 1);
                    break;
                }
                else continue;
            case POS_D_CANCEL:
                SetPort(save_graf);
                DisposDialog(pos_dialog);
                return;
            default:
                continue;
        }
        break;
    }
    SetPort(save_graf);
    DisposDialog(pos_dialog);
    move_map(&box, mk_long(mouse_point));
}

/* Calculate the new origin of the map from the position of a point
 * within the box, and initialize the map.
 */
```

```
move_map(box, place)
    Rect *box;
    long place;
{
    Point point;
    int side = box->right - box->left;              /* Assume it is square */
    WindowPtr window = hello_window;                /* For now only one window */
    register map_handle map = (map_handle)GetWRefCon(window);
    struct cx_num new_origin;
    register int x, y;
    Rect content;

    point = *(Point *)&place;
    point.h = (point.h - box->left) - side / 2;
    point.v = side / 2 - (point.v - box->top);
    new_origin.real = (double)point.h / (double)50;
    new_origin.imag = (double)point.v / (double)50;
    (*map)->start_at = new_origin;
    (*map)->last_x = (*map)->last_y = 0;
    (*map)->x_offset = (*map)->y_offset = 0;
    for (x = 0; x < (*map)->x_dim; x++)
    {   for (y = 0; y < (*map)->y_dim; y++)
            VALUE(map, x, y) = NO_VALUE;
    }
    content = window->portRect;
    content.bottom -= BAR_WIDTH;
    content.right -= BAR_WIDTH;
    InvalRect(&content);
    EraseRect(&content);
    ValidRect(&content);
    adjust_bars(window);
}

/* A support routine for the positioning dialog. Here we draw our current
 * position.
 */
draw_pos_box(box)
    Rect *box;
{
    int side = box->right - box->left;    /* Assume it is square */

    FrameRect(box);
    MoveTo(box->left + side / 2, box->top);
    Line(0, side - 1);
    MoveTo(box->left, box->top + side / 2);
    Line(side - 1, 0);
    MoveTo(box->left + side / 2 + 3, box->top + side / 2 + 12);
    DrawText("(0,0)", 0, 5);
    draw_map_rects(box);
}

/* Draw a scaled-down box showing our current map's position in the larger
 * scheme of things
 */
draw_map_rects(box)
    Rect *box;
{
    Rect rect;
    double x, y;
    int side = box->right - box->left;    /* Assume it is square */
    WindowPtr window = FrontWindow();
    map_handle map;
```

```
     for(; window; window = (WindowPtr)((WindowPeek)window)->nextWindow)
     {   if (my_window(window))
         {   map = (map_handle)GetWRefCon(window);
             x = (*map)->start_at.real;
             y = (*map)->start_at.imag;
             rect.top = (side / 2) - (int)(y * 50) + box->top;
             rect.left = (side / 2) + (int)(x * 50) + box->left;
             rect.bottom = rect.top +
                    (int)((*map)->step * (*map)->scale * (*map)->y_dim * 50);
             rect.right = rect.left +
                    (int)((*map)->step * (*map)->scale * (*map)->x_dim * 50);
             FillRect(&rect, gray);
             FrameRect(&rect);
         }
     }
}

/* Mark the new position. The pen mode is patCopy after this routine
 * is called. If "final" is non-zero, cur_position is used as a new
 * origin for the map.
 */
new_position(where, final)
    long where;
{
    static int position_valid = 0;
    static long cur_position;

    PenMode(patXor);
    if (position_valid)
        x_marks_new_spot(cur_position);
    x_marks_new_spot(where);
    cur_position = where;
    position_valid = 1;
    PenMode(patCopy);
    if (final)
        position_valid = 0;
}

/* Draws an "+" at the specified spot in the current pen mode. So if the
 * mode is patXor, this routine can be used to erase old spots.
 */
x_marks_new_spot(spot)
    long spot;
{
    Point point;

    point = *(Point *)&spot;
    MoveTo(point.h - 2, point.v);
    Line(4, 0);
    MoveTo(point.h, point.v - 2);
    Line(0, 4);
}

/* Fill in the map. Real numbers go left to right, increasing.
 * Imaginary numbers go top to bottom, decreasing. We calculate a value
 * for a point if: 1) It has no value; 2) It would be visible at the
 * current resolution OR we have already finished calculating all the
 * visible points.
 */
fill_in_map(window)
    WindowPtr window;
{
```

```
        register map_handle map;
        register double step;
        register int x, y, scale, scale_ratio;
        PicHandle pict;
        struct cx_num where;

        if (!window) return;
        map = (map_handle)GetWRefCon(window);
        step = (*map)->step;
        x = (*map)->last_x; y = (*map)->last_y;
        scale = (*map)->scale;
        scale_ratio = (*map)->view_scale / scale;
        for (; x < (*map)->x_dim; x++)
        {   for (; y < (*map)->y_dim; y++)
            {       if (VALUE(map, x, y) == NO_VALUE &&
                        (scale_ratio == 1 ||
                            !(x % scale_ratio || y % scale_ratio)))
                {   where.real = (*map)->start_at.real + (x * step * scale);
                    where.imag = (*map)->start_at.imag - (y * step * scale);
                    if ((VALUE(map, x, y) = calc_value(&where)) != NO_VALUE)
                    {   paint_point(window, x, y);
                        (*map)->last_x = x;  (*map)->last_y = y;
                        (*map)->modified;
                    }
                    else return;
                }
            }
            y = 0;   /* Start another column */
        }
}

/* Check if a point is inside the Mandelbrot Set. If the magnitude
 * of the complex number has not exceeded 2 in "white_max" iterations,
 * it is likely IN the mandelbrot set. Otherwise it lies outside and
 * the the number of iterations it took to determine this is used to
 * select a pattern for that point. We check for pending events every
 * 128 iterations.
 */
char
calc_value(where)
    register struct cx_num *where;
{
    register double val_real, val_imag, sq_real, sq_imag;
    register int count;
    EventRecord dummy;

    val_real = val_imag = 0.0;
    for (count = 0; count <= white_max; count++)
    {   sq_real = val_real * val_real;
        sq_imag = val_imag * val_imag;
        if ((sq_real + sq_imag) > 4.0) break;
        if (!(count & 0x7F) && EventAvail(everyEvent, &dummy))
            return NO_VALUE;
        val_imag = (val_real * val_imag * 2.0) + where->imag;
        val_real = sq_real - sq_imag + where->real;
    }
    return which_pattern(count);
}

/* Select a pattern based on whether a point is in the Mandlebrot Set, or
 * if it lies outside, how soon was it determined to lie outside.
 */
```

```
        char
which_pattern(count)
{
        if (count > white_max) return BLACK;
        else if (count > lt_gray_max) return WHITE;
        else if (count > gray_max) return LIGHT_GRAY;
        else if (count > dk_gray_max) return GRAY;
        else return DARK_GRAY;
}


paint_point(window, x, y)
        WindowPtr window;
{
        GrafPtr save_graf;
        register map_handle map = (map_handle)GetWRefCon(window);
        register int scale = (*map)->view_scale;
        register int scale_ratio = scale / (*map)->scale;
        register int inval_x = (x - (*map)->x_offset) / scale_ratio,
                inval_y = (y - (*map)->y_offset) / scale_ratio;
        Rect rect, content;

        content = window->portRect;
        content.bottom -= BAR_WIDTH; content.right -= BAR_WIDTH;
        inval_x *= scale; inval_y *= scale;
        SetRect(&rect, inval_x, inval_y, inval_x + scale, inval_y + scale);
            if (SectRect(&rect, &content, &rect))
                {           GetPort(&save_graf);
                            SetPort(window);
                            InvalRect(&rect);
                            BeginUpdate(window);
                            plot_one(map, x, y);
                            EndUpdate(window);
                            SetPort(save_graf);
                }
}


plot_map(window)
        WindowPtr window;
{
        register map_handle map = (map_handle)((WindowPeek)window)->refCon;
        register int scale_ratio = (*map)->view_scale / (*map)->scale;
        register int x, y;
        for (x = 0; x < (*map)->x_dim; x += scale_ratio)
        {   for (y = 0; y < (*map)->y_dim; y += scale_ratio)
                    plot_one(map, x, y);
        }
}

/* Plot one point in the map. If clipping has not be set up for the
 * map window, a rectangle may be provided to clip an individual point
 * to.
 */
plot_one(map, x, y)
        map_handle map;
        register int x, y;
{
        register int fill_with = VALUE(map, x, y);
        register int scale = (*map)->scale;
        register int view_scale = (*map)->view_scale;
        Rect to_fill;

        x -= (*map)->x_offset; y -= (*map)->y_offset;
```

```
        x *= scale; y *= scale;
        SetRect(&to_fill, x, y, x + view_scale, y + view_scale);
        switch(fill_with)
        {   case BLACK: FillRect(&to_fill, black); break;
            case WHITE: FillRect(&to_fill, white); break;
            case LIGHT_GRAY: FillRect(&to_fill, ltGray); break;
            case GRAY: FillRect(&to_fill, gray); break;
            case DARK_GRAY: FillRect(&to_fill, dkGray); break;
            case NO_VALUE:
                break;
        }
}


/* Exit the program cleanly */
finish()
{
    ExitToShell();
}
```

file_menu.c

```
#include "mandelbrot.h"

extern WindowPtr hello_window;
extern WindowRecord w_record;
extern Point get_put;

do_new()
{
        if (hello_window) return;
        make_window(hello_window = (WindowPtr)&w_record);
}

do_open()
{
        register WindowPtr window = (WindowPtr)&w_record;
        register map_handle map;
        register OSErr error = noErr;
        register ControlHandle scroll_bar;
        int file_refnum;
        SFReply reply;
        SFTypeList types;

        if (hello_window) return;
        types[0] = MANM;
        SFGetFile(mk_long(get_put), 0L, 0L, 1, types, 0L, &reply);
        if (!reply.good) return;
        if (error = FSOpen(reply.fName, reply.vRefNum, &file_refnum))
                return;
        if (!(map = read_in_map(file_refnum))) return;
        if (error = FSClose(file_refnum)) return;
        (*map)->save_volume = reply.vRefNum;
        SetWRefCon(window, (long)map);
        ShowWindow(window);
        move_bars(window);
        adjust_bars(window);
        InvalRect(&window->portRect);
        hello_window = window;
```

```
/* Read in the map header structure first to determine how many columns
 * of map data there are and how long those columns are.
 */
map_handle
read_in_map(file_refnum)
{
        map_handle map = (map_handle)NewHandle((Size)sizeof(struct map));
        Size size = sizeof(struct map);
        register Handle column;
        register int x;
        OSErr error = noErr;

        if (!map) return (map_handle)0L;
        HLock(map);
        error = FSRead(file_refnum, &size, *map);
        HUnlock(map);
        if (error) return (map_handle)0L;
        SetHandleSize(map,
                sizeof(struct map) + ((*map)->x_dim * sizeof(Handle)));
        size = (*map)->y_dim;
        for (x = 0; x < (*map)->x_dim; x++)
        {       column = NewHandle((Size)(*map)->y_dim);
                if (!column) return (map_handle)0L;
                HLock(column);
                error = FSRead(file_refnum, &size, *column);
                HUnlock(column);
                (*map)->map_values[x] = column;
        }
        (*map)->last_x = (*map)->last_y = 0;
        (*map)->x_offset = (*map)->y_offset = 0;
        return map;
}


/* Close windows: If the window is a DA's, close the DA, otherwise
 * check if the map has been saved, and close the map window.
 */
do_close()
{
        WindowPeek front_window = (WindowPeek)FrontWindow();
        map_handle map;

        if (!front_window) return;
        if (!my_window(front_window))
        {       CloseDeskAcc(front_window->windowKind);
                return;
        }
        map = (map_handle)GetWRefCon(front_window);
        if ((*map)->modified)
        {       switch (save_check())
                {       case SC_CANCEL: return;
                        case SC_YES:    if (do_save(SAVE) == SAVE_CANCEL)
return;
                        case SC_NO:                     break;
                }
        }
        HideWindow(front_window);
        hello_window = 0L;
        free_map(map);
}


/* Loops through the columns of the map, disposing of the handles to the
 * columns, then disposes of the map structure's handle.
```

```
        */
free_map(map)
        register map_handle map;
{
        register int x;

        for (x = 0; x < (*map)->x_dim; x++)
                DisposHandle((*map)->map_values[x]);
        DisposHandle(map);
}

save_check()
{
        return CautionAlert(256, 0L);
}

do_save(save_type)
{
        WindowPtr window = foremost_window();
        SFReply reply;
        OSErr error;
        map_handle map;
        int file_refnum;
        static char **prompt = 0L;

        if (!window) return SAVE_CANCEL;
        map = (map_handle)GetWRefCon(window);
        if (!(*map)->save_file[0] || save_type == SAVE_AS)
        {       if (!prompt) prompt = GetResource(STR_, SAVE_AS_PROMPT);
                SFPutFile(mk_long(get_put), *prompt, (*map)->save_file, 0L,
                        &reply);
                if (!reply.good) return SAVE_CANCEL;
                error = FSOpen(reply.fName, reply.vRefNum, &file_refnum);
                if (error == fnfErr)
                {       error = Create(reply.fName, reply.vRefNum, MNAP, MANM);
                        if (error) goto save_error;
                        error = FSOpen(reply.fName, reply.vRefNum,
&file_refnum);
                        if (error) goto save_error;
                }
                else if (error) goto save_error;
                pstring_assign((*map)->save_file, reply.fName);
                store_map(map, file_refnum);
                if (error = FSClose(file_refnum)) goto save_error;
        }
        else
        {       error = FSOpen((*map)->save_file, (*map)->save_volume,
                        &file_refnum);
                if (error == fnfErr)
                {       error = Create((*map)->save_file, (*map)->save_volume,
                                MNAP, MANM);
                        if (error) goto save_error;
                        error = FSOpen((*map)->save_file, (*map)->save_volume,
                                &file_refnum);
                        if (error) goto save_error;
                }
                else if (error) goto save_error;
                store_map(map, file_refnum);
                if (error = FSClose(file_refnum)) goto save_error;
        }
        return 0;
save_error:
```

```
                (*map)->save_file[0] = 0;
                SysBeep(10);
                return SAVE_CANCEL;
        }


/* Copy the second pascal string argument into the first */
pstring_assign(to, from)
                char *to, *from;
{
                char *end = from + *from + 1;

                for (*to++ = *from++; from < end;)
                        *to++ = *from++;
}


/* Write the map structure and handles to columns in one write, and then
 * loop through the columns, writing each out. Here the handles are locked
 * because the FSWrite call expects a pointer.
 */
store_map(map, file_refnum)
                register map_handle map;
{
                long size = sizeof(struct map);
                OSErr error = noErr;
                register int x;

                HLock(map);
                if (error = FSWrite(file_refnum, &size, *map)) goto no_write;
                HUnlock(map);
                for (x = 0, size = (*map)->y_dim; x < (*map)->x_dim; x++)
                {       HLock((*map)->map_values[x]);
                        error = FSWrite(file_refnum, &size, *((*map)->map_values[x]));
                        if (error) goto no_write;
                        HUnlock((*map)->map_values[x]);
                }
                (*map)->modified = 0;
                return;
 no_write:
                SysBeep(5);
                return;
}


do_print()
{
                WindowPtr window = hello_window;
                THPrint print_record;
                TPPrPort port_ptr;

                if (!window) return;
                PrDrvrOpen();
                PrintDefault(&print_record);
                (void)PrValidate(&print_record);
                PrCtlCall(iPrDevCtl, lPrReset, 0L, 0L);
                port_ptr = PrOpenDoc(&print_record, 0L, 0L);
                PrOpenPage(port_ptr, 0L);
                PrCtlCall(iPrBitsCtl, &window->portBits, &window->portRect,
                        lPaintBits);
                PrClosePage(port_ptr);
                PrCloseDoc(port_ptr);
                PrDrvrClose();
}
```

```
do_revert()
{
}

/* Quit, check if the map has been saved */
do_quit()
{
        int sc_reply;
        WindowPtr map_window = foremost_window();
        map_handle map;

        if (!map_window) finish();
        map = (map_handle) GetWRefCon(map_window);
        if (!(*map)->modified) finish();
        if ((sc_reply = save_check()) == SC_YES)
        {        if (do_save(SAVE) == SAVE_CANCEL) return;
        }
        else if (sc_reply == SC_CANCEL) return;
        else finish();
```

Mandelbrot. r

```
* Resource compiler file for the Mandelbrot set mapper
Mandelbrot.rsrc
RSRCRCMP

Type WIND
  ,256(36)
  Mandelbrot Map
  45 128 296 384
  Visible GoAway
  0
  0

* Scroll bars have rectangles chosen to fit properly in the above window
Type CNTL
  ,256
  vertical scroll bar
  -1 241 157 257
  Visible
  16
  0
  0 50 0

  ,257
  horizontal scroll bar
  156 -1 172 242
  Visible
  16
  0
  0 50 0

Type MENU
  ,1
  \14

  ,256
  File
```

```
      New
      Open...
      Close
      Save
      Save As...
      Revert
      (-
      Print
      (-
      Quit

  ,257
  Edit
    Undo
    (-
    (Cut
    Copy
    Paste
    Clear

  ,258
  Map
    Resolution...
    Magnification...
    Positioning...

Type DLOG
  ,256
  No title
  100 181 220 331
  Visible NoGoAway
  3
  0
  256


Type DITL
  ,256
  6

  button
  90 60 115 140
Cancel

  button
  90 10 115 50
OK

  radioButton
  5 10 25 140
Coarse

  radioButton
  25 10 45 140
Medium

  radioButton
  45 10 65 140
Fine
```

```
   radioButton
   65 10 85 140
Extra Fine


Type DLOG
   ,257
   No title
   30 120 240 392
   Visible NoGoAway
   3
   0
   257


Type DITL
   ,257
   3

   button
   110 210 135 267
Cancel

   button
   75 210 100 250
OK

   userItem
   5 5 205 205

Type STR
   ,256
Save as:

Type ALRT
   ,256
   100 100 250 400
   258
   5555

type DITL
   ,258
   4
   Button
   115 5 141 95
Cancel

   Button
   115 105 141 195
Yes

   Button
   115 205 141 295
No

   StatText Enabled
   15 90 47 250
Save before closing?
```

Chapter Ten

Debugging

This chapter covers the topic of debugging in general, and debugging Macintosh programs in specific. You will find:

- What you need to know about debugging.
- What kind of debuggers are available.
- How debuggers are used in general.
- A list of Macintosh error numbers.
- Which are the most common bugs in Macintosh programs.
- How to create and execute a test plan.

How to Prepare for Debugging

Debugging is the most intellectually demanding part of programming. It is also the most difficult to teach. Many software engineering curriculums leave out debugging, or slight it in favor of techniques that help to get programs working correctly in the first place. If it has not happened to you already, you will realize that debugging skill is the most important skill involved in getting programs done in a short amount of time.

While debugging is learned through experience, there are some things you can do to prepare yourself for your first experiences debugging Macintosh programs. You ought to be familiar with the 68000 instruction set. The chapter in this book on Macintosh hardware provides a brief overview. You do not need to have written 68000 assembly-language code in order to read it; keep a 68000 reference manual handy. When you encounter an instruction you don't know about, look it up. You should also familiarize yourself with your compiler's conventions for global variable access, parameter passing, and register use.

Common conventions followed by Macintosh programming languages and in assembly-language programming are as follows: The register a7 is used to point to the top of the stack. The stack grows from higher to lower addresses. The global data area of your program is pointed to by the a5 register. The link instruction is used in conjunction with register a6 to build stack frames. Familiarity with these conventions will enable you to find global variables, examine the stack, and better figure out what piece of C source code corresponds to the machine code you are tracing. Your compiler's manual should describe any other conventions used in code generation by that compiler.

This chapter covers debugging on the Macintosh and covers some of the specific characteristics of Macintosh debugging. It also covers some general principles of debugging and the tools you will have at hand. If you do not already have a debugger, get one! It will be your most valuable tool.

Two Major Macintosh Debuggers

There are two major Macintosh debuggers: MacDB, and TMON. The most significant difference between the two of them is the number of Macintoshes it takes to debug a program.

MacDB is split between two Macintoshes: One Macintosh runs the program being debugged along with a debugging *nub* that can set breakpoints and capture system errors and do some other low-level debugging chores. The user interface for MacDB runs on another Macintosh. The two Macintoshes are connected via a cable between the two machines' serial ports. By sending commands through this cable, the debugger's user interface controls the nub in the machine running the program being debugged.

The advantage of this approach is that the debugger is able to take advantage of the Macintosh user interface. It could not do so on the Macintosh being debugged. The debugger's nub also takes up very little space in the machine being debugged. The user interface of MacDB also cannot be damaged by an errant program, making it easier to use on some kinds of bugs. The main disadvantage is that it takes two Macintoshes to debug.MacDB is published by Apple Computer and is available at Apple dealers.

TMON is a debugger that requires only one machine. It is installed in the Macintosh's memory and remains there, inactive, until some event occurs that causes it to wake up. Applications can be launched and terminated without disrupting TMON. The TMON user interface is not like most Macintosh applications because the ROM toolkit cannot be used by two programs at once, and in the case of TMON it is already in use by the program being debugged.

TMON has a pleasant enough user interface, though, and the fact that it works with one Macintosh makes it convenient. For software writers with only one Macintosh, TMON is the only usable debugger.

TMON cannot be protected from damage if a buggy program overwrites the memory TMON occupies, but TMON can detect that such damage has occurred. Thus bugs that cause TMON to be overwritten are more difficult to find because the tools to examine the aftermath of the program error might not be working. But these programs can be traced to the point at which damage occurs.TMON is available from ICOM Simulations Inc., 626 Wheeling Road, Wheeling, Illinois, 60090.

Some compilers may come with their own debuggers. Compiler-specific debuggers have some advantages in that they know how the corresponding compiler passes arguments to subroutines.

Basic Concepts in Debugging

Tracing, breakpointing, dumping, and disassembling are the fundamental activities of debugging. Disassembly is an integral part of almost all debugging activity. To tell you what part of a program you are looking at, your debugger translates the assembled program back into assembler mnemonics, substituting, where it can, symbolic names for offsets, labels, and locations in global storage.

Tracing means following the program, instruction by instruction, through execution. Tracing often leads you right to the bug. To use tracing effectively with C, you will need to get used to the kind of code your compiler generates so that you can tell where you are in the source listing as you trace. The 68000 has a processor mode that allows the debugger to step a program one instruction at a time. This means that even ROM routines can be traced.

Breakpointing involves replacing instructions in the program with breakpoints. The debugger does this for you, so all you see is the effect of the program stopping and the debugger waking up to tell you where the program has stopped. Breakpoints let you run a program at full speed up to a section of the program that you suspect has a bug.

Tracing and breakpoints can be used in combination to zero in on a bug. By setting breakpoints around where you think the buggy code is executed, you can cut down on the amount of tracing you have to do to find the bug.

Dumps of sections of memory can reveal invalid values. Three places to look in the Macintosh when it is running a program that you are debugging are:

- The top of the stack. Register a7 usually points to the top of the stack.
  One way to see if the stack is being correctly maintained is to check to see if a plausible address is at the top of the stack just before an RTS instruction is executed.
- The application's global variables. Register a5 usually points to an application's global variables.
- Low memory. This is where the Macintosh system puts its global variables.

Deep S___

When a fundamental error has occurred and the processor cannot continue executing a program, the processor branches to an error handler. On the Macintosh, the error handler determines which error occurred and displays the error number on the screen. This is the only point where the usually user-friendly Macintosh reverts to displaying numbers where an explanatory phrase would be much more helpful.

Errors that bring programs to a halt are called DS errors. And I think you know why.

The following table lists the error code numbers and describes the errors that cause them to be displayed:

Error	Explanation
1	Bus error. This *should* never happen on a Macintosh. The Macintosh hardware is designed so that bus transactions

always appear to have succeeded, no matter what actually happened.

2   Address error. The processor tried to read an instruction or a 16-bit word of data from an odd address. This can occur if a character pointer is cast to an integer pointer while it has an odd value.

3   Illegal instruction. The processor tried to decode data as an instruction. This usually results from the wrong data used as a return address in a subroutine.

4   Divide by zero. One of the divide instructions was executed with a divisor of 0.

5   Bounds check failed. The CHK instruction found a register out of bounds. C does no bounds-checking, so this error should be rare.

6   Overflow trap. *if* the V bit in the status register is set and a TRAPV instruction is executed, this trap occurs.

7   Priviledge violation. The Macintosh always runs in system mode in which all instructions are permitted. To generate a priviledge violation, the status register would have to be modified to put the processor in user mode. The status register can be set explicitly with a MOVE instruction or as a side effect of the RTE instruction. Invalid information on the stack could cause the RTE instruction to put the wrong value in the status register.

8   Trace exception. Another symptom of a status register being loaded with invalid data. See the description of error 7.

9   Line 1010 exception. This means that the Toolbox trap handler has stopped functioning.

10   Line 1111 exception. This group of traps is often used to set breakpoints. If an unexpected line 1111 trap occurs, it is equivalent to an illegal instruction. See error 3.

11   Miscellaneous exception. Caused by all other 68000 exceptions.

12   Unimplemented trap. This error is reported when the trap dispatcher cannot find a Toolbox trap. It may mean the dispatcher is broken or that the equivalent of an illegal instruction error has occurred. See error 3.

13   Spurious interrupt. This error is reported when there is no interrupt handler for an interrupt. This usually means that the interrupt table has been overwritten.

14   I/O system error. This occurs when an I/O queue element contains bad data.

15   Segment loader error. This means the segment loader attempted to read in a segment and failed. This can be caused by an error in the resource compiler file that puts an application's CODE resources together.

16   Floating-point error.

17–24   Failed to load pack 0 to 7, respectively. This means that these packages are not present in the system file being used.

25   Out of memory.

26   Failed loading segment 0. This means that the application file was incorrectly made or has been corrupted.

27   Bad file map. An inconsistency in a file operation was detected. This may mean the volume being accessed has been corrupted.

28   Stack overflow. The "stack sniffer" has detected that the stack has collided with a heap, usually the application heap.

32–53   Memory manager errors.

41   The Finder could not be found. It may have been removed or the volume it is on has been corrupted.

100   Failed to mount the startup volume. Another symptom of a corrupted file system.

The Most Common Bugs

Programming the Macintosh in C yields a telltale set of bugs that differ from those found in assembly language and Pascal programming. The commonest kind of bug in C programs in general is the family of bugs that arises from mismatched parameters. Mismatched parameters occur when subroutines or Toolbox traps are passed more or fewer parameters than they require or inappropriate parameters.

In Macintosh programming, mismatched parameter bugs are more common, nastier and more varied in their manifestations, and more difficult to track down than in other environments. They occur when programmers forget how many parameters a routine takes, whether a default value is -1 or 0, what size a parameter is, or that a parameter is a VAR parameter and, in C, must be explicitly passed by reference. These bugs are difficult to find because they often manifest themselves inside the Toolbox trap that was supplied with flawed information.

If a session with the debugger reveals that your program fails inside a Toolbox trap, a parameter mismatch should be your first suspicion. Check the parameters being passed to the routine that fails. Also check subroutine parameters being passed between routines in your own code. Because the caller of a C routine manipulates the stack, C programs can mask parameter mismatch across one or more calls. Pascal routines and the stack-based Toolbox traps split stack manipulation between the caller and the called routine, so a parameter mismatch is likely to cause immediate failure, typically an illegal instruction or address error upon returning when the RTS instruction loads an invalid address into the program counter.

When you suspect a parameter mismatch, make sure all the following conditions hold true:

- The number of parameters is correct.
- The size of the parameters is correct. A common error is to pass an integer constant when a long constant is required.
- The parameter is passed in the correct form. Pascal VAR parameters require that a pointer to a parameter value be passed. Make sure that you have correctly read the description of the routine you are calling.

Testing

When you are happy with the way your program works, wait! Do not go sell it or distribute it to people who will be relying on it. Test it. All responsible software developers put their software through (at least) two testing phases. These testing phases are typically called alpha and beta.

The purpose of testing is to find bugs. The hard part is getting the bugs described clearly. Bug reports should contain a desciption of what occurred and information about the setting in which the behavior occurred. If possible, the person reporting a bug should describe not only what happened, but how to make it happen again.

Alpha testing is the first testing phase. Alpha releases are usually released to technically adept users who understand the purpose of the application and who probably understand how some or all of the application was designed and implemented. Preparing an alpha release involves preliminary testing on all the configurations the software will run on and the preparation of the first draft of the application's documentation.

Alpha testing should tell you if you have made any fundamental errors, whether performance is adequate, and whether the documentation correctly corresponds to the way the program works. Testing on a variety of configurations is vital. You should plan on testing with a Macintosh 512k, and a Macintosh Plus, both with and without hard disks.

Alpha testing should proceed acording to a test plan. A test plan is a set of exercises designed to bring out any weak spots in a program: How does it behave when it runs out of memory? How does it behave when windows are shrunk or expanded to extremes? What if the program's current save-file is deleted through a desk accessory? Usually such provocative use of a program will uncover many errors and their remedies will improve the robustness of the program in general.

If you are left with a sheaf of unresolved problems with your alpha release, you may want to cancel the beta release and spend some time fixing the problems so that the beta release does not have to be accompanied by work-around hints and a bug list. Do not try to fix the problems with your alpha release while the beta release is being tested. If you find you have time on your hands during the beta release, count yourself among the fortunate!

Beta testing is the second phase of testing. Beta testing simulates the conditions under which the software will be sold or distributed. In other respects beta testing is like alpha testing – you are looking for bugs. The number of beta testers should be greater than the number of alpha testers, ideally including the alpha test group in its entirety. In addition, the beta testers should include representatives of the target group of users. Beta testing is probably the most nerve-wracking experience you will go through as a developer. The deadlines for publication are looming, and you are dealing with a large group of testers, some of whom cannot be relied on to describe their problems in clear terms. To make beta testing go more smoothly, use your cadre of alpha testers to help the less computer-savvy beta testers characterize the problems they run into.

The most valuable kind of beta tester is the *power user*. The power user often is not a programmer at all. Instead, the power user pushes applications like spreadsheets to their limits. Power users are valuable because they often do things with an application that the designer and author had no idea anyone would want to do.

Testing Macintosh software differs from testing other kinds of software because it is event driven. Event-driven software can have an infinite variety of interactions with the user, so it is not always possible to test every eventuality. Because of this difference, clear bug reporting is of paramount importance. You will have to rely on your testing phases and your careful selection of testers to exercise the software enough to find the obscure bugs.

Points to Consider

1) If the Macintosh reports that it attempted to execute an illegal instruction, how could the flow of the program reach an illegal instruction?

2) Two programs have the same parameter mismatch bug. One is written in Pascal, the other in C. Will the bug manifest itself differently? Why?

3) Unlike most systems that run UNIX, the Macintosh has one address space. How does this make debugging more difficult? How does it make it easier?

Part II

Reference Handbook

- **QuickDraw**
- **Event Manager**
- **Window Manager**
- **Dialog Manager**
- **Memory Manager**
- **Menu Manager**
- **Control Manager**
- **Text Edit**
- **Standard File Package**
- **File Manager**
- **Font Manager**
- **Print Manager**
- **Resource Manager**
- **Toolbox Utilities**
- **Desk Manager**
- **Scrap Manager**
- **Segment Loader**

QUICKDRAW

QuickDraw is the basis of all activity on the Macintosh screen.

By combining a set of data structures to represent graphic objects, with routines that perform calculations on those objects, QuickDraw draws and forms a comprehensive graphics environment.

QuickDraw can fill a region with a pattern, calculate whether a point lies in a region, and represent that region in a data structure whether it has been drawn on the screen or not. QuickDraw provides these tools in multiple coordinate systems, so that whole graphics environments can be moved around the screen. QuickDraw provides all of the tools used by the Window Manager, but it is not a windowing system in and of itself.

The Window Manager uses QuickDraw calculations to tell what parts of the screen should be clipped to. However, the illusion of scraps of paper on a desktop is created by the Window Manager, not by QuickDraw alone.

The most important QuickDraw data structure is the region. Regions can represent objects of any shape. Since QuickDraw can perform all of its fundamental calculations on regions (such as the calculations that determine the overlap of graphics and clipping calculations), QuickDraw has a qualitative advantage over most graphics environments that deal only in rectangles and not abitrary shapes.

This is one reason why the Macintosh user interface looks more sophisticated than most other windowed user interfaces.

Constants

```
#define srcCopy        0
#define srcOr          1
#define srcXor         2
#define srcBic         3
#define notSrcCopy     4
#define notSrcOr       5
#define notSrcXor      6
#define notSrcBic      7
#define patCopy        8
#define patOr          9
#define patXor         10
#define patBic         11
#define notPatCopy     12
#define notPatOr       13
#define notPatXor      14
#define notPatBic      15

#define normalBit      0
#define inverseBit     1
#define redBit         4
#define greenBit       3
#define blueBit        2
```

```
#define cyanBit          8
#define magentaBit       7
#define yellowBit        6
#define blackBit         5

#define BlackColor       33
#define whiteColor       30
#define redColor         205
#define greenColor       341
#define blueColor        409
#define cyanColor        273
#define magentaColor     137
#define yellowColor      69

#define picLParen        0
#define picRParen        1

#define frameMode        0
#define paintMode        1
#define eraseMode        2
#define invertMode       3
#define fillMode         4

#define bold             0x01
#define italic           0x02
#define underline        0x04
#define outline          0x08
#define shadow           0x10
#define condense         0x20
#define extend           0x40
```

Data Structures

```
typedef unsigned char Byte;
typedef char SignedByte;
typedef char *Ptr;
typedef Ptr *Handle;
typedef int (*ProcPtr)();
typedef unsigned int Boolean;


typedef char QDByte;
typedef QDByte *QDPtr;
typedef QDPtr *QDHandle;
typedef char *Str255;
typedef unsigned char Pattern[8];
typedef int Bits16[16];


typedef unsigned int Style;
```

```
struct FontInfo
{       int  ascent;
        int  descent;
        int  widMax;
        int  leading;
};

typedef struct FontInfo FontInfo;

struct Point
{       int v;
        int h;
};

typedef struct Point Point;

struct Rect
{       int top;
        int left;
        int bottom;
        int right;
};

typedef struct Rect                     Rect;

struct BitMap
{       QDPtr baseAddr;
        int rowBytes;
        Rect bounds;
};

typedef struct BitMap BitMap;

struct Cursor
{       Bits16 data;
        Bits16 mask;
        Point hotSpot;
};

typedef struct Cursor Cursor;

struct Region
{       int picSize;
        Rect picFrame;
};

typedef struct Picture Picture;
typedef struct Picture *PicPtr;
typedef struct Picture **PicHandle;

struct Polygon
{       int polySize;
        Rect polyBBox;
```

```
                Point polyPoints[1];
};

typedef struct Polygon Polygon;
typedef struct Polygon *PolyPtr;
typedef struct Polygon **PolyHandle;

struct QDProcs
{           QDPtr textProc;
            QDPtr lineProc;
            QDPtr rectProc;
            QDPtr rRectProc;
            QDPtr RoundRectProc;
            QDPtr arcPRoc;
            QDPtr polyProc;
            QDPtr rgnProc;
            QDPtr bitsProc;
            QDPtr commentProc;
            QDPtr txMeasProc;
            QDPtr getPicProc;
            QDPtr putPicProc;
};


typedef struct QDProcs QDProcs;
typedef struct QDProcs *QDProcsPtr;

struct GrafPort
{           int device;
            BitMap portBits;
            Rect portRect;
            RgnHandle visRgn;
            RgnHandle clipRgn;
            Pattern bkPat;
            Pattern fillPat;
            Point pnLoc;
            Point pnSize;
            int pnMode;
            Pattern pnPat;
            int pnVis;
            int txFont;
            Style txFace;
            int txMode;
            int txSize;
            int spExtra;
            long fgColor;
            long bkColor;
            int colrBit;

            int patStretch;
            QDHandle picSave;
            QDHandle rgnSave;
            QDHandle polySave;
```

```
        QDHandle grafProcs;
};

    typedef struct GrafPort GrafPort;

    typedef struct GrafPort *GrafPtr;
```

The following global variables are used by Quickdraw. These are not low-memory globals. Most compilers provide pre-allocated space for these variables. This support parallels that of the Lisa Pascal development system.

```
GrafPtr thePort;
Pattern white;
Pattern black;
Pattern ltGray;
Pattern dkGray;
Cursor arrow;
BitMap screenBits;
long randSeed;
```

If your compiler does not pre-define these variables, you will have to do so yourself. If you define them, they must be in the above order so that Quickdraw's initialization call works correctly.

Functions

GrafPort Routines

```
    void    InitGraf (globalPtr)
            QDPtr globalPtr;
```

InitGraf should be called one time only, at the beginning of your program. InitGraf initializes the Quickdraw global variables. These global variables, and their initial values are:

Type	Variable	Initial Value
GrafPtr	thePort	NULL
Pattern	white	all-white pattern
Pattern	black	all-black pattern
Pattern	gray	50% gray pattern
Pattern	ltGray	25% gray pattern
Pattern	dkGray	75% gray pattern
Cursor	arrow	pointing arrow cursor
BitMap	screenbits	Macintosh screen (0,0,512,342)
long	randSeed	1

The parameter globalPtr tells Quickdraw where these global variables are stored. C programmers should use &thePort for this parameter.

```
void    OpenPort (gp)
        GrafPtr gp;
```

OpenPort is called before using a new grafPort. It will allocate space for the visRgn and clipRgn (by calling NewRgn), initialize the fields of the grafPort, and make the grafPort the current port by calling SetPort(gp).

The initial values given to grafPort are:

Type	Field	Initial value
int	device	0
BitMap	portBits	screenBits (from InitGraf)
Rect	portRect	screenBits.bounds(0,0,512,342)
RgnHandle	visRgn	handle to rectangular region (0,0,512,342)
RgnHandle	clipRgn	handle to rectangular region (-30000,-30000,30000,30000)
Pattern	bkPat	white
Pattern	fillPat	black
Point	pnLoc	(0,0)
Point	pnSize	(1,1)
int	pnMode	patCopy
Pattern	pnPat	black
int	pnVis	0 (visible)
int	txFont	0 (system font)
Style	txFace	normal
int	txMode	srcOr
int	txSize	0 (Font Manager decides)
int	spExtra	0
long	fgColor	blackColor
long	bkColor	whiteColor
int	colrBit	0
int	patStretch	0
QDHandle	picSave	NULL
QDHandle	rgnSave	NULL
QDHandle	polySave	NULL
QDProcsPtr	grafProcs	NULL

```
void    InitPort (gp)
        Grafptr gp;
```

InitPort sets the fields of gp's grafPort to the above initial values. InitPort next calls SetPort (gp), making gp's grafPort the current port. Note that the grafPort must have already been opened with OpenPort, as InitPort does not allocate space for visRgn and clipRgn.

```
void    ClosePort (gp)
        GrafPtr gp;
```

ClosePort frees the memory used by the grafPort's visRgn and ClipRgn.


```
void    SetPort (gp)
        GrafPtr gp;
```

SetPort will make gp's grafPort the current port. It does this by setting thePort (the global GrafPtr) equal to gp.


```
void    GetPort (gp)
        GrafPtr *gp;
```

GetPort gets the current port and returns it via gp.


```
void    GrafDevice (device)
        int device;
```

GrafDevice sets thePort's device field equal to the device parameter. This number tells which logical output device is to be used for the current grafPort. Device = 0 is the Macintosh screen. This is used by the Font Manager.


```
void    SetPortBits (bm)
        BitMap *bm;
```

SetPortBits sets the portBits field of the current grafPort to bm. Since drawing is done in the bit image pointed to by bm, be sure the fields in bm are set up correctly before you call SetPortBits. Drawing is not confined to the piece of memory displayed on the screen. You can set up bitmaps to act as output buffers or as off-screen images.


```
void    PortSize (width, height)
        int width, height;
```

PortSize is normally called only by the Window Manager. It changes the size of the current grafPort's portRect. The top left corner remains in the same location. The bottom right corner is adjusted so that the rectangle is of a specified width and height. PortSize does not change what is on the screen.


```
void    MovePortTo (leftGlobal, topGlobal)
        int leftGlobal,topGlobal;
```

MovePortTo is normally called only by the Window Manager. MovePortTo changes the current portRect's location with respect to portBits.bounds.

PortRect is moved so that its top left corner is leftGlobal and topGlobal units are from the top left corner of portBits.bounds. MovePortTo does not affect anything currently on the screen but it will affect future activity in the port.

```
void    SetOrigin (h,v)
        int h,v;
```

SetOrigin sets the coordinates of the top left corner of portRect to (h,v). Calling SetOrigin won't change the current screen but it will affect any future drawing in the port.

```
void    SetClip (rgn)
        RgnHandle rgn;
```

SetClip changes the clipRgn of the current grafPort to a region just like the one with the handle rgn. This is done by copying rgn to clipRgn. Since a copy is made, clipRgn can be changed without changing rgn.

```
void    GetClip (rgn)
        RgnHandle rgn;
```

GetClip copies the current grafPort's clipRgn to the region rgn. An actual copy is made: rgn can be changed and it will not affect clipRgn.

```
void    ClipRect (r)
        Rect *r;
```

ClipRect copies the rectangle r to the clipRgn of the current grafPort making a rectangular clipping region.

```
void    BackPat (pat)
        Pattern Pat;
```

BackPat makes pat the background pattern of the current grafPort.

Cursor Handling

To keep track of calls to HideCursor and ShowCursor, QuickDraw maintains a global variable known as the cursor level. If the cursor level is zero, then the cursor is visible. When the cursor level is below zero the cursor is invisible. ShowCursor never raises the cursor level above 0.

```
void    InitCursor ( )
```

InitCursor gives you the predefined arrow cursor and sets the cursor level to 0.

```
void    SetCursor (crsr)
        Cursor *crsr;
```

SetCursor changes the current cursor to crsr. If the cursor is visible, this change will occur immediately. If the cursor is hidden, you'll see the new cursor when the cursor is uncovered.

```
void    HideCursor ( )
```

HideCursor makes the cursor invisible. The bits where the cursor was are restored. HideCursor also decrements the cursor level. Calls to HideCursor should be balanced with calls to ShowCursor.

```
void    ShowCursor ( )
```

ShowCursor increments the cursor level if it is below 0 and displays the cursor when the cursor level becomes 0.

```
void    ObscureCursor ( )
```

ObscureCursor temporarily hides the cursor. The cursor will reappear the moment that the mouse is moved. ObscureCursor does not change the cursor level.

Pen and Line Drawing

```
void    HidePen ( )
```

HidePen will decrement the pnVis field of the current grafPort. Drawing will not occur on the screen if pnVis is negative. This procedure is called by OpenRgn, OpenPicture and OpenPoly so that regions, pictures and polygons can be defined without appearing on screen. Calls to HidePen should be balanced by calls to ShowPen.

```
void    ShowPen ( )
```

ShowPen increments the pnVis field of the current grafPort. When pnVis is 0, on-screen drawing becomes visible. The pnVis field can become greater than 0, so calls to ShowPen should be balanced by calls to HidePen. ShowPen is called by

CloseRgn, ClosePicture, and ClosePoly, thus balancing calls to HidePen made by OpenRgn, OpenPicture and OpenPoly.

```
void    GetPen (pt)
        Point *pt;
```

GetPen gets the location of the pen and returns it in pt. Pt is in the local coordinate system of the current grafPort.

```
void    GetPenState (pnState)
        PenState *pnState;
```

GetPenState gets the location, size, pattern and mode of the current grafPort's pen and stores this information in pnState.

```
void    SetPenState (pnState)
        PenState *pnState;
```

SetPenState sets the location, size, pattern and mode of the current grafPort's pen equal to the values stored in pnState.

```
void    PenSize (width, height)
        int width, height;
```

PenSize sets the dimensions of the pen in the current grafPort, making the graphics pen the specified width and height.

```
void    PenMode (mode)
        int mode;
```

PenMode sets the pnMode of the current grafPort to mode. This field variable specifies the mode through which the pnPat is transferred to the bitMap. The pattern transfer mode can be one of:
```
patCopy
patXor  notPatCopy
notPatXor
patOr   patBic
notPatOr
notPatBic
```

If a source transfer mode or negative value is in the mode field, than no transfer is done. The current pen mode can be found at thePort->pnMode.

```
void      PenPat (pat)
          Pattern pat;
```

PenPat sets the pattern (black, white, gray, dkGray, ltGray) used by the graphics pen in the current graphics port to pat. The current pattern can be found at thePort->pnPat.

```
void      PenNormal ( )
```

PenNormal resets the graphics pen to the initial value. After calling PenNormal, pnSize is (1,1), pnMode is patCopy, and pnPat is black.

```
void      MoveTo (h, v)
          int h, v;
```

MoveTo is a non-drawing procedure. It places the pen at the current grafPort's local coordinates (h, v).

```
void      Move (dh, dv)
          int dh, dv;
```

Move moves the pen relative to it's current location without doing any drawing. If (h,v) is the current location, Move calls MoveTo(h+dh,v+dv).

```
void      LineTo (h,v)
          int h, v;
```

LineTo draws a line from the current location to the point (h,v). The pen remains at (h,v).

```
void      Line (dh, dv)
          int dh, dv;
```

Line draws a line by calling LineTo (h+dh, v+dv) where (h,v) is the current location of the pen. The pen remains at (h+dh, v+dv).

Text Drawing

```
void      TextFont (font)
          int font;
```

TextFont sets the font of the current grafPort to a given font number. You can find the current font at thePort->txFont.

```
void    TextFace (face)
        Style face;
```

TextFace sets the style for the current grafPort to face. Face can be one (or the sum of more than one) of the predefined style constants: bold, italic, underline, outline, shadow, condense, extend.

To get this style	Face should be
bold	bold
bold & italic	bold+italic
current value & italic	thePort->txFace+italic
current value & not italic	thePort->txFace+italic
normal	0

```
void    TextMode (mode)
        int mode;
```

TextMode sets the current grafPort's text transfer mode to the given mode. Mode should be one of the following source transfer modes: srcOr, srcXor or srcBic.

```
void    TextSize (size)
        int size;
```

TextSize sets the current grafPort's text size to the number of points given by size.

For best results, use a size the Font Manager has available. Otherwise the available size will be scaled. Even multiples of an available size are the second best choice. If size is zero, the Font Manager picks whichever available size is closest to the system font size and uses that size.

```
void    SpaceExtra (extra)
        int extra;
```

SpaceExtra is used to implement right and left justified text.

Extra specifies the number of pixels that each space will be widened by in the following lines of text to be drawn. Typically this is the difference between the length of the line of text (in pixels) and the space between the margins, divided by the number of spaces in the line.

By padding each space with this number of pixels the line will occupy all of the space between the margins.

```
void    DrawChar (ch)
        char ch;
```

DrawChar draws the character ch using the current font, style, size and source transfer mode. The left end of the character's base line is at the pen location, and the horizontal coordinate of the pen's location is increased by the character's width. The font's "missing" symbol is drawn if the character is not available in the font.

```
void    DrawString (s)
        Str255 s;
```

DrawString draws the string given by s. DrawString calls DrawChar for each character in the string.

```
void    DrawText (textBuf, firstByte, byteCount)
        QDPtr textBuf;   int firstByte, byteCount;
```

DrawText draws byteCount characters from a text buffer. The first character drawn is the character at location firstByte.

TextBuf points to the text buffer. The characters are drawn to the right of the pen's location. The pen ends up to the right of the last character.

```
void    GetFontInfo (info)
        FontInfo *info;
```

GetFontInfo gets the ascent, descent, width of widest character, distance between descent of a line and ascent of the line below it. This information, given in pixels, is placed into the fields of info. It is based on the current font, size and style.

Drawing in Color

```
void    ForeColor (color)
        long color;
```

ForeColor sets the foreground color to color.

```
void    BackColor (color)
        long color;
```

BackColor sets the background color to color.

```
void    ColorBit (whichBit)
        int whichBit;
```

ColorBit tells QuickDraw which bit plane to draw in. This is used to support color devices with up to 32 bits of color information per pixel.

Calculations with Rectangles

```
void    SetRect (r, left, top, right, bottom)
        Rect *r;   int left, top, right, bottom;
```

SetRect sets the coordinates of the rectangle r to (left, top, right, bottom).

```
void    OffsetRect (r, dh, dv)
        Rect *r;   int dh, dv;
```

OffsetRect performs a translation of the position of the rectangle r in the coordinate plane. The rectangle is moved dh horizontal and dv vertical units.

```
void    InsetRect (r, dh, dv)
        Rect *r;   int dh, dv;
```

InsetRect allows you to shrink or expand the rectangle r. The rectangle will be centered at the same location, but the sides will move inward by dv (or out if dv is negative). The top and bottom will move toward the center by dh (or they will move out if dh is negative). If dh or dv causes the width or height to become less than 1, then r is set to the empty rectangle: (0,0,0,0).

```
Boolean            SectRect (srcRectA, srcRectB, dstRect)
        Rect *srcRectA, *srcRectB, *dstRect;
```

SectRect will give the intersection of two rectangles, srcRectA and srcRectB. The intersection rectangle is dstRect. If srcRectA and srcRectB do not intersect, then dstRect is (0,0,0,0) and SectRect is false.

If srcRectA and srcRectB touch only along an edge or at a corner, then they are not intersecting rectangles. Remember lines and points are infinitely small on the Macintosh.

```
void    UnionRect (srcRectA, srcRectB, dstRect)
        Rect *srcRectA, *srcRectB, *dstRect;
```

UnionRect computes coordinates for rectangle dstRect: the smallest rectangle which encloses srcRectA and srcRectB.

```
Boolean            PtInRect (pt, r)
        long pt;   Rect *r;
```

PtInRect will be true if the pixel below and to the right of pt is inside rectangle r. If this pixel is not inside r, PtInRect will be false.

```
void    Pt2Rect (ptA,  ptB, dstRect)
        long ptA, ptB;  Rect *dstRect;
```

Pt2Rect calculates coordinates for dstRect so that it is the smallest rectangle enclosing PtA and PtB.

```
void    PtToAngle (r, pt, angle)
        Rect *r;   long pt;   Int *angle;
```

PtToAngle will calculate the integer angle (0 to 359 °) from the center of the rectangle r to the line from the center to the point pt.

The angle is measured clockwise (12 o'clock = 0°, 3 o'clock = 90°, 6 o'clock = 180°, 9 o'clock = 270°). All other angles are measured relative to the rectangle. The line which goes from the center through the top right corner is 45°. The line through the bottom right corner is 135°.

You can see these are not true angles, but these angles are the ones to use when doing calculations with arcs and wedges.

```
Boolean     EqualRect (rectA, rectB)
            Rect *rectA, *rectB;
```

EqualRect will be TRUE if rectA and rectB are the same (they have the same boundary coordinates), FALSE if they are not.

```
Boolean     EmptyRect (r)
            Rect *r;
```

EmptyRect will be TRUE if r is an empty rectangle, FALSE if it's not.

An empty rectangle is one where the top coordinate is less than or equal to the bottom coordinate, or the right coordinate is less than or equal to the left coordinate.

Graphic Operations on Rectangles

```
void    FrameRect (r)
        Rect *r;
```

FrameRect uses the current graphics pen to draw a hollow outline just inside rectangle r. The location of the pen is not changed by FrameRect.

If a region is open and being formed, then the outside outline of the new rectangle is added to the region's boundary.

```
void    PaintRect (r)
        Rect *r;
```

PaintRect fills the rectangle r with the current grafPort's pnPat, using the current pnMode. The pen location is not changed.

```
void    EraseRect (r)
        Rect *r;
```

EraseRect fills the rectangle r with the background pattern using patCopy mode. The pen is not used, it's location does not change.

```
void    InvertRect (r)
        Rect *r;
```

InvertRect toggles all the pixels inside rectangle r: all white pixels become black, all black pixels become white.

```
void    FillRect (r, pat)
        Rect *r;   Pattern pat;
```

FillRect uses patCopy mode to fill rectangle r with pattern pat.

Graphic Operations on Ovals

```
void    FrameOval (r)
        Rect *r;
```

FrameOval uses the characteristics of the current graphics pen to draw a hollow outline inside the oval that fits inside rectangle r. The pen location does not change after calling FrameOval.

FrameOval will add the outside outline of the oval to the boundary of an open region.

```
void    PaintOval (r)
        Rect *r;
```

PaintOval fills the oval determined by rectangle r with the current pnPat using the current pnMode. The location of the pen is not changed in PaintOval.

```
void    EraseOval (r)
        Rect *r;
```

EraseOval paints the oval determined by r with the background pattern using the patCopy mode. The pen location doesn't change.

```
void    InvertOval (r)
        Rect *r;
```

InvertOval changes all the pixels inside the oval determined by r: all white pixels become black pixels and all black pixels become white pixels. The pen is not moved.

```
void    FillOval (r, pat)
        Rect *r;   Pattern pat;
```

FillOval uses patCopy mode to fill the oval determined by r with the given pattern. FillOval does not affect the pen location.

Graphic Operations on Rounded-Corner Rectangles

```
void    FrameRoundRect (r, ovalWidth, ovalHeight)
        Rect *r;   int ovalWidth, ovalHeight;
```

FrameRoundRect uses the attributes of the current graphics pen to draw a hollow outline just inside the rounded-corner rectangle determined by r, ovalWidth and ovalHeight. FrameRoundRect does not change the pen's location.

For open regions, the outside outline of this rounded-corner rectangle is added to the region's boundary.

```
void    PaintRoundRect (r, ovalWidth, ovalHeight)
        Rect *r;   int ovalWidth, ovalHeight;
```

PaintRoundRect uses the mode and pattern of the current graphics pen to paint the specified rounded-corner rectangle. PaintRoundRect will not change the pen's location.

```
void    EraseRoundRect (r, ovalWidth, ovalHeight)
        Rect *r;   int ovalWidth, ovalHeight;
```

EraseRoundRect will use patCopy mode to paint the specified round-cornered rectangle with the current grafPort's background pattern. EraseRoundRect will not affect the pen's location.

```
void    InvertRoundRect (r, ovalWidth, ovalHeight)
        Rect *r;   int ovalWidth, ovalHeight;
```

InvertRoundRect will change all the pixels inside the rounded-corner rectangle determined by r, ovalWidth and ovalHeight. All the black pixels will be changed to white, all white pixels will be changed to black. This procedure has no affect on the pen's position.

```
void    FillRoundRect (r, ovalWidth, ovalHeight, pat)
        Rect *r;   int ovalWidth, ovalHeight;   Pattern pat;
```

FillRoundRect will paint the specified rounded-corner rectangle with the pattern pat. FillRoundRect uses patCopy mode—it does not change the pen's location.

Graphic Operations on Arcs and Wedges

QuickDraw Definition: ARC—Arcs used by QuickDraw are determined by three components:
1. the rectangle they are contained in
2. the angle the arc starts at
3. the angle the arc ends at


```
void    FrameArc (r, startAngle, arcAngle)
        Rect *r;   int startAngle, arcAngle;
```

FrameArc will use the characteristics of the current graphics pen to draw a hollow outline just inside of the specified arc. The pen location remains the same.
For open regions, FrameArc is unlike any of the other frame procedures in that it does *not* add to the boundary of the region.


```
void    PaintArc (r, startAngle, arcAngle)
        Rect *r;   int startAngle, arcAngle;
```

PaintArc uses the current pnPat and pnMode to paint the wedge bounded by the given arc. PaintArc does not change the pen's location.


```
void    EraseArc (r, startAngle, arcAngle)
        Rect *r;   int startAngle, arcAngle;
```

EraseArc paints the wedge with bkPat using patCopy mode. EraseArc does not change the pen's location.


```
void    InvertArc (r, startAngle, arcAngle)
        Rect *r;   int startAngle, arcAngle;
```

InvertArc changes all of the pixels contained in the associated wedge. Each white pixel becomes a black pixel, each pixel that was black becomes white.
InvertArc does not change the pen's location.

```
void    FillArc (r, startAngle, arcAngle, pat)
        Rect *r;   int startAngle, arcAngle;      Pattern pat;
```

FillArc uses patCopy to paint the given wedge with the specified pattern.

Calculations with Regions

All the descriptions of the region functions assume the reader is familiar with QuickDraw regions.


```
RgnHandle                              NewRgn ( )
```

NewRgn is called when you want to define a new region. Heap space is allocated for the new region, the region starts off as the empty region (0,0,0,0), and a handle to the region is returned.

NewRgn *must* be called for a region before that region can be used.


```
void    DisposeRgn (rgn)
        RgnHandle rgn;
```

DisposeRgn frees the memory used by rgn's region. When you no longer need the region, call DisposeRgn to get rid of it.


```
void    CopyRgn (srcRgn, dstRgn)
        RgnHandle srcRgn, dstRgn;
```

CopyRgn copies srcRgn to the region with handle dstRgn.


```
void    SetEmptyRgn (rgn)
        RgnHandle rgn;
```

SetEmptyRgn reinitializes rgn to the empty region (0,0,0,0).


```
void    SetRectRgn (rgn, left, top, right, bottom)
        RgnHandle rgn;   int left, top, right, bottom;
```

SetRectRgn wipes out rgn's current structure, and makes the region the rectangle given by left, top, right, and bottom. If the specified rectangle is an empty rectangle, rgn becomes the empty region (0,0,0,0).

```
void    RectRgn (rgn, r)
RgnHandle rgn;    Rect *r;
```

RectRgn wipes out rgn's current structure, and makes the region the rectangle specified by r. If r is an empty rectangle, rgn becomes the empty region.


```
void    OpenRgn ( )
```

OpenRgn lets QuickDraw know you're going to define a region. QuickDraw begins saving information about all lines and framed shapes you draw until CloseRgn is called. The information QuickDraw saved is then organized into a region.
OpenRgn calls HidePen, so no drawing appears on screen while a region is being defined (you can get around that by calling ShowPen just after OpenRgn).


```
void    CloseRgn (dstRgn)
RgnHandle dstRgn;
```

CloseRgn signals QuickDraw that it has all the lines and framed shapes you want in the region. The collected information is organized into a region which is accessible using dstRgn.
CloseRgn calls ShowPen—this balances OpenRgn's HidePen call.


```
void    OffsetRgn (rgn, dh, dv)
RgnHandle rgn;    int dh, dv;
```

OffsetRgn moves region rgn dh units in the horizontal direction, dv units vertically. This will not affect the screen.
OffsetRgn is a very efficient method for translational movement of the region. The region is stored relative to it's bounding rectangle, so only the rectangle needs to be changed.


```
void    InsetRgn (rgn, dh, dv)
RgnHandle rgn;    int dh, dv;
```

InsetRgn moves the boundary of rgn's region in or out, thus shrinking or expanding the region. The boundary is moved toward the center: dh horizontally and dv vertically. Negative dh and dv cause movement away from the center.


```
void    SectRgn (srcRgnA, srcRgnB, dstRgn)
RgnHandle srcRgnA, srcRgnB, dstRgn;
```

SectRgn calculates the region that is the intersection of the two regions srcRgnA and srcRgnB. DstRgn tells QuickDraw where to store the resulting region. DstRgn can be equal to either srcRgnA or srcRgnB.

```
void    UnionRgn (srcRgnA, srcRgnB, dstRgn)
        RgnHandle srcRgnA, srcRgnB, dstRgn;
```

UnionRgn calculates the region which is the union of regions srcRgnA and srcRgnB. DstRgn is the resulting region. DstRgn can be equal to either srcRgnA or srcRgnB.

```
void    DiffRgn (srcRgnA, srcRgnB, dstRgn)
        RgnHandle srcRgnA, srcRgnB, dstRgn;
```

DiffRgn calculates a new region by subtracting srcRgnB from srcRgnB. The resulting region is stored at dstRgn. DstRgn can be equal to either srcRgnA or srcRgnB. If srcRgnA is the empty region, dstRgn automatically becomes an empty region.

```
void    XorRgn (srcRgnA, srcRgnB, dstRgn)
        RgnHandle srcRgnA, srcRgnB, dstRgn;
```

XorRgn makes dstRgn the union of srcRgnA and srcRgnB minus the intersection of srcRgnA and srcRgnB. DstRgn can be equal to either srcRgnA or srcRgnB.

```
Boolean        PtInRgn (pt, rgn)
        Point pt;  RgnHandle rgn;
```

PtInRgn is TRUE if the pixel below and to the right of point pt is in the region rgn. Otherwise PtInRgn is FALSE.

```
Boolean        RectInRgn (r, rgn)
        Rect *r;   RgnHandle rgn;
```

RectInRgn is TRUE if the intersection of the rectangle r and the region rgn contains at least one bit. If the intersection is empty, RectInRgn is FALSE.

```
Boolean        EqualRgn (rgnA, rgnB)
        RgnHandle rgnA, rgnB;
```

EqualRgn tests if regions are equal. Two regions must have the same size, shape and location to be considered equal. EqualRgn returns TRUE when rgnA is equal to rgnB, otherwise EqualRgn returns FALSE.

```
Boolean        EmptyRgn (rgn)
        RgnHandle rgn;
```

EmptyRgn returns TRUE when rgn is the empty region. EmptyRgn is FALSE if rgn is not empty.

Graphic Operations on Regions

```
void    FrameRgn (rgn)
        RgnHandle rgn;
```

FrameRgn uses characteristics of the current grafPort's pen to draw an outline just inside rgn's boundary. The frame is as wide and as tall as the pen, but it does not go outside of the region.

```
void    PaintRgn (rgn)
        RgnHandle rgn;
```

PaintRgn paints region rgn onto the current grafPort using the current pnPat and pnMode.

```
void    EraseRgn (rgn)
        RgnHandle rgn;
```

PaintRgn paints region rgn onto the current grafPort using the current bkPat PatCopy mode.

```
void    InvertRgn (rgn)
        RgnHandle rgn;
```

InvertRgn toggles all the pixels inside region rgn: all white pixels are switched to black, all black pixels are switched to white.

```
void    FillRgn (rgn, pat)
        RgnHandle rgn;    Pattern pat;
```

FillRgn uses PatCopy mode to fill the region rgn with pattern pat.

Bit Transfer Operations

```
void    ScrollRect (r, dh, dv, updateRgn)
        Rect *r;    int dh, dv;    RgnHandle updateRgn;
```

ScrollRect moves all the visible bits in rectangle r (the bits contained in r, visRgn, clipRgn, portRect and portBits.bound) a distance of dh in the horizontal direction, dv in the vertical. Bits scrolled outside of the area are gone. Vacated positions are filled with pattern bkPat, and this area becomes the updateRgn.

```
void    CopyBits (srcBits, dstBits, srcRect, dstRect,
                  mode, maskRgn)
        BitMap *srcBits, *dstBits;   Rect *srcRect, *dstRect;
        int mode;    RgnHandle maskRgn;
```

CopyBits copies a bit image from one bitMap (srcBits) to another (dstBits) using the given transfer mode.

SrcRect specifies a rectangle in srcBits that is to be copied. Use the srcBits.bounds coordinate system when specifying srcRect.

DstRect is the rectangle in dstBits where the bit image will be transferred. DstRect is in the dstBits.bounds coordinate system. If srcRect and dstRect arc not the same size, the bit image will be scaled to fit the dstRect.

MaskRgn is in the the dstBits.bounds coordinate system. The bit image is always clipped to the region given by maskRgn. If you don't want to clip to a region, then use NULL for maskRgn.

Pictures

```
PicHandle    OpenPicture (picFrame)
        Rect *picFrame;
```

OpenPicture returns a handle to a new picture with picFrame as the picture frame. The picture is now open. Until the picture is closed, all drawing routines and picture comments are part of the picture.

Drawing does not normally occur on screen when a picture is open because OpenPicture calls HidePen. You can change this by calling ShowPen just after the picture has been opened.

While a picture is open, you can trick QuickDraw into doing some drawing that is not part of the picture. To do this, you need to get the current grafPort's picSave value and save it. Then give picSave a NULL value: QuickDraw thinks it's not saving a picture. Now drawing is not included in the picture. To resume making the picture, restore picSave's previous value.

```
void    ClosePicture ( )
```

ClosePicture tells QuickDraw the current picture is done. ClosePicture's call to ShowPen balances OpenPicture's HidePen.

```
void    PicComment (kind, dataSize, dataHandle)
        int kind, datasize;    QDHandle dataHandle;
```

PicComment is used to insert application-specific information into a QuickDraw picture. DataHandle can point to anything. DataSize is the size (in bytes) of the data. Kind can be used by the application to keep track of different types of picture comments.

```
void    DrawPicture (myPicture, dstRect)
        Pichandle myPicture;  Rect *dstRect;
```

DrawPicture draws myPicture in the current grafPort. The picture is scaled to dstRect. Any picture comments in myPicture are passed along to the procedure referenced through the grafProcs field of the current grafPort.

```
void    KillPicture (myPicture)
        Pichandle myPicture;
```

KillPicture gets rid of myPicture. Any memory used by myPicture is released. Call KillPicture only if you do not want to use myPicture again.

Calculations with Polygons

```
PolyHandle    OpenPoly ( )
```

OpenPoly opens a new polygon and returns a handle to it.

HidePen is called so the drawing will not appear on the screen. While the polygon is open, QuickDraw saves information about calls to line-drawing routines: endpoints of the lines are used to define the polygon. To close the polygon, call ClosePoly.

To draw lines while a polygon is open but not have them included in the polygon: get the current grafPort's polySave field and save this value. Set polySave to NULL. While polySave is NULL QuickDraw will not add to the polygon.

To resume making the polygon, restore polySave to the previous value.

```
void    ClosePoly ( )
```

ClosePoly closes the open polygon. The bounding rectangle polyBox is computed. ShowPen is called to restore on-screen drawing.

```
void    KillPoly (poly)
        PolyHandle poly;
```

KillPoly gets rid of the polygon with handle poly. All memory used for the polygon is released. Be sure you no longer need poly before you kill it.

```
void    OffsetPoly (poly, dh, dv)
        PolyHandle poly;   int dh, dv;
```

OffsetPoly translates poly on the coordinate plane. It moves a distance of dh horizontal and dv vertical units. OffsetPoly is a efficient method of moving the polygon—all points are stored relative to the starting point, so only one change is made.

Graphic Operations on Polygons

```
void    FramePoly (poly)
        PolyHandle poly;
```

FramePoly uses the current grafPort's pen to draw an outline just inside the poly. Because the pen is to the right and below the point, the outline will be outside of the polyBBox.

```
void    PaintPoly (poly)
        PolyHandle poly;
```

PaintPoly paints the polygon poly using the pnPat and pnMode of the current grafPort.

```
void    ErasePoly (poly)
        PolyHandle poly;
```

ErasePoly paints polygon poly using the current grafPort's bkPat and the patCopy transfer mode.

```
void    InvertPoly (poly)
        PolyHandle poly;
```

InvertPoly inverts all bits in polygon poly. If a bit is white it becomes black, if it's black, it is changed to white.

```
void    FillPoly (poly, pat)
        PolyHandle poly;    Pattern pat;
```

FillPoly paints polygon poly with pattern pat using patCopy transfer mode.

Calculations with Points

```
void    AddPt (srcPt, dstPt)
        Point srcPt, *dstPt;
```

AddPt adds the coordinates of srcPt to dstPt and stores the result in dstPt.

```
void    SubPt (srcPt, dstPt)
        Point srcPt,*dstPt;
```

SubPt subtracts the coordinates of srcPt from dstPt and stores the result in dstPt.

```
void    SetPt (pt, h, v)
        Point *pt;   int h,v;
```

SetPt makes pt a point with coordinates h and v.

```
Boolean      EqualPt (ptA, ptB)
        Point ptA, ptB;
```

EqualPt is TRUE if ptA has the same coordinates as ptB. EqualPt is FALSE when ptA is not equal to ptB.

```
void    LocalToGlobal (pt)
        Point *pt;
```

LocalToGlobal transforms point pt from the current grafPort's coordinate system to the global coordinate system.

```
void    GlobalToLocal (pt)
        Point *pt;
```

GlobalToLocal transforms the point pt from the global coordinate system to the current grafPort's coordinate system.

Miscellaneous Utilities

```
int     Random ( )
```

Random returns an integer between -32768 and 32767. The integer is from a uniform pseudo-random distribution. The seed for this function is the global variable randSeed. RandSeed is initialized to 1 by InitGraf.

```
Boolean      GetPixel (h, v)
        int h, v;
```

GetPixel is TRUE when the pixel cooresponding to the point (h,v) is black, FALSE when the pixel is white. H and v should be in the current grafPort's coordinate system.

GetPixel doesn't check if the pixel actually belongs to the current grafPort. You can do this by calling PtInRgn (pt, thePort->visRgn).

```
void    StuffHex (thingPtr, s)
        QDPtr thingPtr;    Str255 s;
```

StuffHex allows you to poke bits into a data structure. The bit sequence is given by s—a string of hexadecimal digits. The bits are placed into the memory accessed by thingPtr.

StuffHex pokes the bits with no questions asked. *You* have to make sure the bit sequence is not longer than it should be.

```
void    ScalePt (pt, srcRect, dstRect)
        Point *pt;    Rect *srcRect, *dstRect;
```

ScalePt scales a width and height in srcRect to the width and height it would be in dstRect if srcRect where scaled to dstRect. The width and height in srcRect are given by pt. Upon return pt is equal to the width and height in dstRect.

```
void    MapPt (pt, srcRect, dstRect)
        Point *pt;    rect *srcRect, *dstRect;
```

MapPt takes point pt in srcRect and changes it to the point it would be in dstRect if srcRect where scaled to dstRect.

```
void    MapRect (r, srcRect, dstRect)
        Rect *r, *srcRect, *dstRect;
```

MapRect changes r from a rectangle in srcRect to the rectangle it would be if srcRect where scaled to dstRect. This is done by calling MapPt for the top left and bottom right corners of the rectangle.

```
void    MapRgn (rgn, srcRect, dstRect)
        RgnHandle rgn;    Rect *srcRect, *dstRect;
```

MapRgn changes rgn from a region in srcRect to the region it would be if srcRect where scaled to dstRect. MapRgn accomplishes this by calling MapPt for all the points in the region.

```
void    MapPoly (poly, srcRect, dstRect)
        PolyHandle poly;    Rect *srcRect, *dstRect;
```

MapPoly changes poly from a polygon in srcRect to the polygon it would be if srcRect where scaled to dstRect. MapPoly accomplishes this by calling MapPt for all the points in the polygon.

Customizing QuickDraw Operations

Each grafPort has a set of routines associated with it that QuickDraw uses for the lowest level operations. These are the only QuickDraw routines that actually modify the locations in a bitmap. By changing these routines, QuickDraw can be customized for drawing on external graphics devices such as the Imagewriter.

```
void    SetStdProcs (procs)
        QDProcs *procs;
```

SetStdProcs is used to change the low-level QuickDraw routines of the current graf port. QDProcs points to a structure full of function pointers pointing to the new low-level funtions.

```
void StdText (byteCount, textBuf, numer,denom)
        int byteCount;    QDPtr textBuf;    Point numer, denom;
```

StdText implements text drawing. TextBuf points to the text to be drawn. Bytecount is the number of bytes of text to be drawn. Numer and denom specify scaling factors.

```
void    StdLine (newPt)
        Point newPt;
```

Stdline implements line drawing from the current pen location to newPt.

```
void    StdRect (verb, r)
        GrafVerb verb;    Rect *r;
```

StdRect implements all drawing operations on rectangles. Verb specifies the operation, e.g. fill, invert, frame, etc.

```
void    StdRRect (verb, r, ovalWidth, ovalHeight)
        GrafVerb verb;    Rect *r;    int ovalWidth, ovalHeight;
```

StdRRect implements all drawing operations on round-cornered rectangles.

```
void    StdOval (verb, r)
        GrafVerb verb;   Rect *r;
```

StdOval implements all drawing operations on ovals.


```
void    StdArc (verb, r, startAngle, arcAngle)
        GrafVerb verb;   Rect *r;   int startAngle, arcAngle;
```

StdArc implements all drawing operations on arcs.


```
void    StdPoly (verb, poly)
        GrafVerb verb;   PolyHandle poly;
```

StdPoly implements all drawing operations on polygons.


```
void    StdRgn (verb, rgn)
        GrafVerb verb;   RgnHandle rgn;
```

StdRgn implements all drawing operations on regions.


```
void    StdBits (srcBits,srcRect,dstRect,mode,maskRgn)
        BitMap *srcBits;  Rect *srcRect,*dstRect;  int mode;
        RgnHandle maskRgn;
```

StdBits implements bit transfer between the bitmaps. StdBits scales the image if the source and destination rectangles have different dimensions.

Mode specifies the transfer mode, e.g. xor, or, and, etc. The bit transfer is clipped to within MaskRgn.


```
void    StdComment (kind, dataSize, dataHandle)
        int kind, dataSize;   QDHandle dataHandle;
```

StdComment inserts comments in the current open picture.


```
int     StdTxMeas (byteCount,textBuf,numer,denom,info)
        int byteCount; QDPtr textBuf; Point numer,denom; FontInfo *info;
```

StdTxMeas measures text width as though the text had been drawn using StdText.

```
void    StdGetPic (dataPtr, byteCount)
        QDPtr dataPtr;   int byteCount;
```

StdGetPic is used to access QuickDraw pictures. It retrieves bytecount bytes from the current open picture and puts them in the location pointed to by dataPtr.

```
void    StdPutPic (dataPtr, byteCount)
        QDPtr dataPtr;   int byteCount;
```

StdPutPic stores information in the current open picture.

EVENT MANAGER

The *Event Manager* drives all Macintosh applications.

Unlike most systems where programs read from input streams that might be files or devices such as a keyboard, Macintosh programs react to a stream of events. These events may be caused by keystrokes, mouse button clicks, ejected disks, updated windows, etc. Without explicitly searching for input from all possible sources, Macintosh applications receive input from one source: the *event queue*.

The event queue is managed and controlled by the Event Manager which provides routines for

- retrieving events from the event queue
- classifying events
- posting events
- removing events from consideration

Constants

```
#define nullEvent        0
#define mouseDown        1
#define mouseUp          2
#define keyDown          3
#define keyUp            4
#define autoKey          5
#define updateEvt        6
#define diskEvt          7
#define activateEvt      8
#define abortEvt         9
#define networkEvt       10
#define driverEvt        11
#define app1Evt          12
#define app2Evt          13
#define app3Evt          14
#define app4Evt          15

#define charCodeMask     0x00FF
#define keyCodeMask      0xFF00

#define nullMask         0x0001
#define mDownMask        0x0002
#define mUpMask          0x0004
#define keyDownMask      0x0008
#define keyUpMask        0x0010
#define autoKeyMask      0x0020
#define updateMask       0x0040
#define diskMask         0x0080
#define activMask        0x0100
#define abortMask        0x0200
```

```
#define networkMask        0x0400
#define driverMask         0x0800
#define app1Mask           0x1000
#define app2Mask           0x2000
#define app3Mask           0x4000
#define app4Mask           0x8000

#define everyEvent    0xFFFF
```

Data Structures

```
struct    EventRecord
{       int what;
        long message;
        long when;
        Point where;
        int modifiers;
};

typedef struct EventRecord EventRecord;

typedef long KeyMap[4];
```

Functions

Accessing Events

```
Boolean GetNextEvent (eventMask, theEvent)
      int eventMask;   EventRecord *theEvent;
```

GetNextEvent will set the event equal to the next available event which is of the type (or types) specified by eventMask. If theEvent was on the event queue it is taken off by GetNextEvent. GetNextEvent will first call SystemEvent (a Desk Manager function) so that the system can intercept any events that it (rather than your application) should respond to.

GetNextEvent will be TRUE if it returns an event your application should deal with. If GetNextEvent is FALSE, there is no event for your application and theEvent is a null event.

```
Boolean EventAvail (eventMask, theEvent)
      int eventMask;   EventRecord *theEvent;
```

EventAvail is the same as GetNextEvent with the exception that theEvent will not be removed from the event queue.

Posting and Removing Events

> void   PostEvent (eventCode, eventMsg)
>   int eventCode;   long eventMsg;

PostEvent posts an event with the type field set to eventCode and the event-message field set to eventMsg. Typically, this is used to post application-events.

> void   FlushEvents (eventMask, stopMask)
>   int eventMask, stopMask;

FlushEvents removes any pending events from the event queue.

Reading the Mouse

> void   GetMouse (mouseLoc)
>   Point *mouseLoc;

GetMouse sets mouseLoc equal to the current mouse location. MouseLoc will be in the current grafPort's local coordinate system.

> Boolean   Button ( )

Button will be TRUE if the mouse button is currently down, FALSE if the button is up.

> Boolean   StillDown ( )

StillDown will be TRUE if the mouse button is down and there are no mouse events in the event queue. This means that the button is still down from the previous mouse-down event. StillDown is FALSE if the mouse button is up or the button is down because of a new mouse-down event.

> Boolean   WaitMouseUp ( )

WaitMouseUp is TRUE if the mouse button is still down from a previous mouse-down event. If the mouse button is down because of a new mouse-down event, WaitMouseUp is FALSE and the mouse-up event associated with the previous mouse-down event will be removed from the event queue. WaitMouseUp is FALSE if the mouse button is currently up.

Reading the KeyBoard and KeyPad

```
void    GetKeys (theKeys)
        KeyMap theKeys;
```

GetKeys sets theKeys equal to the current state of the keyboard and keypad (if there is one).

Miscellaneous Utilities

```
void    SetEventMask (theMask)
        int theMask;
```

This sets the system event mask to theMask. This means that the system will post only those event types that have their corresponding bits set in the mask.

```
long    TickCount ( )
```

TickCount returns the number of ticks since the system was last started up. Ticks are 1/60 of a second.

```
long    GetDblTime ( )
```

GetDblTime will return the threshold time value that should exist between a mouse-up and mouse-down event so that two mouse clicks is considered a double-click. Time is measured in ticks.

```
long    GetCaretTime ( )
```

GetCaretTime returns the number of ticks between blinks of the caret. The caret is used to mark the insertion point in editable text—a vertical bar is the usual caret. If you aren't using TextEdit for editable text, then your application is responsible for making the caret blink.

WINDOW MANAGER

The *Window Manager* is responsible for creating the "desktop metaphor." The Window Manager relies on QuickDraw to provide independent coordinate systems for each window, to clip to boundaries set up by the Window Manager and to do all of the drawing. But without the Window Manager's routines that draw window frames, keep track of which parts of which windows need updating, and which is the active window, Macintosh applications would have a tough time taking advantage of QuickDraw's abilities.

In addition to windowing functions built on top of QuickDraw's grafPort and clipping abilities, the Window Manager provides routines for creating windows based on templates in a resource file, deleting windows, moving, sizing, and titling windows.

Constants

```
#define documentProc    0
#define dBoxProc        1
#define dBoxZero        2
#define mdBoxProc       3
#define rDocProc        16

#define dialogKind      2
#define userKind        8

#define inDesk          0
#define inMenuBar       1
#define inSysWindow     2
#define inContent       3
#define inDrag          4
#define inGrow          5
#define inGoAway        6

#define noConstraint    0
#define hAxisOnly       1
#define vAxisOnly       2

#define wDraw           0
#define wHit            1
#define wCalcRgns       2
#define wNew            3
#define wDispose        4
#define wGrow           5
#define wDrawGIcon      6

#define wNoHit          0
#define wInContent      1
#define wInDrag         2
#define wInGrow         3
#define wInGoAway       4
```

Data Structures

```
typedef struct WindowRecord *WindowPeek;

struct WindowRecord
{        GrafPort port;
         int WindowKind;
         char visible;
         char hilited;
         char goAwayFlag;
         char spareFlag;
         RgnHandle strucRgn;
         RgnHandle contRgn;
         RgnHandle updateRgn;
         Handle windowDefProc;
         Handle dataHandle;
         StringHandle titleHandle;
         int titleWidth;
         Handle controlList;
         WindowPeek nextWindow;
         PicHandle windowPic;
         long refCon;
};

typedef struct WindowRecord WindowRecord;

typedef GrafPtr WindowPtr;
```

Functions

Initialization and Allocation

```
void InitWindows ( )
```

InitWindows must be called once before you use any other Window Manager procedures, since this function initializes the Window Manager. The Window Manager port is created and the desktop is drawn with an empty menu bar.

```
void GetWMgrPort (wPort)
     GrafPtr *wPort;
```

GetWMgrPort sets wPort equal to the Window Manager port.

```
WindowPtr NewWindow (wStorage, boundsRect, title, visible, procID, behind,
goAwayFlag, refCon)
        Ptr wStorage;   Rect *boundsRect;   Str255 title;
        Boolean visible, goAwayFlag;   int procID;   WindowPtr behind;   long refCon;
```

NewWindow creates a new window, adds it to the window list, and returns a windowPtr to the new window. The window structure is initialized using the parameters of NewWindow.

```
        WindowPtr GetNewWindow (windowID, wStorage, behind)
              int windowID;   Ptr wStorage;   WindowPtr behind;
```

GetNewWindow uses resources to create a new window, add it to the window list, and then returns a windowPtr to the new window. WindowID is the resource ID for the new window's template. The window structure is initialized using the information in the window resource.

```
        void    CloseWindow (theWindow)
                WindowPtr theWindow;
```

CloseWindow erases theWindow and removes it from the window list. The memory used by all the data structures associated with theWindow will be freed. CloseWindow will *not* release the memory used by the window record. If you supplied a pointer for wStorage to NewWindow (or GetNewWindow), then CloseWindow (not DisposeWindow) is the way to get rid of this window.

```
        void    DisposeWindow (theWindow)
                WindowPtr theWindow;
```

DisposeWindow calls CloseWindow for theWindow then frees the memory used for theWindow's record. If the window record is on the heap (you created theWindow by using wStorage = NULL) then DisposeWindow is the method to use to get rid of theWindow.

Window Display

```
        void    SetWTitle (theWindow, title)
                WindowPtr theWindow;   Str255 title;
```

SetWTitle sets the title of theWindow 's given title. theWindow 's frame will be redrawn if needed.

```
void    GetWTitle (theWindow, title)
WindowPtr theWindow;    Str255 title;
```

GetWTitle sets title to the title of theWindow.


```
void    SelectWindow (theWindow)
WindowPtr theWindow;
```

SelectWindow makes theWindow the active window. This is done by:
unhighlighting the previously highlighted window; putting theWindow in front of all
other window; highlighting theWindow, and generating an activate event.

Call SelectWindow when you see that there was a mouse-down event in the
content region of an inactive window.


```
void    HideWindow (theWindow)
WindowPtr theWindow;
```

HideWindow makes theWindow invisible. If theWindow is the active window,
then the window behind it (if there is one) becomes the active window.


```
void    ShowWindow (theWindow)
WindowPtr theWindow;
```

ShowWindow makes theWindow visible. If theWindow is already visible, then
ShowWindow has no effect. ShowWindow does not change the window list. The
front-to-back ordering stays the same.

If theWindow is the frontmost window, it gets highlighted (if it's not already
highlighted) and an activate event is generated.


```
void    ShowHide (theWindow, showFlag)
WindowPtr theWindow;    Boolean showFlag;
```

ShowHide gives you another option for showing or hiding windows.   Given
theWindow and showFlag here is what ShowHide will do:

theWindow	showFlag	Result
visible	TRUE	no effect
invisible	TRUE	theWindow is made visible
visible	FALSE	theWindow is made invisible
invisible	FALSE	no effect

ShowHide will not change the active window, so none of the events associated
with the activation process occur when ShowHide is used.

```
void    HiliteWindow (theWindow, fHilite)
        WindowPtr theWindow;    Boolean fHilite;
```

HiliteWindow highlights or unhighlights theWindow, depending on the value of fHilite. Given theWindow and fHilite, here is what HiliteWindow will do:

theWindow	fHilite	Result
highlighted	TRUE	no effect
not highlighted	TRUE	theWindow is highlighted
highlighted	FALSE	theWindow is unhighlighted
not highlighted	FALSE	no effect

Your application should never have to call HiliteWindow, since highlighting of active windows and unhighlighting of deactivated windows is taken care of in SelectWindow.

```
void    BringToFront (theWindow)
        WindowPtr theWindow;
```

BringToFront puts theWindow in front of all other windows. theWindow is redrawn if this action is necessary.

You should never need to call BringToFront since this action is done if you use SelectWindow. If you decide to use BringToFront, then it is up to you to make sure that windows are unhighlighted and highlighted as is appropriate.

```
void    SendBehind (theWindow, behindWindow)
        WindowPtr theWindow, behindWindow;
```

SendBehind is a function which changes the front-to-back ordering of windows. theWindow is placed in back of behindWindow. Any necessary redrawing is done. If behindWindow is NULL, then theWindow goes behind all windows on the window list. If theWindow is the active window, it gets unhighlighted, the new active window (the next visible window on list) gets highlighted and the appropriate activate events are generated.

SendBehind should *not* be used to deactivate a previously active window. Use SelectWindow to do this.

If you want to move theWindow closer to the front (theWindow is already somewhere in back of behindWindow) you'll need to include the following routine just after calling SendBehind:

```
wPeek = *theWindow
PaintOne(wPeek,wpeek->strucRgn)
CalcVis(wPeek)
```

This will ensure that theWindow appears as it should on the screen.

```
WindowPtr FrontWindow ( )
```

FrontWindow will return a pointer to the first visible window in the window list (the active window). If there is no such window, a NULL value is returned.

```
void    DrawGrowIcon (theWindow)
        WindowPtr theWindow;
```

DrawGrowIcon should be called when you get an update or activate event for a window that has a size box in its content region.

If theWindow is the active window, the size box will be drawn. If theWindow is not active, DrawGrowIcon will draw whatever is appropriate to indicate that theWindow cannot be sized at this time. DrawGrowIcon uses the window definition function to determine what it draws.

Mouse Location

```
int     FindWindow (thePt, whichWindow)
        Point thePt;   WindowPtr *whichWindow;
```

FindWindow will tell in which part of which window a mouse-down event occurred.

Call FindWindow with thePt equal to the location (in global coordinates) where the mouse was pressed. If the mouse button was pressed inside a window, then whichWindow will point to that window. If the mouse was not in a window, whichWindow will be NULL. In either case, the return value for FindWindow will be one of the predefined constants: inDesk, inMenu, inSysWindow, inContent, inDrag, inGrow, inGoAway.

```
Boolean TrackGoAway (theWindow, thePt)
        WindowPtr theWindow;   Point thePt;
```

After determining that a mouse-down event has occured in the go-away region of theWindow, your application should call TrackGoAway with thePt set equal to the global coordinates where the mouse button was pressed.

Once called, TrackGoAway takes over highlighting the go-away region when the mouse is inside that area. It will unhighlight it when the mouse is outside of the region. TrackGoAway retains control until the mouse button is released. When the mouse button is released the go-away region is unhighlighted. TrackGoAway will be TRUE if theWindow should go away, and FALSE if it shouldn't go away.

Window Movement and Sizing

```
void    MoveWindow (theWindow, hGlobal, vGlobal, front)
WindowPtr theWindow;    int hGlobal, vGlobal;   Boolean front;
```

MoveWindow moves theWindow to the global coordinates given by hGlobal and vGlobal. This point instructs the screen location to move the top left corner of theWindow's portRect. The size, plane and local coordinate system of theWindow remain the same.

If front is TRUE, then MoveWindow will make theWindow the active window (if it isn't already) by calling SelectWindow.

```
void DragWindow (theWindow, startPt, boundsRect)
    WindowPtr theWindow;    Point startPt;   Rect *boundsRect;
```

After you determine that a mouse-down event occurred in the drag region of theWindow, your application should call DragWindow. Set startPt equal to the location (in global coordinates) where the mouse button was pressed.

Use boundsRect (in global coordinates) to confine movement of theWindow. DragWindow will make a gray outline of theWindow follow the movements of the mouse until the mouse button is released. If the button is released at a point inside of boundsRect, then DragWindow will call MoveWindow to move theWindow to that point.

If the Command key is not being held down, theWindow will become the active window (if it isn't already) by having the front parameter TRUE when MoveWindow is called. If the mouse button is released at a point outside the limit set by boundsRect, then DragWindow has no effect.

```
long    GrowWindow (theWindow, startPt, sizeRect)
    WindowPtr theWindow;    Point startPt;   Rect *sizeRect;
```

GrowWindow should be called after you've found that the mouse button was pressed in theWindow's grow region. Have startPt set equal to the point (in global coordinates) where the mouse-down occurred. Use sizeRect to sets limits for the size of theWindow's portRect as follows:

Coordinate	Used to set:
sizeRect->top	minimum # of pixels in vertical direction
sizeRect->left	minimum # of pixels in horizontal direction
sizeRect->bottom	maximum # of pixels in vertical direction
sizeRect->right	maximum # of pixels in horizontal direction

GrowWindow will have a "grow image" of theWindow follow the mouse until the mouse button is released. A grow image for theWindow is a gray outline of theWindow along with gray outlines of any other feature such as title bar, scroll bars, etc. which indicates the size of theWindow. The grow image is defined by theWindow's definition function.

When the mouse button is released, then GrowWindow returns the size that theWindow will be. If the return value is zero, this indicates the size of theWindow should *not* change.

For non-zero return values, the high-order word is the number of pixels in the vertical direction, the low-order word is the number of horizontal pixels. Your application should now call SizeWindow.

```
void    SizeWindow (theWindow, w, h, fUpdate)
        WindowPtr theWindow;   int w, h;   Boolean fUpdate;
```

If w and h are zero, then SizeWindow does nothing. If w or h are non-zero, then SizeWindow will change the size of theWindow's portRect to the width and height given by w and h. SizeWindow then draws the frame for theWindow using the new size.

The title will be truncated on the right if it doesn't fit in the title bar or centered if it does fit.

If fUpdate is TRUE, then SizeWindow will take care of adding new areas of theWindow's content region to the update region. If fUpdate is FALSE, your application is responsible for doing the right thing.

Update Region Maintenance

```
void    InvalRect (badRect)
        Rect *badRect;
```

InvalRect adds badRect to the update region of the window whose grafPort is the current port. BadRect is in the window's content region and should be specified in the local coordinate system.

```
void    InvalRgn (badRgn)
        RgnHandle badRgn;
```

InvalRgn adds badRgn to the update region of the window whose grafPort is the current port.

```
void    ValidRect (goodRect)
        Rect *goodRect;
```

ValidRect removes goodRect from the update region, where goodRect is in the content region of the window whose grafPort is the current port.

GoodRect should be in local coordinates. The Window Manager will not redraw this rectangle, so using ValidRect gives better performance.

```
void    ValidRgn (goodRgn)
        RgnHandle goodRgn;
```

ValidRgn removes goodRgn from the current update region. This region will not be redrawn during an update.

```
void    BeginUpdate (theWindow)
        WindowPtr theWindow;
```

BeginUpdate should be called when you get an update event for theWindow.

During BeginUpdate, theWindow's visRgn will be replaced with the intersection of the visRgn and the update region.

The update region is then set to be the empty region. After BeginUpdate, you should then draw theWindow's content region (drawing only the visRgn would give same results). The areas of theWindow that require updating will then be drawn. Your next step is to call EndUpdate for theWindow.

```
void    EndUpdate (theWindow)
        WindowPtr theWindow;
```

EndUpdate will restore theWindow's grafPort visRgn which was altered during BeginUpdate.

Miscellaneous Utilities

```
void    SetWRefCon (theWindow, data)
        WindowPtr theWindow;    long data;
```

SetWRefCon sets theWindow's refCon field equal to the given data.

```
long    GetWRefCon (theWindow)
        WindowPtr theWindow;
```

GetWRefCon returns the value stored in theWindow's refCon field.

```
void    SetWindowPic (theWindow, pic)
        WindowPtr theWindow;    PicHandle pic;
```

SetWindowPic sets theWindow's windowPic field equal to pic. This will result in the Window Manager drawing the specified picture instead of generating an update event when the contents are to be drawn.

```
PicHandle GetWindowPic (theWindow)
    WindowPtr theWindow;
```

GetWindowPic returns a handle to the picture that makes up theWindow's contents.

```
long    PinRect (theRect, thePt)
    Rect *theRect;   Point thePt;
```

PinRect can be used to get a point inside theRect which is the projection of thePt onto theRect. The point is returned as a long integer, the high-order word is the vertical component, the low-order word is the horizontal.

The value for the *vertical* is:

thePt->v	if thePt->v is between theRect's top and bottom
theRect->top	if thePt->v is above theRect->top
theRect->bottom	if thePt->v is below theRect->bottom

The *horizontal* component is:

thePt->h	if thePt->h is between theRect's right and left sides
theRect->right	if thePt->h is to the right of theRect->right
theRect->left	if thePt->h is to the left of theRect->left

PinRect sort of "pins" thePt inside theRect.

```
long    DragGrayRgn (theRgn, startPt, limitRect,    slopRect, axis, actionProc)
    RgnHandle theRgn;   Point startPt;  Rect *limitRect, *slopRect;
  int axis;   ProcPtr actionProc;
```

This routine is typically called by DragWindow to drag the outline of the window being moved around the screen, following the movement of the mouse. This routine can be used to drag a gray outline of any region.

Low-Level Routines

The following are low-level routines. They are not normally called by applications but you may find them useful.

```
Boolean CheckUpdate (theEvent)
    EventRecord *theEvent;
```

CheckUpdate is called by the Event Manager. It checks all the visible windows on the window list (going from front to back) and looks for non-empty update regions.

When it finds a non-empty update region, it will look in the window record to see if this window has a picture handle. If it does, then the picture is drawn. If there is no picture handle, an update event for this window is stored in theEvent and CheckUpdate is TRUE. If no such window exists, then CheckUpdate returns FALSE.

```
void    ClipAbove (window)
        WindowPeek window;
```

ClipAbove sets the clipRgn of the Window Manager port so that only what should show (parts not obscured by other windows) for the given window will show.

This is done by intersecting the desktop with the current clipRgn then subtracting the structure regions for all the windows that are in front of the given window.

```
void    SaveOld (window)
        WindowPeek window;
```

SaveOld will save the specified window 's content and structure regions. A call to SaveOld must be balanced by a call to DrawNew.

```
void    DrawNew (window, update)
        WindowPeek window;    Boolean update;
```

DrawNew paints an area white, the area being:

(oldStruct XOR newStruct) AND (oldContent XOR newContent)

where oldStruct and oldContent were both saved during SaveOld (above) and newStruct and newContent are the current structure and content regions. If the parameter update is TRUE then the area is added to this window 's update region.

Do *not* nest SaveOld and DrawNew.

```
void    PaintOne (window, clobberedRgn)
        WindowPeek window;    RgnHandle clobberedRgn;
```

PaintOne will paint the given window clipped to the given clobberedRgn, plus all visible windows in front of this one. It will draw the window's frame, paint any unobscured content region white, then add this content region to the update region. If window is NULL, it is assumed to be the desktop and gets painted gray.

```
void    PaintBehind (startWindow, clobberedRgn )
        WindowPeek startWindow;    RgnHandle clobbered;
```

PaintBehind will call PaintOne for startWindow and all windows behind startWindow. ClobberedRgn is the clip region for all windows.

```
void    CalcVis (window)
        WindowPeek window;
```

CalcVis will determine the visRgn for window. This is the content region minus all structure regions for all windows in front of the given window.

```
void    CalcVisBehind (startWindow, clobberedRgn)
        WindowPeek startWindow;    RgnHandle clobbered;
```

CalcVisBehind will determine the visRgn for startWindow and all windows behind startWindow. All visRgns calculated in this procedure are clipped to clobberedRgn. CalcVisBehind is called after PaintBehind.

DIALOG MANAGER

The *Dialog Manager* is a set of high-level tools that interact with the user. The Dialog Manager uses the Window Manager, the Control Manger, and Text Edit to create and conduct dialogs. Various levels of control over dialogs are available, from "hands-off" operation to modes in which each keystroke is checked by an application's routines.

Constants

```
#define crtlItem        0x04
#define btnCtrl         0x00
#define chkCtrl         0x01
#define radCtrl         0x02
#define resCtrl         0x03
#define statText        0x08
#define editText        0x10
#define iconItem        0x20
#define picItem         0x40
#define userItem        0x00
#define itemDisable     0x80

#define OK              1
#define Cancel          2

#define stopIcon        0
#define noteIcon        1
#define ctnIcon         2

#define volBits         0x3
#define alBit           0x4
#define OKDismissal     0x8
```

Data Structures

```
struct DialogRecord
{       WindowRecord window;
        Handle items;
        TEHandle textH;
        int editField;
        int editOpen;
        int aDefItem;
};

typedef struct DialogRecord DialogRecord;
typedef struct DialogRecord *DialogPeek;
```

```c
typedef WindowPtr        DialogPtr;

struct DialogTemplate
{        Rect boundsRect;
         int procID;
         char visible;
         char filler1;
         char goAwayFlag;
         char filler2;
         long refCon;
         int itemsID;
         Str255 title;
};

typedef struct DialogTemplate DialogTemplate;

typedef struct DialogTemplate *DialogTPtr;

typedef struct DialogTemplate **DialogTHandle;

struct StageList
{        char boldItem;
         char boxDrawn;
         char sound;
};

typedef struct StageList StageList[4];

struct AlertTemplate
{        Rect boundsRect;
         int itemsID;
         StageList stages;
};
```

Functions

Initialization

```c
void     InitDialogs (restartProc)
         ProcPtr restartProc;
```

InitDialogs initializes the Dialog Manager and provides the application with a procedure that will restart the application if a system error occurs. This procedure is given by restartProc. If restartProc is NULL, the application will not restart after a system error.

InitDialogs should be called only once after you have initialized the following: QuickDraw, the Font Manager, the Window Manager, the Menu Manager, TextEdit and the Control Manager. In addition to initializing the Dialog Manager, InitDialogs installs the standard sound procedure and passes empty strings to ParamText (see below).

```
void    ErrorSound (soundProc)
        ProcPtr soundProc;
```

ErrorSound tells the Dialog Manager to use a particular sound procedure for dialogs and alerts. SoundProc points to the sound procedure you want to use. If ErrorSound is not called, the standard sound procedure is used. If soundProc is NULL, there is no sound or blink on the menu bar.

```
void    SetDAFont(fontNum)
        int fontNum;
```

SetDAFont sets the font that will be used for all dialogs and alerts created after SetDAFont is called. FontNum specifies the font to be used. If you don't call this procedure, the system font is used. SetDAFont can not be used to change control titles —these are always in the system font.

Creating and Disposing of Dialogs

```
DialogPtr NewDialog (dStorage, boundsRect, title, visible,
                        procID, behind, goAwayFlag, refCon, items)
        Ptr dStorage;  Rect *boundsRect;  Str255 title;
        Boolean visible, goAwayFlag;  int procID;  WindowPtr behind;
        long refCon;  Handle items;
```

NewDialog creates a new dialog as described by the parameters. NewDialog is a superset of NewWindow, in the way that Dialog Manager is a superset of the Window Manager. The first eight parameters are passed on to NewWindow to create the dialog's window. The rest are used to fill in the dialog itself.

```
DialogPtr GetNewDialog (dialogID, dStorage, behind)
        int dialogID;   Ptr dStorage;   WindowPtr behind;
```

GetNewDialog uses resources to create a dialog. The Resource Manager reads in the dialog resource with the given dialogID, then reads in the item list for the dialog (unless it's already in memory). GetNewDialog then makes a copy of the item list for use by the Dialog Manager.

```
void    CloseDialog (theDialog)
        DialogPtr theDialog;
```

CloseDialog closes a dialog and removes its window from the window list. If the dialog window was automatically allocated, it is disposed of.

```
void    DisposDialog (theDialog)
        DialogPtr theDialog;
```

DisposDialog closes the dialog by calling CloseDialog and frees the memory used by the item list and the dialog record. DisposDialog is used to eliminate dialogs that were allocated on the heap.

```
void    CouldDialog (dialogID)
        int dialogID;
```

CouldDialog puts all the information used by the dialog with the given ID (the dialog's template, window definition function, item list resource, and all it's items defined as resources) into memory, and makes it unpurgeable. By storing these items in memory, the dialog can function when the resource file is unaccessible.

```
void    FreeDialog (dialogID)
        int dialogID;
```

FreeDialog causes the information used by the dialog with a given ID purgeable, thereby undoing the effects of CouldDialog. FreeDialog should be called when the resource file becomes accessible again.

Handling Dialog Events

```
void    ModalDialog (filterProc, itemHit)
        ProcPtr filterProc;   int *itemHit;
```

ModalDialog handles all events which occur while a modal dialog is the active window. When an event involving an enabled dialog item occurs, the event is filtered and handled. ModalDialog then returns with itemHit equal to the number of that item.

ModalDialog polls for events. It calls SystemTask first, (thus supporting desk accessories) then calls GetNextEvent with a mask which excludes disk-inserted events. If the event is a mouse-down event outside the dialog window's content region, ModalDialog beeps and continues polling, otherwise the event is filtered and handled. This continues until an enabled item is handled.

FilterProc filters events in various ways. When filterProc is NULL the standard filter is used, which causes ModalDialog to return 1 if the Return or Enter keys have been hit. When filterProc is not NULL, ModalDialog uses the procedure pointed to by filterProc. If filterProc points to theFilter then the procedure theFilter should be declared as follows:

```
Boolean         theFilter (theDialog, theEvent, itemHit)
        DialogPtr theDialog; EventRecord *theEvent; int *itemHit;
```

```
Boolean IsDialogEvent (theEvent)
    EventRecord *theEvent;
```

IsDialogEvent will tell you whether or not theEvent should be handled as part of a dialog. TheEvent should be handled as part of a dialog if it is: an update or activate event for a dialog window; a mouse-down event in a dialog window's content region; or if theEvent occurred when a dialog window was active. If theEvent is determined to be a dialog event, IsDialogEvent returns TRUE, otherwise IsDialogEvent returns FALSE.

IsDialogEvent is used with modeless dialogs. If your application includes any modeless dialogs, then call IsDialogEvent after calling GetNextEvent. If theEvent is a dialog event, DialogSelect can be called to handle it.

```
Boolean DialogSelect (theEvent, theDialog, itemHit)
    EventRecord *theEvent;  DialogPtr *theDialog;  int *itemHit;
```

DialogSelect is used to handle events involving modeless dialogs. If the routine IsDialogEvent returns TRUE, your program should call DialogSelect to determine whether the event involves an active part of a the current modeless dialog. A pointer to the dialog returns in DialogPtr and the item involved returns in itemHit.

```
void    DlgCut (theDialog)
    DialogPtr theDialog;
```

DlgCut lets you handle the Cut editing command when a modeless dialog is active. If theDialog has any editText items, DlgCut will call TECut with the currently selected editText item.

```
void    DlgCopy (theDialog)
    DialogPtr theDialog;
```

DlgCopy handles the Copy edit command for active modeless dialogs. If theDialog has any editText items, DlgCopy calls TECopy.

```
void    DlgPaste (theDialog)
    DialogPtr theDialog;
```

DlgPaste handles the Paste editing command for active modeless dialogs. It checks if there are any editText items in theDialog, and if so, TEPaste is called.

```
void    DlgDelete (theDialog)
        DialogPtr theDialog;
```

DlgDelete lets you handle the Clear editing event when a modeless dialog is active. DlgDelete will call TEDelete if theDialog has any editText items.

```
void    DrawDialog (theDialog)
        DialogPtr theDialog;
```

DrawDialog draws the theDialog's window. Normally, you won't need to call DrawDialog as DialogSelect and ModalDialog will take care of updating the dialog. However, DrawDialog is useful for displaying dialogs which do not require any response. An example of this would be a window which would tell the user what is happening during lengthy processes.

Invoking Alerts

```
int     Alert (alertId, filterProc)
        int alertID;    ProcPtr filterProc;
```

Alert starts up the alert with the given alertID. The stage of the alert is checked. The current sound procedure is called to make whatever noise is appropriate for this stage of alert. If the alert box should be drawn for this stage, then Alert calls NewDialog to draw the box and ModalDialog (using the given filterProc) to take care of the processing. If the alert box has not been drawn Alert's return value is -1 (or the number of the item hit).

```
int     StopAlert (alertID, filterProc)
        int alertID;    ProcPtr filterProc;
```

StopAlert is the same as Alert except that it draws the Stop icon in the top left corner of the box: in the rectangle (10,20,42,52). To draw the Stop icon, StopAlert uses icon resource with ID = stopIcon.

```
int     NoteAlert (alertID, filterProc)
        int alertID;    ProcPtr filterProc;
```

NoteAlert is the same as Alert, except that it draws the Note icon in the top left corner of the alert box (in the rectangle (10,20,42,52)). To draw the Note icon, NoteAlert uses icon resource with ID = noteIcon.

```
int     CautionAlert (alertID, filterProc)
        int alertID;   ProcPtr filterProc;
```

CautionAlert is like Alert except that the Caution icon is drawn in the upper left corner of the alert box: in the rectangle (10,20,42,52). To draw the Caution icon, CautionAlert uses icon resource with ID = ctnIcon.

```
void    CouldAlert (alertID)
        int alertID;
```

CouldAlert makes sure that all the data needed to do the alert with the given alertID is in memory and is unpurgeable. Call CouldAlert just before situations where the alert could occur while the resource file is inaccessible.

```
void    FreeAlert (alertID)
        int alertID;
```

FreeAlert undoes the effects of CouldAlert. Call FreeAlert (using the same alertID used with CouldAlert) when you no longer need to keep the alert in memory (the resource file is accessible).

Manipulating Items in Dialogs and Alerts

```
void    ParamText (param0, param1, param2, param3)
        Str255 param0, param1, param2, param3;
```

ParamText lets you do string substitution for statText items in alerts and dialogs. For all following alerts and dialogs, the string '^0' will be replaced by param0; '^1' will be replaced by param1; '^2' will be replaced by param2; and '^3' will be replaced by param3. Empty strings should be used as parameters where no substitution is desired.

```
void    GetDItem (theDialog, itemNo, type, item, box)
        DialogPtr theDialog;  int itemNo, *type;  Handle *item;  Rect *box;
```

GetDItem gets information about the itemNo numbered item in theDialog. Type is set to the item type; the item parameter becomes a handle to the item; and box is set equal to the item's display rectangle.

```
void    SetDItem (theDialog, itemNo, type, item, box)
        DialogPtr theDialog;  int itemNo, type;  Handle item;  Rect box;
```

SetDItem sets theDialog's itemNo numbered item to be of the given type. A handle to the item is given by parameter item, and box provides the display rectangle for the item.

```
void    GetIText (item, text)
        Handle item;   Str255 text;
```

GetItext gets the text associated with the item, and returns it through the parameter text. For correct results, item should be a statText or editText item in a dialog box.

```
void    SetIText (item, text)
        Handle item;   Str255 text;
```

SetIText sets the text of a statText or editText item (with handle given by parameter item) in a dialog equal to the text of the text parameter.

```
void    SelIText (theDialog, itemNo, strtSel, endSel)
        DialogPtr theDialog;   int itemNo, strtSel, endSel;
```

SelIText selects text in an editText item numbered itemNo in theDialog.

StrtSel is the position of the first character in the selection range. EndSel is the position of the first character after (but not in) the selection range. The selection range is displayed inverted. If strtSel = endSel, or the item contains no text, this is an insertion point and a blinking vertical bar is displayed.

SelIText is useful if the user makes an error in a edit item of a dialog. The error should report in a alert box, then select the entire text of the item with SelIText. The error will go away when the user retypes the text of the item. This eliminates the need to select the item.

```
int GetAlrtStage ( )
```

GetAlrtStage returns the stage number of the last occurrence of an alert. The stage is a number from 0 to 3.

```
void    ResetAlrtStage ( )
```

ResetAlrtStage sets the stage number of an alert to -1, so the next occurrence of the alert will be as if it were the first.

MEMORY MANAGER

The *Memory Manager* allocates memory for Macintosh programs and data. Many Macintosh data structures are held in relocatable blocks of memory and they are addressed through "handles." Handles point to "master pointers" which in turn point to the relocatable blocks of memory.

When memory is compacted, only the master pointers need to be updated to reflect the new position of relocatable blocks. This memory management scheme prevents available memory from becoming fragmented into pieces too small to be useful.

The Memory Manager provides tools for allocating and freeing memory, for changing the properties of memory—locking it in place for instance—and for creating "heaps" from which memory is allocated.

Constants

```
#define noErr          0
#define memFullErr     −108
#define nilHandleErr   −109
#define memWZErr       −111
#define memPurErr      −112

#define maxSize        0x800000
```

Data Structures

```
typedef long Size;
typedef int MemErr;
typedef struct Zone *THz;

struct Zone
{       Ptr bkLim;
        Ptr purgePtr;
        Ptr hFstFree;
        long zcbFree;
        ProcPtr gzProc;
        int moreMast;
        int flags;
        int cntRel;
        int maxRel;
        int cntNRel;
        int maxNRel;
        int cntEmpty;
        int cntHandles;
        long minCBFree;
```

```
        ProcPtr purgeProc;
        Ptr sparePtr;
        Ptr allocPtr;
        int heapData;
};

typedef struct Zone Zone;
```

Functions

Initialization and Allocation

```
void                    InitApplZone ( )
```

InitApplZone is called by the Segment Loader. When an application is started, the application doesn't need to call this routine. InitApplZone will initialize the application heap zone and make it the current zone.

The initialized zone:
* has size of 64K
* can be expanded by 1K increments if necessary
* has allocated space for 64 master pointers
* can have additional master pointers, added 64 at a time
* has empty pointer for grow zone function (gzProc)

MemError codes: NoErr   no error

```
void    SetApplBase (startPtr)
        Ptr startPtr;
```

SetApplBase is a routine which is normally used only by the system.

The starting address of the application heap zone is changed to the address specified by startPtr, then InitApplZone is called.

The application heap zone starts immediately after the system zone. Changing the starting address of the application heap zone changes the size of the system zone.

Note that the system zone can only be made *bigger*, any attempts to make it smaller will be ignored. Using an address larger than the one at the end of the system zone of startPtr will result in a bigger system zone.

MemError codes: NoErr
no error

```
void    InitZone (pGrowZone, cMoreMasters, limitPtr, startPtr)
        ProcPtr pGrowZone;  int cMoreMasters;  Ptr limitPtr, startPtr;
```

InitZone creates a new heap zone and makes this the current zone. The new heap zone will be initialized with its header and trailer. The first byte of this new zone is the address specified by startPtr.

LimitPtr specifies the address of the zone trailer's first byte. The parameter pGrowZone is a pointer to the grow zone routine for this zone. Whenever this zone needs to allocate master pointers, cMoreMasters tells how many master pointers should be allocated.

The new zone is located at ORD(startPtr) to ORD(limitPtr)+11. The zone has a 52-byte header and each master pointer takes up 4 bytes. The usable space (which cannot be less than zero) is calculated using:

ORD(limitPtr) - ORD(startPtr) - 52 - 4*cMoreMasters

This space will decrease as more master pointers are allocated.

MemError codes: NoErr
no error

```
void    SetApplLimit (zoneLimit)
        Ptr zoneLimit;
```

SetApplLimit sets a size limit for application heap zone. This limit is specified by zoneLimit (a Ptr, not a byte count). The application zone can grow up to the byte just before zoneLimit, but no further. If it happens that the zone is already beyond zoneLimit, then it will not grow any larger.

MemError codes: NoErr
no error

```
void    MaxApplZone ( )
```

MaxApplZone gives you a maximum sized application heap zone. The maximum size will reflect any size limitaions you may have set with SetApplLimit

MemError codes: NoErr
no error

```
void MoreMasters ( )
```

MoreMasters will allocate another block of master pointers in the current heap zone. Call this function early in an application to avoid heap fragmentation.

MemError codes: NoErr   no error
                       memFullErr   memory too full

Heap Zone Access

THz GetZone ( )

GetZone will return a pointer to the current heap zone.

MemError codes: NoErr   no error

void   SetZone (hz)
        THz hz;

SetZone sets the zone specified by hz to be the current zone.

MemError codes: NoErr   no error

THz   ApplicZone ( )

ApplicZone will return a pointer to the original application heap zone.

MemError codes: NoErr   no error

Allocating and Releasing Relocatable Blocks

Handle NewHandle (logicalSize)
        Size logicalSize;

NewHandle is used to get a handle to a relocatable block of logicalSize bytes in the current heap zone. This new block is unlocked and unpurgeable. If it can't get a block of logicalSize, then NewHandle returns a NULL value. But before it will return a NULL, NewHandle will try every trick it knows: compacting the heap zone, increasing its size, purging blocks, and calling its grow zone function.

MemError codes: NoErr   no error
                       memFullError   Not enough room in zone

void   DisposHandle (h)
        Handle h;

DisposHandle frees the memory used by the relocatable block accessed through handle h. Any other handles which access the same block as h become invalid.

MemError codes: NoErr   no error
                       memWZErr   attempt to operate on a free block

```
Size    GetHandleSize (h)
        Handle h;
```

GetHandleSize will return the number of bytes used by the relocatable block whose handle is h. GetHandleSize will return a 0 in case of error.

MemError codes: NoErr   no error
                       nilHandleErr   empty master pointer
                       memWZErr   attempt to operate on a free block

```
void    SetHandleSIze (h, newSize)
        Handle h;   Size newSize;
```

SetHandleSize will set the logical size of the relocatable block with handle h to the number of bytes given by newSize. Do not try to increase the size of a locked block using SetHandleSize.

MemError codes: NoErr   no error
                       memFullErr   memory too full
                       nilHandleErr   empty master pointer
                       memWZErr   attempt to operate on a free block

```
Thz     HandleZone (h)
        Handle h;
```

HandleZone will return a handle to whichever heap zone contains the relocatable block with handle h. If h is empty, then the current zone is the return value. If an error occurs, you should ignore HandleZone 's return value.

MemError codes: NoErr   no error
                       memWZErr   attempt to operate on a free block

```
Handle RecoverHandle (p)
        Ptr p;
```

RecoverHandle returns a handle to the relocatable block that Ptr p points to.

MemError codes: NoErr   no error
(This error code may not work in C. D0 is not changed in assembler.)

```
void    ReallocHandle (h, logicalSize)
        Handle h;   Size logicalSize;
```

ReallocHandle allocates a relocatable block of logicalSize bytes. Then handle h's master pointer is updated to point to this newly allocated block. ReallocHandle will work whether or not h is an empty pointer. If h is not empty, the block associated with h will be released before the new block is allocated.

MemError codes:	NoErr	no error
	memFullErr	memory too full
	memWZErr	attempt to operate on a free block
	memPurErr	locked block

Allocating and Releasing Non-Relocatable Blocks

```
Ptr NewPtr (logicalSize)
      Size logicalSize;
```

NewPtr tries to create a nonrelocatable block of logicalSize bytes from the current heap zone. If successful, NewPtr returns a pointer to this block. If unsuccessful NewPtr returns a NULL pointer.

NewPtr will attempt the following before returning a NULL pointer: compacting the current zone, increasing the zone's size, purging blocks, and calling its grow function if there is one.

| MemError codes: | NoErr | no error |
| | memFullErr | memory too full |

```
void DisposPtr (p)
      Ptr p;
```

DisposPtr frees the memory used by the nonrelocatable block pointed to by p. All pointers to this block are useless after DisposPtr, so they should no longer be used for this purpose.

| MemError codes: | NoErr | no error |
| | memFullErr | memory too full |

```
Size GetPtrSize (p)
      Ptr p;
```

GetPtrSize returns the logical size (in bytes) used by the nonrelocatable block which p points to. GetPtrSize will return size = 0 if there is an error.

| MemError codes: | NoErr | no error |
| | memWZErr | attempt to operate on a free block |

```
void SetPtrSize (p, newSize)
     Ptr p;   Size newSize;
```

SetPtrSize will change the logical size of p's nonrelocatable to the number of bytes specified by newSize. Do not use SetPtrSize to increase size of a locked block.

MemError codes:	NoErr	no error
	memFullErr	memory too full
	memWZErr	attempt to operate on a free block

```
THz PtrZone (p)
     Ptr p;
```

PtrZone will return a pointer to the heap zone which contains the block that p points to. Ignore the return value in case of error.

MemError codes:	NoErr	no error
	memWZErr	attempt to operate on a free block

Freeing Space on the Heap

```
long FreeMem ( )
```

FreeMem will return the total number of free bytes in the current heap zone. This number is usually greater than the amount of space that can be allocated to fragmentation.

MemError codes:	NoErr	no error

```
Size MaxMem (grow)
     Size *grow;
```

MaxMem will compact the current heap zone, purge all purgeable blocks, then return the number of bytes contained in its largest contiguous area.

If the current heap is the original application heap zone, then grow is set equal to the maximum number of bytes which the zone can grow. For all heap zones other than the original application heap zone, grow is set equal to 0.

MaxMem will not expand the zone, nor does it call the grow function.

```
Size CompactMem (cbNeeded)
     Size cbNeeded;
```

CompactMem will move forward all relocatable blocks (as best as possible) until a contiguous block of at least cbNeeded bytes is found or the whole zone has been compacted. When it is done compacting, CompactMem will return the number of bytes available in the zone's largest contiguous free block.

MemError codes: NoErr   no error

```
Size ResrvMem (cbNeeded)
Size cbNeeded;
```

ResrvMem will create (but not allocate) a block of cbNeeded bytes as close as possible to the beginning of the current zone. In order to do this, ResrvMem will move other blocks upward in memory, expand the zone, or purge blocks from the zone.

ResrvMem should be used if you have a relocatable block that will be locked for long periods of time. Because ResrvMem creates the block near the beginning of the heap zone, this block will easily be skipped over if the zone is compacted, thus reducing the possibility of fragmentation. You won't need to call ResrvMem for non-relocatable blocks, as NewPtr automatically calls it.

MemError codes: NoErr   no error
                        memFullErr   memory too full

```
void PurgeMem (cbNeeded)
     Size cbNeeded;
```

PurgeMem will sequentially purge relocatable, unlocked, purgeable blocks from the current heap zone until it frees a contiguous block of at least cbNeeded bytes or until the entire zone is purged.

MemError codes: NoErr   no error
                        memFullErr   memory too full

```
void EmptyHandle (h)
     Handle h;
```

EmptyHandle does nothing if h is already empty. For non-empty h, EmptyHandle will free the memory occupied by the relocatable block having handle h.

The master pointer associated with this purged block returns a NULL value, but the pointer to this master pointer (a.k.a. handles to this block) will remain valid—empty, but valid. If the block is reallocated, the master pointer will point to this new block and all handles will work correctly.

MemError codes: NoErr   no error
                        memWZErr   attempt to operate on a free block
                        memPurErr   locked block

Properties of Relocatable Blocks

```
void HLock (h)
     Handle h;
```

HLock locks the relocatable block pointed to by h. It does this by setting the master pointer's lock bit. Once locked, a block cannot be moved. HLock has no effect if the block is already locked.

MemError codes:	NoErr	no error
	nilHandleErr	empty master pointer
	memWZErr	attempt to operate on a free block

```
void HUnlock (h)
     Handle h;
```

HUnlock will unlock the h's relocatable block by clearing the lock bit in the master pointer. This allows the block to be moved in its heap zone if necessary. HUnlock has no effect if the block is already unlocked.

MemError codes:	NoErr	no error
	nilHandleErr	empty master pointer
	memWZErr	attempt to operate on a free block

```
void HPurge (h)
     Handle h;
```

HPurge will mark the relocatable block with handle h as purgeable by setting the purge bit in the master pointer. If this block is already purgeable, HPurge has no effect.

MemError codes:	NoErr	no error
	nilHandleErr	empty master pointer
	memWZErr	attempt to operate on a free block

```
void HNoPurge (h)
     Handle h;
```

HNoPurge will clear the purge bit in h's master pointer, indicating that this block in not to be purged. If the block is already unpurgeable, then HNoPurge has no effect.

MemError codes:	NoErr	no error
	nilHandleErr	empty master pointer
	memWZErr	attempt to operate on a free block

Utility Routines

```
void BlockMove (sourcePtr, destPtr, byteCount)
     Ptr sourcePtr, destPtr;   Size byteCount;
```

BlockMove moves a block of byteCount contiguous bytes from the address sourcePtr to address destPtr. BlockMove just moves the block—it doesn't care where from or where to, and it doesn't update any pointers.

MemError codes: NoErr   no error

```
Ptr TopMem ( )
```

TopMem returns a pointer to the address which is one byte beyond the last byte of RAM.

MemError codes: NoErr   no error

```
MemErr MemError ( )
```

MemError returns the result code due to the last Memory Manager routine that was called.

MENU MANAGER

The *Menu Manager* controls the contents of the Macintosh's pull-down menus. Using Menu Manager routines, menus can be created, deleted, and their contents changed. The Menu Manager can also process keyboard equivalents to menu commands. Menu commands can be turned off if they are inactive in certain contexts.

Constants

```
#define noMark            0
#define commandMark      17
#define checkMark        18
#define diamondMark      19
#define appleSymbol      20

#define mDrawMsg          0
#define mChooseMsg        1
#define mSizeMsg          2

#define textMenuProc      0
```

Data Structures

```
struct      MenuInfo
{    int    menuId;
     int    menuWidth;
     int    menuHeight;
     Handle menuProc;
     unsigned  long  enableFlags;
     Str255  menuData;
{;

typedef  struct  MenuInfo  MenuInfo;

typedef  struct MenuInfo   *MenuPtr;

typedef  struct  MenuInfo  **MenuHandle;
```

Functions

Initialization and Allocation

```
void    InitMenus ( )
```

InitMenu will initialize the Menu Manager by allocating a relocatable block on the heap (large enough for the largest menu list) and redrawing the empty menu bar (InitWindows will draw the menu bar the first time). Call InitMenus only once, other routines (see below) should be used if your application requires new menus.

```
MenuHandle NewMenu (menuID, menuTitle)
        int menuID;    Str255 menuTitle;
```

NewMenu creates an empty menu with the specified menuID and menuTitle then returns a handle to the new menu. This new menu is set up to use the standard menu definition procedure. For applications, menuID should be positive. Negative menu IDs are for desk accessories and no menu can use zero for a menu ID.

Once you've created the new menu, your application should: add items to the menu (see AppendMenu and AddResMenu); add the menu to the menu list (InsertMenu); then redraw the changed menu bar (DrawMenuBar).

When you no longer need a menu you've created using NewMenu, use DisposeMenu to free the memory occupied by the menu.

```
MenuHandle GetMenu (resourceID)
        int resourceID;
```

GetMenu will read the menu with resourceID from the resource file into a menu record in memory. If this menu has a non-standard definition procedure, the procedure is read from the resource file into memory.

A handle to the procedure goes into the menu record.

A handle to the menu is returned by GetMenu.

The menu has items but it is not on the menu list. To use it, add it to the menu list using InsertMenu, then redraw the menu bar by calling DrawMenuBar.

Memory used by this menu can be freed by using ReleaseResource—a Resource Manager procedure.

```
void    DisposeMenu (theMenu)
        MenuHandle theMenu;
```

DiposeMenu releases memory used by theMenu, when it is a menu created by using NewMenu.

Forming the Menus

```
void    AppendMenu (theMenu, data)
        MenuHandle theMenu;    Str255 data;
```

AppendMenu adds an item (or items) to theMenu created from NewMenu or GetMenu. The text for the menu item(s) is given in the string data, where the following meta-characters are interpreted as specified:

Character	Meaning
; or Return	separates items
^	followed by an icon number, adds icon to item
!	followed by a character, marks item with character
<	followed by B,I,U,O, or S to set style as bold, italic, underline, outline or shadow (only 1 style setting per item)
/	followed by a character, sets keyboard for item
(	disables item

Once an item is on the menu, it is there to stay. You cannot remove items from the menu or change their order. The menu list doesn't need to contain TheMenu, AppendMenu works for any menu.

```
void    AddResMenu (theMenu, theType)
        MenuHandle theMenu;    ResType theType;
```

AddResMenu gets all items of theType that it can find, and appends them to theMenu. Items of theType are found by searching through all the open resource files. Once found, they are added to theMenu as enabled items, without any icons, marks, and in the normal style.

Resources with names that begin with . or % are *not* appended to theMenu during AddResMenu. This makes the resources of theType available, which will not appear on theMenu.

```
void    InsertResMenu (theMenu, theType, afterItem)
        MenuHandle theMenu; resType theType;    int afterItem;
```

InsertResMenu does the same thing that AddResMenu does, but it allows you to specify where in theMenu items of theType will occur. The afterItem parameter is used to do this as follows:

If	Then
afterItem = 0	items of theType go before all items
0 < afterUten < last item #	items are inserted after item with item number equal to afterItem
afterItem <= last item #	items are appended to theMenu

Items added to a menu by InsertMenu will be in the reverse order from that used by AddResMenu. To be user friendly, use AddResMenu so the ordering of items in your application is consistent with that of other applications.

Forming the Menu Bar

```
void    InsertMenu (theMenu, beforeID)
        MenuHandle theMenu;    int beforeID;
```

InsertMenu adds theMenu to the menu list. It is inserted before the menu with ID equal to beforeID. TheMenu is added to the end if beforeID is 0 If theMenu is already on the menu list, or if the menu list is full, InsertMenu does nothing.

```
void    DrawMenuBar ( )
```

DrawMenuBar draws the menu bar according to the current menu list. Call DrawMenuBar after any operation (or sequence of operation) which affects the menu list, such as DeleteMenu, InsertMenu, ClearMenu, and SetMenu.

```
void    DeleteMenu (menuID)
        int menuID;
```

DeleteMenu removes the menu with menuID from the menu list. The menu still exists, it's just not on the menu list anymore. If there is no menu with menuID, then DeleteMenu does nothing.

```
void    ClearMenuBar ( )
```

ClearMenuBar removes all menus from the menu list. It does not free any memory, so the menus are still usable.

```
Handle GetNewMBar (menuBarID)
       int menuBarID;
```

GetNewMBar uses the menu bar resource with the given resource ID to create a menu list. A handle to this new list will be returned. GetNewMBar will read in the menuBarID resource if its not already in memory, then it will call GetMenu for each menu that is on this menu list.

The menu list created by GetNewMBar is *not* the current list. To make it the current list, use SetMenuBar (see below).

Handle GetMenuBar ()

GetMenuBar makes a copy of the current menu list, and returns a handle to the copy.

```
void    SetMenuBar (menuList)
        Handle menuList;
```

SetMenuBar makes the *given* menuList the *current* menu list.

Using GetMenuBar and SetMenuBar will allow you to save the current menu list, change the list as needed, and then restore the saved list at some other time.

Choosing from a Menu

```
long    MenuSelect (startPt)
        Point startPt;
```

MenuSelect should be called after determining that a mouse-down event occurred in the menu bar. StartPt is the point returned in the where field of the event record.

```
long    MenuKey (ch)
        char ch;
```

If a key-down event occurs and the command-key is held down, MenuKey should be called.

```
void    HiliteMenu (menuID)
        int menuID;
```

Given a non-zero menuID, HiLiteMenu highlights the specified menu. With menuID zero, the currently highlighted menu is unhighlighted.

Controlling Appearance of Items

```
void    SetItem (theMenu, item, itemString)
        MenuHandle theMenu;    int item;    Str255 itemString;
```

SetItem changes the text of item in theMenu to the given itemString. SetItem does not use meta-characters, so these characters can appear in the item's text.

```
void    GetItem ( theMenu, item, itemString)
        MenuHandle theMenu;   int item;   Str255 itemString;
```

GetItem sets itemString equal to the text of the specified item in theMenu. Like SetItem (above), GetItem does not use meta-characters—so if these characters appear in the text of the item, they'll appear in itemString.

GetItem and SetItem are useful for switching between two menu items which are sort of opposites, such as SHOW FOO and HIDE FOO. If FOO is showing, then HIDE FOO should appear on theMenu. If FOO is not showing, SHOW FOO should be on theMenu.

```
void    DisableItem ( theMenu, item)
        MenuHandle theMenu;   int item;
```

DisableItem disables the specified item in theMenu. Item = 0 will disable theMenu. If theMenu is disabled, all items on it are disabled. Be sure to call DrawMenuBar after disabling theMenu.

Disabled items appear dimmed on theMenu. They cannot be selected and are not highlighted when the cursor moves over them. Disabled menus appear dimmed on the menu bar. When the cursor moves over the disabled menu, the menu drops down and all items in the menu are dimmed. Menus (or menu items) should be disabled when they are not applicable. This will inform users what is, and is not, available to them when they use the program.

```
void    EnableItem ( theMenu, item)
        MenuHandle theMenu;   int item;
```

EnableItem enables the specified item on theMenu. Item = 0 will enable theMenu.

Enabled items are not dimmed, they are highlighted as the cursor moves over them, and they can be selected. Enabled menus should not be dimmed in the menu bar—call DrawMenuBar after enabling theMenu.

```
void    CheckItem ( theMenu, item, checked)
        MenuHandle theMenu;   int item;   Boolean checked;
```

CheckItem checks or unchecks a specified item on theMenu. If checked is TRUE, the item will appear checked and a mark will appear to the left of the item (and it's icon, if any). If checked is FALSE, then the check mark (if there is one) is removed from the item.

```
void    SetItemMark (theMenu, item, markChar)
        MenuHandle theMenu;    int item;    char markChar;
```

SetItemMark will mark a given item on theMenu with the character indicated by markChar. MarkChar can be any character in the system font, or one of the predefined characters (see Constants above). The mark will appear to the left of the item and its icon, if any.

```
void    GetItemMark (theMenu, item, markChar)
        MenuHandle theMenu;    int item;    char *markChar;
```

GetItemMark sets markChar equal to the ASCII value of the character that is marking an item of theMenu. If the item is not marked, then markChar is set to 0.

```
void    SetItemIcon ( theMenu, item, icon)
        MenuHandle theMenu;    int item, icon;
```

SetItemIcon assigns an icon to the given item in theMenu. The parameter icon is an integer from 1 to 255. This integer is the icon number of the icon assigned to the item. This is not the same as the resource ID of the icon. The Menu Manager will add 256 to the icon number to get the resource ID of the icon. It then calls on the Resource Manager to fetch the icon.

```
void    GetItemIcon (theMenu, item, icon)
        MenuHandle theMenu;    int item, *icon;
```

GetItemIcon sets icon equal to the icon number of the icon assigned to the specified item on theMenu. If the item has not icon associated with it, icon is set equal to 0. The icon number is 256 less than the resource ID of the icon.

```
void    SetItemStyle (theMenu, item, chStyle)
        MenuHandle theMenu;    int item;    Style chStyle;
```

SetItemStyle sets the style of the given item on theMenu to the style specified through chStyle.

```
void    GetItemStyle (theMenu, item, chStyle)
        MenuHandle theMenu;    int item;    Style *chStyle;
```

GetItemStyle sets chStyle to the style used by the given item in theMenu.

Miscellaneous Utilities

```
void    SetMenuFlash (count)
        int count;
```

SetMenuFlash sets the number of itmes a selected menu item will flash equal to the parameter count. Count should be an integer between 0 and 3—values greater than 3 will be too slow, count of 0 will disable flashing.

Set MenuFlash is used by the control panel—don't use this in your application.

```
void    CalcMenuSize (theMenu)
        MenuHandle theMenu;
```

CalcMenuSize calculates and stores the horizontal and vertical dimensions of theMenu. CalcMenuSize is called automatically the the Menu Manager after every call to AppendMenu, SetItem, SetItemIcon, and SetItemStyle.

```
int     CountMItems (theMenu)
        MenuHandle theMenu;
```

CountMItems returns the number of items in theMenu.

```
MenuHandle GetMHandle (menuID)
        int menuID;
```

GetMHandle returns a handle to the menu having the specified menuID, if this menu is on the menu list. If this menu is not on the menu list, NULL is returned.

```
void    FlashMenuBar (menuID)
        int menuID;
```

FlashMenuBar inverts the menu bar title of the menu having the given menuID. If this menu is not on the menu list (so it's not on the menu bar) or if menuID = 0, then entire menu bar is inverted.

CONTROL MANAGER

The *Control Manager* provides a set of high-level tools (such as buttons and scroll-bars), and a set of low-level interfaces for creating new kinds of controls. Controls range in complexity from buttons that may be "pressed" or "toggled" to more elaborate controls such as scroll bars. Complex controls such as scroll bars are a composite of buttons and indicators, each of which is responsive to the mouse in different ways. The Control Manager sorts out activity in these complex controls and calls on your application's routines to react to the way such a control is used.

The Control Manager also defines a protocol that can be followed to create new controls. By creating a control definition function that correctly follows the Control Managers rules, you can add new controls to the Control Manager's repertiore.

Constants

```
/* Control definition IDs */
#define pushButProc      0
#define checkBoxProc     1
#define radioButProc     2
#define useWFont         8
#define scrollBarProc    16


/* Part Codes:  part code 128 is reserved for special use by the Control
     Manager.  Don't use 128 for parts of your controls. */
#define inButton         10
#define inCheckBox       11
#define inUpButton       20
#define inDownButton     21
#define inPageUp         22
#define inPageDown       23
#define inThumb          129

/* Constraints for DragControl */
#define noConstraint     0
#define hAxisOnly        1
#define vAxisOnly        2

/* Messages to use when defining your own controls */
#define drawCntl         0
#define testCntl         1
#define calcCrgns        2
#define initCntl         3
#define dispCntl         4
#define posCntl          5
#define thumbCntl        6
#define dragCntl         7
#define autoTrack        8
```

Data Structures

```
typedef struct ControlRecord **                    ControlHandle;

struct ControlRecord {
        ControlHandle nextControl;    /* next control */
        WindowPtr contrlOwner;        /* control's window */
        Rect    contrlRect;           /* rectangle bounds */
        char    contrlVis;            /* TRUE if visible */
        char    contrlHilite;         /* highlight status */
        int     contrlValue;          /* current setting */
        int     contrlMin;            /* minimum setting */
        int     contrlMax;            /* maximum setting */
        Handle  contrlDefProc;        /* control definition function */
        Handle  contrlData;           /* data used by contrlDefProc */
        ProcPtr contrlAction;         /* default action routine */
        long    contrlRfCon;          /* reference value */
        Str255  contrlTitle;          /* control's title */
};

typedef  struct  ControlRecord  ControlRecord;
typedef  struct  ControlRecord  *ControlPtr;
```

Functions

Initialization and Allocation

```
ControlHandle NewControl (theWindow, boundsRect,title, visible, value,
                          min,max,procID,refCon )
    WindowPtr theWindow; Rect *boundsRect;  Str255 title;
    Boolean visible; int value, min, max, procID;  long refCon;
```

NewControl creates a control which is added to the beginning of theWindow's control list. A handle to the new control is returned. The values passed to NewControl are placed into the fields of the control record. Highlighting is off, and there is no default action (contrlAction is NULL).

The newly created control will be in theWindow, therefore any coordinates for the control should be in theWindow's local coordinate system. The rectangle that encloses the control is boundsRect. This rectangle also determines the control's size and location. For standard controls, note the following:

- Simple buttons fit the rectangle exactly. Be sure you have at least a 20 point difference between the top and bottom of the rectangle. You will need this space so that the tallest characters will fit.

- Check boxes and radio buttons need at least a 16 point top to bottom difference.

- Normally, scroll bars are 16 pixels wide so you should have at least a 16 point difference between the top and bottom (or left and right) coordinates. If the difference is less than 16, the scroll bars will be scaled to fit in the rectangle.

The control's title (if it has one) is the string variable "title." If the title is too long to fit in the control's rectangle, then it will be truncated (for simple buttons, the title will be centered and truncated on both ends; for check boxes and radio buttons, the title will be truncated on the right).

If the parameter visible is TRUE, then NewControl draws the control. NewControl does not wait for an update event. The control will be drawn immediately in the window.

The value parameter gives the initial setting for the control. The minimum and maximum parameters define the range of the control. If the control is a button-type (or one that does not have an initial value and for which a range is meaningless), then it does not matter what values you send as parameters. If the control is an on-or-off type (check box or radio button), then minimum should be zero (the control is off) and maximum should be one (the control is on). The initial value must be either on or off.

procId is the control definition ID of the control. This tells the Control Manager the resource ID of the definition function of the control. You can use one of the predefined controls, or define your own.

The control's reference value is RefCon. This structure element is reserved for your application. Your application can set and use RefCon. It is not used by other Macintosh routines.

```
ControlHandle GetNewControl ( controlID, theWindow)
         int controlID; WindowPtr theWindow;
```

GetNewControl has the same end result as NewControl, but accomplishes these feats using resources. GetNewControl uses the resource controlID to create a control, adds the control to the beginning of theWindow's control list, and returns a handle to the newly created control.

```
void    DisposeControl (theControl)
        ControlHandle theControl;
```

Calling DisposeControl will cause the following actions: theControl will be removed from the screen, it will be taken off its window's control list, and all memory used by the control and any data structures associated with it will be freed.

```
void    KillControls(theWindow)
        WindowPtr theWindow;
```

KillControls will eliminate all the controls in theWindow's control list. It does this by calling DisposeControl for each control on theWindow's control list.

Control Display

```
        void    SetCTitle (theControl,title)
ControlHandle  theControl; Str255  title;
```

SetCTitle will set theControl's title to the string you send it, and the control will be redrawn.

```
        void    GetCTitle (theControl,title)
        ControlHandle  theControl; Str255  title;
```

GetCTitle gets theControl's title and returns it in the string title.

```
        void HideControl (theControl)
            ControlHandle  theControl;
```

If theControl is invisible, then HideControl will do nothing. If theControl is visible, then calling HideControl will make it invisible.

The region theControl occupied in the control's window will be filled with the window's background pattern. The rectangle which enclosed theControl is added to the window's update region, making whatever may have been obscured by the control visible again.

```
        void    ShowControl (theControl)
        ControlHandle  theControl;
```

ShowControl will draw theControl in its window. TheControl may be partially or even totally obscured by overlapping windows or other objects. If ShowControl is called for a control which is already visible, ShowControl has no effect.

```
        void    DrawControls (theWindow)
        WindowPtr  theWindow;
```

DrawControls draws all the visible controls in theWindow. The order in which they appear will be the reverse of the order they were created. The first control will appear last (also foremost) in theWindow. Window Manager routines do not generate calls to DrawControls. So if you get an update event for a window which has controls, make sure your application calls DrawControls.

```
        void    HiliteControl (theControl, hiliteState)
        ControlHandle  theControl; int hiliteState;
```

HiliteControl will change the way theControl is highlighted. The value of hiliteState (0 to 255) will determine the change in highlighting:

- A zero value means no highlighting.

- If hiliteState is between 1 and 253, it represents a part code indicating which part of the control is to be highlighted.

- A hiliteState value of 254 or 255 means that the control is to be made inactive and gets the 'inactive' highlighting scheme. If the value is 254, you will be able to detect a mouse click inside the control, if the value is 255, you will not be able to.

HiliteControl will generate a call to the control definition function, redrawing the control with the new highlight state.

Mouse Location

```
int     TestControl (theControl,thePoint)
        ControlHandle  theControl;  Point thePoint;
```

TestControl will test which part of theControl contains thePoint. ThePoint is expected to be in the local coordinates of theControl's window.

For visible and active controls:

TestControl will test which part of theControl contains thePoint. If thePoint is not in theControl, 0 is the return value. If it is inside theControl, then the part code corresponding to thePoint is returned.

For inactive but visible controls:

If theControl has hiliteState 254, TestControl returns 254. If the hiliteState is 255 then TestControl returns 0.

TestControl returns 0 when theControl is invisible.

```
int FindControl (thePoint,theWindow,whichControl)
        Point thePoint; WindowPtr theWindow; ControlHandle *whichControl;
```

FindControl will determine which (if any) of theWindow's controls the mouse-down event occured in. Call FindControl after learning that the mouse button was pressed in the content region of a window which has controls.

theWindow is the window where the mouse button was pressed. thePoint is where the mouse button was pressed and it is in theWindow's local coordinate system. If the mouse button was pressed:

- a visible, active control, whichControl is set to the control handle of the control. The part code of the part containing thePoint is returned.

- a visible, inactive control with 254 highlighting, whichControl is set to the control handle of that control, and 254 is the value returned by FindControl.

- an invisible control, an inactive control with 255 highlighting, or not in any control, whichControl is NULL and 0 is returned.

- an invisible window, or if thePoint is not actually in theWindow (these things won't happen if you called FindWindow) then whichControl gets the NULL value and 0 is returned.

```
int TrackControl (theControl,startPt,actionProc)
    ControlHandle theControl; Point startPt; ProcPtr actionPtr;
```

TrackControl tracks the movements of the mouse and takes all the appropriate actions for theControl. Appropriate actions are, of course, dependent on the type and part of theControl. TrackControl will keep tracking until the mouse button is released.

You should call TrackControl after you found out (using FindControl) that the mouse button was pressed in a visible, active control. theControl is the control handle of the visible, active control and startPt is the point in the control where the mouse button was first pressed (startPt is in the local coordinate system of theControl's window).

If highlighting is apropos, TrackControl will do that. It'll also undo the highlighting before returning.

If the mouse button is released (with the mouse in the same part that it was when tracking began), then the part code for that part is returned and the current value is stored. Your application should now take actions appropriate for the part and its new value. If the mouse is not in the same part, then a zero value is returned and the value remains the same. If this is the case, then your application should take no action as a result of tracking.

Suppose startPt is in an indicator. A gray outline of the indicator will be dragged by the mouse (TrackControl does this by calling DragGrayRgn—a Window Manager utility function). When the mouse button is released, the indicator is repositioned using theControl's definition function. The relative position of the indicator is used to calculate (and store) the new setting. Your application is responsible for doing the right thing with this new value.

You can have TrackControl do more than highlighting and dragging by passing different values through actionProc. If you send:

- a NULL pointer, then there are no additional actions. This is the right thing to do for simple buttons, radio buttons, and the thumb of a scroll bar.

- a pointer to an action procedure, then you can have some action performed until the mouse button is released.

- a –1 (0xFFFFFFFF), then TrackControl will look in theControl's record for the default action procedure. If the default action procedure is a procedure pointer, then TrackControl will use that action procedure. If the default action procedure has a – 1 value (0xFFFFFFFF) then TrackControl will call the control definition function to take action. If the default action is a NULL pointer, then TrackControl does nothing.

Control Movement and Sizing

```
void    MoveControl (theControl,h,v)
        ControlHandle theControl;  int h,v;
```

MoveControl will move theControl to a new location inside theControl's window. The new location is specified (in local coordinates) by h and v. These are the horizontal and vertical coordinates for the top left corner of theControl's bounding rectangle. The bottom right corner of the rectangle is calculated so that theControl is the same size as before. If theControl is visible, it will be hidden at the present location then redrawn at the new location.

```
void DragControl (theControl, startPt, limitRect, slopRect, axis)
        ControlHandle theControl;  Point startPt; Rect limitRect, slopRect;
        int axis;
```

Call DragControl when the mouse button is down inside theControl. A gray outline of theControl will follow the mouse until the mouse button is released. As soon as the mouse is released, theControl is moved (using MoveControl) to the location it was dragged to.

If theControl's definition function has it's own custom drag routine, then DragControl uses the custom drag. If no custom drag is specified, then DragControl calls the Window Manager's DragGrayRgn. DragGrayRgn uses these parameters:

- StartPt is where the mouse button was originally pressed, in the local coordinate system of theControl's window.

- LimitRect bounds the area in which theControl's outline can travel. This area should be the content region of theControl's window, or some subset of that region.

- SlopRect allows the user a bit of sloppiness when dragging theControl. As long as theControl is in SlopRect it will be accepted, but theControl will be moved to a point inside LimitRect.

- Axis will let you constrain the movement of theControl. If axis is 0, there is no constraint. If axis is 1, then there can only be horizontal movement. If axis is 2, only vertical movement is allowed.

```
void    SizeControl (theControl, w, h)
        ControlHandle theControl;  int w,h;
```

This function will change the size of theControl's enclosing rectangle. The parameters w and h specify the width and height (in pixels) of the rectangle. The top left corner of theControl will remain in the same location—the bottom right corner will be adjusted accordingly. If theControl is visible, it will be hidden, then redrawn in the new size.

Control Setting and Range

```
void    SetCtlValue (theControl, theValue)
        ControlHandle theControl; int theValue;
```

SetCtlValue will set theControl's value to theValue and theControl will be redrawn. If theControl is a scroll bar, the thumb will be redrawn in the correct position. For on-or-off type controls (check boxes and radio buttons), a value of 1 will draw theControl in the on position, a value of 0 will draw it as being off.

If theValue is out of theControl's range, theControl is set to it's maximum or the minimum value, whichever is closest to theValue.

```
int     GetCtlValue (theControl)
        ControlHandle theControl;
```

This function will return theControl's current setting.

```
void    SetCtlMin (theControl, minValue)
        ControlHandle theControl;  int minValue;
```

SetCtlMin changes the minimum range setting for theControl. If the current value of the control is below the new minimum value, then theControl's value is set at the new minimum. SetCtlMin redraws theControl, showing the new values.

```
int GetCtlMin (theControl)
        ControlHandle theControl;
```

GetCtlMin returns the minimum setting for theControl.

```
void    SetCtlMax (theControl, maxValue)
        ControlHandle theControl;  int maxValue;
```

SetCtlMax sets theControl's the maximum value equal to maxValue. If the current value is greater than maxValue, then the value is set equal to maxValue. SetCtlMax redraws theControl with it's new values.

```
int GetCtlMax (theControl)
        ControlHandle theControl;
```

GetCtlMax will return the maximum setting of theControl.

Miscellaneous Utilities

```
void    SetCRefCon (theControl,data)
        ControlHandle theControl;  long data;
```

SetCRefCon will set theControl's reference value equal to the parameter data.

```
long    GetCRefCon (theControl)
        ControlHandle theControl;
```

GetCRefCon returns theControl's reference value.

```
Void    SetCtlAction (theControl, actionProc)
        ControlHandle theControl;  ProcPtr actionProc;
```

SetCtlAction will set theControl's default action procedure equal to the parameter actionProc.

```
ProcPtr GetCtlAction (theControl)
    ControlHandle theControl;
```

The value returned by GetCtlAction is whatever is in the default action field of theControl's control record. If there is a default action procedure for theControl, then a pointer to this procedure will be the return value.

TEXTEDIT

TextEdit provides a uniform way for users to enter text. TextEdit is often used indirectly, as part of a dialog that the Dialog Manager conducts or, as part of a Standard File Package dialog. Because all Macintosh applications use TextEdit, all of the editing capabilities used to correct mistakes in entering text are uniform throughout all Macintosh applications.

Constants

```
#define teJustLeft      0
#define teJustCenter    1
#define teJustRight    -1
```

Data Structures

```
typedef char Chars[32001];
typedef Chars *CharsPtr;
typedef Chars **CharsHandle;

struct TERec
{       Rect destRect;
        Rect viewRect;
        int lineHeight;
        int firstBL;
        int selStart;
        int selEnd;
        int just;
        int length;
        Handle hText;
        int txFont;
        int txFace;
        int txMode;
        int txSize;
        GrafPtr inPort;
        int crOnly;
        int nLines;
        int lineStarts[32001];
};

typedef struct TERec TERec;

typedef struct TERec *TEPtr;

typedef struct TERec **TEHandle;
```

Functions

Initialization

    void TEInit ()

TEInit allocates a handle for the application's scrap. This serves to initialize TextEdit. Call TEInit just once at the beginning of the program.

    TEHandle TENew (destRect, viewRect)
    Rect destRect, viewRect;

TENew sets up and initializes an edit record with the destination rectangle equal to destRect, and the view rectangle equal to the given viewRect. A handle to the edit record is returned.

The edit record created by TENew uses the environment of the current grafPort, so destRect and viewRect should be given in these units. The edit record is set up to be left justified and single spaced with insertion point at position 0. TENew also allocates a handle to the text.

TENew must be called once for each edit record.

Manipulating Edit Records

    void TESetText (text, length, hTE)
    Ptr text;   long length;   TEHandle hTE;

TESetText changes the text in hTE's edit record to the text given by parameter text. The text is length characters long. The selection range is an insertion point at the end of the text. Call TEUpdate to show that text has been changed.

    CharsHandle TEGetText (hTE)
    TEHandle hTE;

TEGetText returns a handle to the text in hTE 's edit record.

    void TEDispose (hTE)
    TEHandle hTE;

TEDispose frees the memory used for hTE: memory used by both the text and the edit record. Call TEDispose when you are totally done using an edit record.

Editing

```
void  TEKey (key, hTE)
      char key;   TEHandle hTE;
```

TEKey replaces hTE 's selection range with a character given by key, and then places an insertion point after that character.

If the selection range is only an insertion point, the character is inserted, and the insertion point is positioned just after the inserted character.

```
void TECut (hTE)
      TEHandle hTE;
```

TECut cuts the selected range from hTE's text and puts it into the scrap. Whatever was in the scrap before is totally replaced by the selected range. If the selected range is an insertion point, the scrap will be emptied.

```
void TECopy (hTE)
      TEHandle hTE;
```

TECopy copies hTE's selected range onto the scrap, completely replacing the scrap's contents. When TECopy is called with an empty selected range (and insertion point), the scrap becomes empty.

```
void TEPaste (hTE)
      TEHandle hTE;
```

TEPaste replaces hTE's selected range with a copy of the scrap, and positions the insertion point just beyond the last character copied from the scrap. For empty scrap, TEPaste deletes the selected range. For empty selected range (insertion point), TEPaste inserts the scrap.

```
void TEDelete (hTE)
      TEHandle hTE;
```

TEDelete deletes the hTE's selected range but does not place it in the scrap. If the select range is an insertion point, TEDelete does nothing.

```
void TEInsert (text, length, hTE)
      Ptr text;   long length;   TEHandle hTE;
```

TEInsert inserts text into hTE's text, placing it just before hTE's selected range (or insertion point). The length parameter gives the number of characters to be inserted.

Note that TEInsert does not delete the selected range, thus making it possible for your application to support the Undo command.

Selected Range and Justification

```
void TESetSelect (selStart, selEnd, hTE)
    long selStart, selEnd;   TEHandle hTE;
```

TESetSelect sets hTE's selected range to the range given by selStart and selEnd. To do this, TESetSelect unhighlights the current selected range (if any), then highlights the new select range. When selStart equals selEnd, this is an insertion point. The caret is displayed and there is no highlighting.

Legal values for selStart and selEnd are from 0 to 65535. If selEnd is beyond the last character, then the position of the last character plus 1 is used for selEnd.

```
void TESetJust (j, hTE)
    int j;   TEHandle hTE;
```

TESetJust sets the justification for hTE to the justification specified by j. J must be one of the following: teJustLeft, teJustCenter, teJustRight.

To show the new justification, your application should call TEUpdate after calling TESetJust.

Mice and Carets

```
void TEClick (pt, extend, hTE)
    Point pt;   Boolean extend;   hTE TEHandle;
```

TEClick is used for setting the selected range through mouse-down events. TEClick should be called when a mouse-down event occurs in hTE's view rectangle.

Pt is the location where the mouse button was pressed, but pt must be in local coordinates (the event record for the mouse-down event gives pt in global coordinates, so call GlobalToLocal for TEClick)! If the shift key was down at the time the mouse button was pressed, then extend should be TRUE, indicating this is an extended selection. If the shift key was not down, extend should be FALSE.

Once control is passed to TEClick, it takes care of highlighting the selected range. The selected range expands or shrinks, according to the movements of the mouse. TEClick also takes care of word selection when a double click occurs.

```
void TEIdle (hTE)
     TEHandle hTE;
```

TEIdle checks to see if it is time for the blinking caret at hTE's insertion point to blink again. To maintain a constant blinking frequency, your application should call TEIdle often. But don't worry about calling TEIdle too often, TextEdit is set up so that blinking will never occur more often than a minimum time period (this minimum time period can be adjusted on the control panel).

```
void TEActivate (hTE)
     TEHandle hTE;
```

TEActivate highlights the selected range in hTE's view rectangle. If the selected range is an insertion point, a blinking caret is displayed at the insertion point.

TEActivate should be called whenever a text editing window becomes active.

```
void TEDeactivate (hTE)
     TEHandle hTE;
```

TEDeactivate is the opposite of TEActivate: it unhighlights the selected range in hTE's view rectangle, or removes the blinking caret if the selected range is an insertion point.

TEDeactivate should be called whenever a text editing window becomes inactive.

Text Display

```
void TEUpdate (rUpdate, hTE)
     Rect *rUpdate;   TEHandle hTE;
```

TEUpdate redraws hTE's text inside the rUpdate rectangle, where rUpdate is given in the grafPort's coordinates. Using hTE's viewRect for rUpdate will cause hTE's entire view rectangle to be redrawn

TEUpdate should be called whenever an update event occurs: after calling BeginUpdate and before calling EndUpdate (see Window Manager for descriptions of BeginUpdate and EndUpdate).

```
void TextBox (text, length, box, j)
     Ptr text;   long length;   Rect *box;   int j;
```

TextBox draws the given text in the rectangle specified in local coordinates by box. The text has length number of characters and is drawn according to the justification specified by j, j being one of the following: teJustLeft, teJustCenter or teJustRight.

Note that TextBox does not use any edit record. It is just used for drawing text.

Advanced Routines

```
void TEScroll (dh, dv, hTE)
    int dh, dv;   TEHandle hTE;
```

TEScroll scrolls the text in hTE's viewRect. The amount scrolled is specified in pixels by dh and dv: positive dh moves the text to the right, negative dh moves the text to the left; positive dv moves the text up, negative dv moves the text down.

Call TEUpdate with hTE's viewRect to show results of scrolling.

```
void TECalText (hTE)
    TEHandle hTE;
```

TECalText recalculates the beginnings of all the lines of text in hTE and updates hTE's lineStarts array.

TECalText should be called after any operation which changes the number of characters per line, such as changing the destination rectangle, or the hText field.

STANDARD FILE PACKAGE

The *Standard File Package* provides a uniform way for users to select files for opening and saving to. If does not actually open the files, or save them. The File Manager is used for those functions.

Constants

```
#define putDlgID        -3999
#define putSave         2
#define putCancel       5
#define putEject        6
#define putName         7

#define getDlgID        -4000
#define getCancel       3
#define getEject        5
#define getDrive        6
#define getNmList       7
#define getScroll       8
```

Data Structures

```
struct SFReply
{       char good;
        char copy;
        OSType fType;
        int vRefNum;
        int version;
        char fName[63];
};

typedef Struct SFReply SFReply;
typedef OSType SFTypeList[4];
```

Functions

```
void SFPutFile (where, prompt, origName, dlgHook, reply)
        Point where;  Str255 prompt, origName; ProcPtr dlgHook;
        SFReply *reply;
```

SFPutFile uses a standard file dialog to get the name of a file from the user. Typically, this file is used to save the current document.

Where is the position of the top left corner of the dialog.

Prompt provides brief application specific instructions. If the document came from a file, OrigName should be the name of that file.

DlgHook lets you specify a function to be called after each time ModalDialog is called while the standard file dialog is on the screen. This lets you filter input to the standard file dialog.

Reply holds the information returned from the dialog.

```
void SFPPutFile (where, prompt, origName, dlgHook, reply, dlgID,
            filterProc)
        Point where;  Str255 prompt, origName; ProcPtr dlgHook;
        SFReply *reply;  int dlgID;  ProcPtr filterProc;
```

SFPPutFile works like SFPutFile with two differences: it allows you to use a different dialog template with resource ID dlgID, and allows you to specify filterProc as a filter procedure for calls to ModalDialog.

```
void SFGetFile (where, prompt, fileFilter, numTypes, typeList, dlgHook,
            reply);
        Point where;   Str255 prompt;  ProcPtr fileFilter;  int numTypes;
        SFTypeList typeList; ProcPtr dlgHook;  SFReply *reply;
```

SFGetFile uses a standard file dialog to display a list of files of the types specified in typeList. This is typically used in opening documents.

Where is the location of the upper left corner of the dialog on the screen.

Prompt gives brief instructions to the user.

FileFilter allows you to specify a function that can be used to further qualify files for display.

DlgHook is a procedure that is called after each call to ModalDialog.

Reply holds the information returned from the dialog.

```
void SFPGetFile (where, prompt, fileFilter, numTypes, typeList, dlgHook,
            reply, dlgID, filterProc);
        Point where;   Str255 prompt;  ProcPtr fileFilter;  int numTypes;
        SFTypeList typeList; ProcPtr dlgHook;  SFReply *reply; int dlgID;
        ProcPtr filterProc;
```

SFPGetFile works like SFGetFile with two differences: it allows you to use a different dialog template with resource ID dlgID, and allows you to specify filterProc as a filter procedure for calls to ModalDialog.

FILE MANAGER

The *File Manager* provides tools for opening, closing, creating, deleting, reading, and writing files. The File Manager has two sets of routines: one is a set of high-level routines that are easy to use and do most of what many of the applications need to do. The more complex "parameter-block" routines are so-named because they take a data structure known as a parameter-block as their argument. These routines allow more complete control over the file system, and in some cases, where several file-system routines must be called in sequence to find information about a file, they can be more efficient.

Constants

```
#define fHasBundle     0x20
#define fInvisible     0x40

#define fTrash         -3
#define fDeskTop       -2
#define fDisk          0

#define fsAtMark       0
#define fsFromStart    1
#define fsFromLEOF     2
#define fsFromMark     3

#define fsCurPerm      0
#define fsRdPerm       1
#define fsWrPerm       2
#define fsRdWrPerm     3
```

Data Structures

```
typedef long OSType;
typedef int OSErr;

struct Finfo
{       OSType fdType;
        OSType fdCreator;
        int fdFlags;
        Point fdLocation;
        int fdFldr;
};

typedef struct Finfo Finfo;
```

```
struct ioParam
{       int ioRefNum;
        SignedByte ioVersNum;
        SignedByte ioPermssn;
        Ptr ioMisc;
        Ptr ioBuffer;
        long ioReqCount;
        long ioActCount;
        int ioPosMode;
        long ioPosOffset;
};

Struct fileParam
{       int ioFRefNum;
        SignedByte ioFVersNum;
        SignedByte filler1;
        int ioFDirIndex;
        SignedByte ioFlAttrib;
        SignedBye ioFlVersNum;
        Finfo ioFlFndrInfo;
        long ioFlNum;
        int ioFlStBlk;
        long ioFlLgLen;
        long ioFlPyLen;
        int ioFlRStBlk;
        long ioFlRLgLen;
        long ioFlRPyLen;
        long ioFlCrDat;
        long ioFlMdDat;
};

struct volumeParam
{       long filler2;
        int ioVolIndex;
        long ioVCrDate;
        long ioVLsBkUp;
        int ioVAtrb;
        int ioVNmFls;
        int ioVDirSt;
        int ioVBlLn;
        int ioVNmAlBlks;
        long ioVAlBlkSiz;
        long ioVClpSiz;
        int ioAlBlSt;
        long ioVNxtFnum;
        int ioVFrBlk;
};
```

```c
struct drvQElRec
{       struct drvQElRec *drvLink;
        int drvFlags;
        int drvRefNum;
        int drvFSID;
        int  drvBlkSize;
};

union OpParamType
{           int sndVal;
            int asncConfig;
            struct
            {       Ptr asncBPtr;
                    int asncBLen;
            } asyncInBuff;
            struct
            {       unsigned char fXOn;
                    unsigned char fCTS;
                    char xon;
                    char  xoff;
                    unsigned char errs;
                    unsigned char evts;
                    unsigned char fInX;
                    unsigned char null;
            } asyncShk;
            struct
            {       Ptr fontRecPtr;
                    int fontCurDev;
            } fontMgr;
            Ptr diskBuff;
            long asyncNBytes;
            struct
            {       int asncs1;
                    int asncs2;
                    int asncs3;
            } asyncStatus;
            struct
            {       int dskTrackLock;
                    long dskInfoBits;l
                    struct drvQElRec         dskQElem;
                    int dskPrime;
                    int dskErrCnt;
            } diskStat;
};

typedef union OpParamType OpParamType;

typedef union OpParamType *OpParamPtr;
```

```
struct cntrlParam
{         int csRefNum;
          int csCode;
          OpParamType csParam;
};

struct ParamBlkRec
{         struct ParamBlkRec *ioLink;
          int ioType;
          int ioTrap;
          Ptr ioCmdAddr;
          ProcPtr ioCompletion;
          int ioResult;
          char *ioNamePtr;
          int ioVRefNum;
          union
          {         struct ioParam iop;
                    struct fileParam fp;
                    struct volumeParam vp;
                    struct cntrlParam cp;
          } u;
};

typedef struct ParamBlkRec ParamBlkRec;

typedef struct ParamBlkRec *ParmBlkPtr;
```

Functions: High-Level

Accessing Volumes

```
OSErr GetVInfo (drvNum, volName, vRefNum, freeBytes)
      int drvNum,*vRefNum;  OSStrPtr volName;  long *freeBytes;
```

GetVInfo gets the name, volume reference number, and number of bytes available for the volume in drive drvNum. The information is returned through parameters volName, vRefNum, and freeBytes.

Result Codes:	noErr	no error
	nsvErr	no such volume error
	paramErr	bad drive number

```
OSErr GetVol (volName, vRefNum)
      OSStrPtr volName;  int*vRefNum;
```

GetVol gets the default volume's name and reference number, and returns them through volName and vRefNum.

Result Codes: noErr   no error
                           nsvErr   no such volume error

OSErr SetVol (volName, vRefNum)
       OSStrPtr volName; int vRefNum;

SetVol makes the volume specified by volName or vRefNum the default volume.

Result Codes: noErr   no error
                           bdNamErr   bad volume name
                           nsvErr   no such volume error
                           paramErr   no default volume

OSErr FlushVol (volName, vRefNum)
       OSStrPtr volName; int vRefNum;

FlushVol writes the descriptive information and volume buffer contents for the
volume specified by volName or vRefNum.

Result Codes: noErr   no error
                           bdNamErr   bad volume name
                           extFSErr   external file system
                           ioErr   disk I/O error
                           nsDrvErr   no such drive error
                           nsvErr   no such volume error
                           paramErr   no default volume

OSErr UnmountVol (volName, vRefNum)
       OSStrPtr volName; int vRefNum;

UnmountVol unmounts the volume given by volName or vRefNum. It calls
FlushVol for the volume, closes all the volume's open files, and releases any memory
used by the volume.
       You should not unmount the startup volume.

Result Codes: noErr   no error
                           bdNamErr   bad volume name
                           extFSErr   external file system
                           ioErr   disk I/O error
                           nsDrvErr   no such drive error
                           nsvErr   no such volume error
                           paramErr   no default volume

```
OSErr Eject (volName, vRefNum)
     OSStrPtr volName;  int vRefNum;
```

Eject is called to eject the volume with the given volName or vRefNum. First it calls FlushVol to flush the volume, the volume goes offline and then gets ejected.

Result Codes:	noErr	no error
	bdNamErr	bad volume name
	extFSErr	external file system
	ioErr	disk I/O error
	nsDrvErr	no such drive error
	nsvErr	no such volume error
	paramErr	no default volume

Changing File Contents

```
OSErr Create (fileName, vRefNum, creator, fileType)
     OSStrPtr fileName;  int vREfNUm;  OSType creator, fileType;
```

Create makes a new (unlocked and empty) file on the volume with vRefNum reference number. The new file's name, type and creator are given by parameters fileName, fileType and creator. The file's modification and creation dates are set to the date on the system clock.

Result Codes:	noErr	no error
	bdNamErr	bad volume name
	dupFNErr	duplicate file name error
	dirFulErr	directory full error
	extFSErr	external file system
	ioErr	disk I/O error
	nsvErr	no such volume error
	vLckdErr	software volume lock
	wPrErr	hardware volume lock

```
OSErr FSOpen (fileName, vRefNum, refNum)
     OSStrPtr fileName;  int vRefNum, *refNum;
```

FSOpen opens the file with the given fileName on the volume specified by vRefNum. An access path that has the same read/write permission as the file is created for the file. RefNum is set equal to the access path's reference number.

Result Codes:	noErr	no error
	bdNamErr	bad volume name
	extFSErr	external file system

fnfErr	file not found error
ioErr	disk I/O error
nsvErr	no such volume error
opWrErr	file already open for writing
tmfoErr	too many files open error

```
OSErr FSRead (refNum, count, buffPtr)
    int refNum; long *count; Ptr buffPtr;
```

FSRead reads data from the open file having refNum as its access path reference number. Starting from the current mark, FSRead tries to read count number of bytes.
The data read in is placed in the buffer pointed to by buffPtr. If the logical end-of-file is encountered before count number of bytes has been read in, the mark is moved to the end-of-file, count is set to the number of bytes actually read in, and an end-of-file error is returned.

Result Codes:

noErr	no error
eofErr	end-of-file error
extFSErr	external file system
fnfErr	file not found error
ioErr	disk I/O error
paramErr	negative count
rfNumErr	bad reference number

```
OSErr FSWrite ( refNum, count, buffPtr)
    int refNum; long *count; Ptr buffPtr;
```

FSWrite tries to write count number of bytes from the location pointed at by buffPtr to the open file with the access path refNum. Writing in the file begins at the file mark. Count is set equal to the number of bytes actually written to the file.

Result Codes:

noErr	no error
dskFulErr	disk full error
fLckdErr	file locked error
fnOpnErr	file not open error
ioErr	disk I/O error
paramErr	negative count
rfNumErr	bad reference number
vLckdErr	software volume lock
wPrErr	hardware volume lock
wrPermErr	write permission error

```
OSErr GetFPos (refNum, filePos)
    int refNum;  long *filePos;
```

GetFPos gets the file marker for the file with access path refNum. FilePos is set equal to the current marker position.

Result Codes:	noErr	no error
	extFSErr	external file system error
	fnOpnErr	file not open error
	ioErr	disk I/O error
	rfNumErr	bad reference number

```
OSErr SetFPos (refNum, posMode, posOff)
    int refNum, posMode;  long posOff;
```

SetFPos lets you set the file marker for the file with the given access path refNum. The placement of the mark is determined by posMode and posOff. PosMode is a position in the file, and posOff is an offset from that position.

If PosMode is:	then mark will be posOff bytes
fsAtMark	at the mark, posOff is ignored
fsFromStart	offset from start of file
fsFromLEOF	offset from logical end-of-file
fsFromMark	offset from mark

Result Codes:	noErr	no error
	eofErr	end-of-file error
	extFSErr	external file system error
	fnOpnErr	file not open error
	ioErr	disk I/O error
	posErr	position is before start of file
	rfNumErr	bad reference number

```
OSErr GetEOF (refNum, logEOF)
    int refNum;  long *logEOF;
```

GetEOF gets the logical end-of-file for the file with refNum access path and sets logEOF equal to this number.

Result Codes:	noErr	no error
	extFSErr	external file system error
	fnOpnErr	file not open error
	ioErr	disk I/O errors
	rfNumErr	bad reference number

```
OSErr SetEOF (refNum, logEOF)
     int refNum;  long logEOF;
```

SetEOF sets the logical end-of-file for the file with the access path refNum. The logical end-of-file is set to logEOF If logEOF is beyond the physical end-of-file, another block of the volume is allocated for the file. If there is not enough room to set the specified logical end-of-file, a disk full error is returned and no change is made. If logEOF is 0, all space used by the file is released.

Result Codes:

noErr	no error
dskFulErr	disk full error
extFSErr	external file system error
fLckdErr	file locked error
fnOpnErr	file not open error
ioErr	disk I/O error
rfNumErr	bad reference number
vLckdErr	software volume lock
wPrErr	hardware volume lock
wrPermErr	write permission error

```
OSErr Allocate (refNum, count)
     int refNum;  long *count;
```

Allocate tries to add count bytes to the file with access path reference number refNum. If count is not a multiple of the block allocation size, it is rounded up to the next multiple, and this number of bytes is added to the file.

If there are not enough bytes available on the volume, whatever space is available is allocated for the file, and Allocate returns a disk full error. Count is set to the number of bytes actually allocated. The physical end-of-file is set one byte beyond the last byte allocated.

Result Codes:

noErr	no error
dskFulErr	disk full error
fLckdErr	file locked error
fnOpnErr	file not open error
ioErr	disk I/O error
rfNumErr	bad reference number
vLckdErr	software volume lock
wPrErr	hardware volume lock
wrPermErr	write permission error

```
OSErr FSClose (refNum)
        int refNum;
```

FSClose closes the file with access path reference number refNum. The file's access path is removed, the volume's buffer contents are written to the volume, and the file directory information is updated.

Note that not all information stored on the volume is correct until FlushVol is called for the volume.

Result Codes:	noErr	no error
	extFSErr	external file system
	fnfErr	file not found error
	fnOpnErr	file not open error
	ioErr	disk I/O error
	nsvErr	no such volume error
	rfNumErr	bad reference number

Changing Information About Files

```
OSErr GetFInfo (fileName, vRefNum, fndrInfo)
        OSStrPtr fileName;  int refNum;  FInfo *fndrInfo;
```

GetFInfo gets the Finder's information for the file with name fileName and volume number given by vRefNum. The information is returned in fndrInfo.

Result Codes:	noErr	no error
	bdNamErr	bad file name
	extFSErr	external file system
	fnfErr	file not found error
	ioErr	disk I/O error
	nsvErr	no such volume error
	paramErr	no default volume

```
OSErr SetFInfo (fileName, vRefNum, fndrInfo)
        OSStrPtr fileName;  int refNum;  FInfo fndrInfo;
```

SetFInfo changes the Finder's information about the file with the given fileName on the volume referenced by vRefNum. The Finder information is set to that given by fndrInfo.

Result Codes:	noErr	no error
	extFSErr	external file system
	fLckdErr	file locked error
	fnfErr	file not found error
	ioErr	disk I/O error

nsvErr	no such volume error
vLckedErr	software volume lock
wPrErr	hardware volume lock

OSErr SetFLock (fileName, vRefNum)
    OSStrPtr fileName; int refNum;

SetFLock locks the fileName file on the volume referenced by vRefNum. Currently used access paths are not affected by the lock.

Result Codes:	noErr	no error
	extFSErr	external file system
	fnfErr	file not found error
	ioErr	disk I/O error
	nsvErr	no such volume error
	vLckedErr	software volume lock
	wPrErr	hardware volume lock

OSErr RstFLock (fileName, vRefNum)
    OSStrPtr fileName; int refNum;

RstFLock unlocks the file with the given fileName on the volume referenced by vRefNum. Currently used access paths are not affected.

Result Codes:	noErr	no error
	extFSErr	external file system
	fnfErr	file not found error
	ioErr	disk I/O error
	nsvErr	no such volume error
	vLckedErr	software volume lock
	wPrErr	hardware volume lock

OSErr Rename (oldName, vRefNum, newName)
    OSStrPtr oldName, newName; int vRefNum;

Rename can change the names of files and volumes. If oldName is a file name, then the file's name is set to the newName (currently used access paths are unaffected by the change).

If oldName is a volume name and vRefNum is the volume's reference number, then the volume is given the newName.

Result Codes:	noErr	no error
	bdNamErr	bad name error
	dirFulErr	directory full error
	dupFNErr	duplicate file name error

extFSErr	external file system
fLckedErr	file locked error
fnfErr	file not found error
fsRnErr	file system renaming error
ioErr	disk I/O error
nsvErr	no such volume error
paramErr	no default volume
vLckedErr	software volume lock
wPrErr	hardware volume lock

```
OSErr FSDelete (fileName, vRefNum)
     OSStrPtr fileName;  int refNum;
```

FSDelete removes the file named fileName from the vRefNum volume. FSDelete removes both forks of the file.

Result Codes:

noErr	no error
bdNamErr	bad name error
extFSErr	external file system
fBsyErr	file busy error
fLckedErr	file locked error
fnfErr	file not found error
ioErr	disk I/O error
nsvErr	no such volume error
vLckedErr	software volume lock
wPrErr	hardware volume lock

Functions: Low-Level

Initialization

```
void    InitQueue ()
```

InitQueue removes all but the present File Manager call from the I/O queue.

Accessing Volumes

```
OSErr PBMountVol (paramBlock)
     ParmBlkPtr paramBlock;
```

PBMountVol mounts the volume in the drive numbered ioVRefNum, and ioVRefNum is set to the volume's reference number. If no other volumes have been mounted, this volume becomes is the default volume. PBMountVol is always synchronous.

Result Codes:

noErr	no error
bdMDBErr	bad master directory block
extFSErr	external file system
ioErr	disk I/O error
mFulErr	memory full error
noMacDskErr	not a Macintosh disk error
nsDrvErr	no such drive error
paramErr	bad drive number
volOnLinErr	volume already on-line

```
OSErr PBGetVInfo (paramBlock, async)
     ParmBlkPtr paramBlock;  Boolean async;
```

PBGetVInfo gets information about a specific volume. The File Manager determines the volume in question by checking ioVolIndex as follows:

- when ioVolIndex is positive, ioVolIndex is used to determine the volume.
- when ioVolIndex is negative, ioNamePtr and ioVRefNum are used to determine the volume.
- when ioVolIndex is zero, ioVRefNum is used to determine the volume. When this happens, ioVRefNum is set to the volume reference number and ioNamePtr returns the volume's name.

Result Codes:

noErr	no error
nsvErr	no such volume error
paramErr	no default volume

```
OSErr PBGetVol (paramBlock, async)
     ParmBlkPtr paramBlock;  Boolean async;
```

PBGetVol returns the default volume's reference number in ioVRefNum and its name in ioNamePtr.

Result Codes:

noErr	no error
nsvErr	no such volume error

```
OSErr PBSetVol (paramBlock, async)
     ParmBlkPtr paramBlock;  Boolean async;
```

PBSetVol makes the volume pointed to by ioNamePtr or ioVRefNum the default volume. The volume must be mounted before it can become the default volume.

Result Codes:

noErr	no error
bdNamErr	bad volume name

nsvErr	no such volume error
paramErr	no default error

```
OSErr PBFlshVol (paramBlock, async)
        ParmBlkPtr paramBlock; Boolean async;
```

PBFlshVol flushes the volume given by ioNamePtr or ioVRefNum. Flushing a volume consists writing the following items to the volume: descriptive information, volume buffer contents, all the volume's access path buffers, and the modification date (which is the current time).

Result Codes:

	noErr	no error
	bdNamErr	bad volume name
	extFSErr	external file system
	ioErr	disk I/O error
	nsDrvErr	no such drive error
	nsvErr	no such volume error
	paramErr	no default volume

```
OSErr PBUnmountVol (paramBlock)
        ParmBlkPtr paramBlock;
```

PBUnmountVol unmounts the volume given by ioNamePtr or ioVRefNum. To unmount a volume, the File Manager flushes the volume, closes all open files on the volume, and releases all memory used for the volume. PBUnmountVol is always synchronous.

Your application should not allow the startup volume to be unmounted.

Result Codes:

	noErr	no error
	bdNamErr	bad volume name
	extFSErr	external file system
	ioErr	disk I/O error
	nsDrvErr	no such drive error
	nsvErr	no such volume error
	paramErr	no default volume

```
OSErr PBOffLine (paramBlock, async)
        ParmBlkPtr paramBlock; Boolean async;
```

PBOffLine takes the volume indicated by ioNamePtr or ioVRefNum and places it off-line. Taking a volume off-line means flushing the volume and releasing most of the memory used by the volume—only 94 bytes of descriptive information will remain in memory.

Result Codes:

	noErr	no error
	bdNamErr	bad volume name

extFSErr	external file system
ioErr	disk I/O error
nsDrvErr	no such drive error
nsvErr	no such volume error
paramErr	no default volume

```
OSErr PBEject (paramBlock, async)
      ParmBlkPtr paramBlock;  Boolean async;
```

PBEject ejects the volume indicated by ioNamePtr or ioVRefNum after it has been taken off-line by calling PBOffLine.

Result Codes:

noErr	no error
bdNamErr	bad volume name
extFSErr	external file system
ioErr	disk I/O error
nsDrvErr	no such drive error
nsvErr	no such volume error
paramErr	no default volume

Changing File Contents

```
OSErr PBCreate (paramBlock, async)
      ParmBlkPtr paramBlock;  Boolean async;
```

PBCreate creates a new unlocked and empty file on the volume indicated by ioVRefNum. The name of the new file is given by ioNamePtr, its version number is given by ioVersNum. The file's creation and modification dates are set to the current time as given by the system clock.

After creating the file, your application should call PBSetFinfo to provide the Finder with information about the file.

Result Codes:

noErr	no error
bdNamErr	bad volume name
dupFNErr	duplicate file name
dirFulErr	directory full error
extFSErr	external file system
ioErr	disk I/O error
nsvErr	no such volume error
vLckdErr	software volume lock
wPrErr	hardware volume lock

```
OSErr PBOpen (paramBlock, async)
     ParmBlkPtr paramBlock;  Boolean async;
```

This is the low-level routine for opening files. The path-reference is returned in the ioVRefNum field of the parameter block rather than through an integer pointer as in the FSOpen call.

Result Codes:	noErr	no error
	bdNamErr	bad volume name
	extFSErr	external file system
	fnfErr	file not found error
	ioErr	disk I/O error
	mFulErr	memory full error
	nsvErr	no such volume error
	opWrErr	file already opened for writing
	tmfoErr	too many files open

```
OSErr PBOpenRF (paramBlock, async)
     ParmBlkPtr paramBlock;  Boolean async;
```

Identical to the PBOpen call, except that the resource fork is opened.

Result Codes:	noErr	no error
	bdNamErr	bad volume name
	extFSErr	external file system
	fnfErr	file not found error
	ioErr	disk I/O error
	mFulErr	memory full error
	nsvErr	no such volume error
	opWrErr	file already opened for writing
	permErr	no permission to read file
	tmfoErr	too many files open

```
OSErr PBRead (paramBlock, async)
     ParmBlkPtr paramBlock;  Boolean async;
```

PBRead tries to read ioReqCount bytes from the file (with access path number ioRefNum) to the buffer pointed to by ioBuffer.

If you try to read beyond the end-of-file, the file marker is moved to the end-of-file and you'll get an end-of-file error result code. After reading is completed, ioActCount is set to the number of bytes actually read in and ioPosOffset gives the file marker's position.

Result Codes:	noErr	no error
	eofErr	end-of-file error
	extFSErr	external file system

fnOpnErr	file not open error
ioErr	disk I/O error
paramErr	negative ioReqCount
rfNumErr	bad reference number

OSErr PBWrite (paramBlock, async)
    ParmBlkPtr paramBlock; Boolean async;

PBWrite tries to write ioReqCount bytes from the buffer pointed to by ioBuffer to the file with access path reference number ioRefNum. IoPosMode and ioPosOffset together indicate the position in the file where the data is to be written, as follows:

If ioPosMode is:	then writing will begin:
fsAtMark	at the mark, ioPosOffset is ignored
fsFromStart	ioPosOffset bytes from start of file
fsFromLEOF	ioPosOffset bytes from logical end-of-file
fsFromMark	ioPosOffset bytes from mark

After writing, ioActCount is set to the number of bytes actually written, ioPosOffset gives the position of the mark.

Result Codes:		
	noErr	no error
	dskFulErr	disk full error
	fLckdErr	file locked error
	fnOpnErr	file not open error
	ioErr	disk I/O error
	paramErr	negative ioReqCount
	posErr	position beyond end-of-file
	rfNumErr	bad reference number
	vLckedErr	software volume lock
	wPrErr	hardware volume lock
	wrPermErr	no permission to write

OSErr PBGetFPos (paramBlock, async)
    ParmBlkPtr paramBlock; Boolean async;

PBGetFPos sets ioPosOffset to the position of the file mark for the file having access path referenced by ioRefNum. IoReqCount, ioActCount, and ioPosMode are set to zero.

Result Codes:		
	noErr	no error
	extFSErr	external file system
	fnOpnErr	file not open error
	ioErr	disk I/O error
	rfNumErr	bad reference number

```
OSErr PBSetFPos (paramBlock, async)
     ParmBlkPtr paramBlock;  Boolean async;
```

PBSetFPos sets the mark for the file indicated by ioRefNum. The mark is set using ioPosMode and ioPosOffset together as follows:

If ioPosMode is:	then mark will be set:
fsAtMark	at the mark, ioPosOffset is ignored
fsFromStart	ioPosOffset bytes from start of file
fsFromLEOF	ioPosOffset bytes from logical end-of-file
fsFromMark	ioPosOffset bytes from mark

An error will result if you try to set the mark beyond the logical end-of-file.

Result Codes:	noErr	no error
	eofErr	end-of-file error
	extFSErr	external file system
	fnOpnErr	file not open error
	ioErr	disk I/O error
	posErr	position error (before start)
	rfNumErr	bad reference number

```
OSErr PBGetEOF (paramBlock, async)
     ParmBlkPtr paramBlock;  Boolean async;
```

PBGetEOF gets the logical end-of-file for the file indicated by ioRefNum, and returns this value in ioMisc.

Result Codes:	noErr	no error
	extFSErr	external file system
	fnOpnErr	file not open error
	ioErr	disk I/O error
	rfNumErr	bad reference number

```
OSErr PBSetEOF (paramBlock, async)
     ParmBlkPtr paramBlock;  Boolean async;
```

PBSetEOF uses the value in ioMisc to set the logical end-of-file for the open file with access path ioRefNum. If the logical end-of-file if beyond the physical end-of-file, the next free allocation block is added to the file, and then the physical end-of-file is set to the byte just after this block. If there in not enough room on the volume, no change is made and an error is returned. Using ioMisc = 0 will free all the space on the volume used by the file.

Result Codes:	noErr	no error
	dskFulErr	disk full error
	extFSErr	external file system

fLckdErr	file locked error
fnOpnErr	file not open error
ioErr	disk I/O error
rfNumErr	bad reference number
vLckdErr	software volume lock
wPrErr	hardware volume lock
wrPermErr	write permission error

```
OSErr PBAllocate (paramBlock, async)
      ParmBlkPtr paramBlock; Boolean async;
```

PBAllocate tries to add ioReqCount bytes to the file with access path reference number ioRefNum. Actually, the next highest multiple (to ioReqCount) of the block allocation size is added to the file.

If there are not enough bytes available on the volume, then whatever space is available is allocated to the file and PBAllocate returns a disk full error.

IoActCount returns the number of bytes actually allocated. The physical end-of-file is set one byte beyond the last byte allocated.

Result Codes:

noErr	no error
dskFulErr	disk full error
fLckdErr	file locked error
fnOpnErr	file not open error
ioErr	disk I/O error
rfNumErr	bad reference number
vLckdErr	software volume lock
wPrErr	hardware volume lock
wrPermErr	write permission error

```
OSErr PBFlshFile (paramBlock, async)
      ParmBlkPtr paramBlock; Boolean async;
```

PBFlshFile write the contents of the access buffer referenced by ioRefNum to the proper volume, and the file directory is updated. Note that not all information on the volume is correct until the volume is flushed.

Result Codes:

noErr	no error
extFSErr	external file system error
fnfErr	file not found error
fnOpnErr	file not open error
ioErr	disk I/O error
nsvErr	no such volume error
rfNumErr	bad reference number

```
OSErr PBClose (paramBlock, async)
    ParmBlkPtr paramBlock;  Boolean async;
```

PBClose writes the contents of the access path (with ioRefNum reference number) buffer to its associated file and frees the memory used by the access path. Note that not all information on the volume is correct until the volume is flushed.

Result Codes:		
	noErr	no error
	extFSErr	external file system error
	fnfErr	file not found error
	fnOpnErr	file not open error
	ioErr	disk I/O error
	nsvErr	no such volume error
	rfNumErr	bad reference number

Changing Information About Files

```
OSErr PBGetFInfo (paramBlock, async)
    ParmBlkPtr paramBlock;  Boolean async;
```

PBGetFInfo gets Finder information for a file on the volume refered to by ioVRefNum. The File Manager determines which of the volume's files is inquired about by looking at ioFDirIndex.

If ioFDirIndex is positive, the File Manager returns information about the file with ioFDirIndex file number. For non-positive ioFDirIndex, the File Manager returns information about the file with name and version number specified by ioNamePtr and ioVersNum.

IoNamePtr returns a pointer to the file's name (unless IoNamePtr is NULL) and ioRefNum is set to the reference number of the first-found access path for the file.

Result Codes:		
	noErr	no error
	bdNamErr	bad name error
	extFSErr	external file system error
	fnfErr	file not found error
	ioErr	disk I/O error
	nsvErr	no such volume error
	paramErr	no default volume

```
OSErr PBSetFInfo (paramBlock, async)
    ParmBlkPtr paramBlock;  Boolean async;
```

PBSetFInfo sets the information about a file to the information given via paramBlock. The file, on the volume with ioVRefNum reference number, has a name given by ioNamePtr and version number ioVersNum.

Result Codes:

noErr	no error	
bdNamErr	bad name error	
extFSErr	external file system error	
fLckdErr	file locked error	
fnfErr	file not found error	
ioErr	disk I/O error	
nsvErr	no such volume error	
vLckdErr	software volume lock	
wPrErr	hardware volume lock	

OSErr PBSetFLock (paramBlock, async)
    ParmBlkPtr paramBlock; Boolean async;

PBSetFLock locks the file on volume ioVRefNum with name and version number given by ioNamePtr and ioVersNum. The lock does not affect the file's access paths already in use.

Result Codes:

noErr	no error	
extFSErr	external file system error	
fnfErr	file not found error	
ioErr	disk I/O error	
nsvErr	no such volume error	
vLckdErr	software volume lock	
wPrErr	hardware volume lock	

OSErr PBRstFLock (paramBlock, async)
    ParmBlkPtr paramBlock; Boolean async;

PBRstFLock unlocks the file on volume ioVRefNum with name and version number given by ioNamePtr and ioVersNum. This unlocking will not affect access paths already in use for the file.

Result Codes:

noErr	no error	
extFSErr	external file system error	
fnfErr	file not found error	
ioErr	disk I/O error	
nsvErr	no such volume error	
vLckdErr	software volume lock	
wPrErr	hardware volume lock	

```
OSErr PBSetFVers (paramBlock, async)
    ParmBlkPtr paramBlock;  Boolean async;
```

PBSetFVers changes the version number for a file on the volume refered to by ioVRefNum. The file's name and current version number are given by ioNamePtr and ioVersNum. The new version number for the file is set to the number given by ioMisc. This change does not affect any access paths currently in use for the file.

The Resource Manager and Segment Loader will not operate on a file unless its version number is 0.

Result Codes:	noErr	no error
	bdNamErr	bad name error
	dupFNErr	duplicate file error
	extFSErr	external file system error
	fLckdErr	file locked error
	fnfErr	file not found error
	ioErr	disk I/O error
	nsvErr	no such volume error
	paramErr	no default volume
	vLckdErr	software volume lock
	wPrErr	hardware volume lock

```
OSErr PBRename (paramBlock, async)
    ParmBlkPtr paramBlock;  Boolean async;
```

PBRename can be used to change the name of a file or a volume.

If ioNamePtr gives a file name and ioVersNum is it's version number, then PBRename changes the file name to the name pointed to by ioMisc. If ioNamePtr is the name of a volume or ioVRefNum is the reference number to a volume, the volume's name is changed to the name pointed to by ioMisc.

Renaming will not affect access paths currently in use.

Result Codes:	noErr	no error
	bdNamErr	bad name error
	dirFulErr	directory full error
	dupFNErr	duplicate file name error
	extFSErr	external file system
	fLckedErr	file locked error
	fnfErr	file not found error
	fsRnErr	file system renaming error
	ioErr	disk I/O error
	nsvErr	no such volume error
	paramErr	no default volume
	vLckedErr	software volume lock
	wPrErr	hardware volume lock

```
OSErr PBDelete (paramBlock, async)
     ParmBlkPtr paramBlock;  Boolean async;
```

PBDelete removes the file with name given by ioNamePtr and version number
ioVersNum from the ioVRefNum volume. PBDelete removes both forks of the file.

Result Codes:

noErr	no error
bdNamErr	bad name error
extFSErr	external file system
fBsyErr	file busy error
fLckedErr	file locked error
fnfErr	file not found error
ioErr	disk I/O error
nsvErr	no such volume error
vLckedErr	software volume lock
wPrErr	hardware volume lock

FONT MANAGER

The *Font Manager* provides tools for getting information about typefaces and managing font resources. The Font Manager is seldom called directly — other Toolbox Managers use fonts and provide interface routines for selecting fonts.

Constants

/* Font Numbers */

```
#define systemFont    0
#define applFont      1
#define newYork       2
#define geneva        3
#define monaco        4
#define venice        5
#define london        6
#define athens        7
#define sanFran       8
#define toronto       9
```

/* Font Types */

```
#define propFont  0x9000
#define fixedFont 0xB000
#define fontWid   0xACB0
```

Data Structures

```
struct  FMInput
{    int    family;
     int    size;
     char   face;
     char   needBits;
     int    device;
     Point numer;
     Point denom;
};

typedef  struct  FMInput  FMInput;

struct  FMOutput
{    int    errNum;
     Handle   fontHandle;
     Byte bold;
     Byte italic;
     Byte ulOffset;
```

```
        Byte ulShadow;
        Byte ulThick;
        Byte shadow;
        SignedByte  extra;
        Byte ascent;
        Byte descent;
        Byte widMax;
        SignedByte  leading;
        Byte unused;
        Point  numer;
        Point  denom;
};

typedef struct FMOutput FMOutput;

typedef struct FMOutput *FMOutPtr;

struct  FontRec
{     int    fontType;
      int    FirstChar;
      itn    lastChar;
      int    widMax;
      int    kernMax;
      int    nDescent;
      int    fRectMax;
      int    chHeight;
      int    owTLoc;
      int    ascent;
      int    descent;
      Int    leading;
      int    rowWords;
};

typedef struct FontRec FontRec;
```

Functions

Initializing the Font Manager

```
        void    InitFonts ( )
```

InitFonts gets the Font Manager ready for use. It also reads the system font into memory if it's not already there. You must call InitFonts once before calling any Toolbox routine that uses the Font Manager.

Getting Font Information

```
        void    GetFontName (fontNum, theName)
                int fontNum;    Str255 theName;
```

GetFontName sets theName equal to the name of the font whose font number is fontNum. TheName will be an empty string if there is no font having the given fontNum.

```
void    GetFNum (fontName, theNum)
        Str255 fontName;   int *theNum;
```

GetFNum sets theNum to equal the font number of the font whose name is fontName. If there is no font with the given fontName, theNum becomes 0.

```
Boolean                 RealFont (fontNum, size)
        int fontNum, size;
```

RealFont will tell you whether or not a given font is available in a particular size. Specify the font you're interested in by setting fontNum equal to the font's font number, and set size equal to the size you want. RealFont looks through all the open resource files: if the font is available in the given size, RealFont will return TRUE, otherwise it will be FALSE.

Keeping Fonts in Memory

```
void    SetFontLock (lockFlag)
        Boolean lockFlag;
```

SetFontLock makes the most recently used font either purgeable or unpurgeable. If lockFlag is TRUE, the font will be locked (unpurgeable). If lockFlag is FALSE, the font is made purgeable (unlocked).

Advanced Routine

```
FMOutPtr                SwapFont (inRec)
        FMInput *inRec;
```

SwapFont returns information about a version of a font which is specified in the Font Manager input record inRec. The information is returned via a Font Manager output record, which is pointed to by SwapFont's return value. The information SwapFont makes available is used mostly by QuickDraw routines.

PRINT MANAGER

The *Print Manager* enables applications to use QuickDraw to plot their output to a printer.

The Print Manager defines the interface to all printing devices. This interface consists of functions that start and end printing jobs and tell the printer that a page is beginning or has ended. The bulk of the Macintosh printing interface is actually QuickDraw. Once a printing job is begun, QuickDraw can be used in much the same way it is used to draw on the screen.

Constants

```
#define lMemFullErr     -108
#define noErr           0

#define bDraftLoop      0
#define bSpoolLoop      1
#define bUser1Loop      2
#define bUser2Loop      3

#define iPrBitsCtl      4
#define lScreenBits     0
#define lPaintBits      1
#define iPrIOCtl        5
#define iPrEvtCtl       6
#define iPrEvtAll       0x0002fffd
#define iPrEvtTop       0x0001fffd
#define iPrDevCtl       7
#define lPrReset        0x00010000
#define lPrPageEnd      0x00020000
#define lprLineFeed     0x00030000
#define iFMgrCtl        8

#define iPFMaxPgs       128
#define iPrPgFract      120
#define iPrAbort        128
#define iPrRelease        2
#define lPfType         'PFIL'
#define lPfSig          'PSYS'

#define sPrDrvr         ".Print"
#define iPrDrvrRef      -3
#define lPrintType      'PREC'
#define iPrintDef       0
#define iPrintLst       1
#define iPrintDrvr      2
#define iMyPrDrvr       0xe000
#define iPStrRFil       0xe000
```

```
#define iPStrPFil      0xe001
#define iPrStlDlg      0xe000
#define PrJobDlg       0xe001
#define feedCut        0
#define feedFanFold    1
#define feedMechCut    2
#define feedOther 3

#define scanTB         0
#define scanBT         1
#define scanLR         2
#define scanRL         3
```

Data Structures

```
typedef char TStr80[81]
typedef TsStr80 *TPstr80;
typedef Rect TPRect;

struct TPrPort
{       GrafPort gPort;
        QDProcs gProcs;
};

typedef struct TPrPort TPrPort;

typedef struct TPrPort *TPPrPort;

union TPPort
{       GrafPtr pGPort;
        TPPrPort pPrPort;
};

typedef union TPPort    TPPort;

struct TPrInfo
{       int iDev;
        int iVRes;
        int iHRes;
        Rect rPage;
};

typedef struct TPrInfo TprInfo;

typedef unsigned char TFeed;

typedef int TWord;

struct TPrStl
{       TWord wDev;
        int iPageV;
```

```
                int iPageH;
                SignedByte bPort;
                TFeed feed;
};

typedef struct TPrStl     TPrStl;

struct TPrJob
{       int iFstPage;
        int iLstPage;
        int iCopies;
        SignedByte bJDocLoop;
        char fFromUsr;
        ProcPtr pIdleProc;
        TPStr80 pFileName;
        int iFileVol;
        SignedByte bFileVers;
        SignedByte bJobX;
};

typedef struct TPrJob TPrJob;

typedef unsigned char TScan;

struct TPrXInfo
{       int iRowBytes;
        int iBandV;
        int iBandH;
        int iDevBytes;
        int iBands;
        SignedByte bPatScale;
        SignedByte bUlThick;
        SignedByte bUlOffset;
        SignedByte bUlShadow;
        TScan scan;
        SignedByte bXInfoX;
};

typedef struct TPrXInfo TPrXInfo;

struct TPrint
{       int iPrVersion;
        TPrInfo prInfo;
        Rect rPaper;
        TPrStl prStl;
        TPrInfo prInfoPT;
        TPrXinfo prXInfo;
        TPrJob prJob;
        int printX[19];
};

typedef struct TPrint TPrint;
```

```
typedef struct TPrint *TPPrint;

typedef struct TPrint **THPrint;

struct TPrStatus
{       int iTotPages;
        int iCurPage;
        int iTotCopies;
        int iCurCopy;
        int iTotBands;
        int iCurBand;
        char fPgDirty;
        char fImaging;
        THPrint hPrint;
        TPPrPort pPrPort;
        PicHandle hPic;
};

typedef struct TPrStatus TPrStatus;
```

Functions

Initialization and Termination

```
void PrOpen ( )
```

PrOpen prepares the Printing Manager for use by opening the Printer Driver and the printer resource file. If this is not possible, PrError indicates a Resource Manager error occurred and PrOpen does nothing.

```
void PrClose ( )
```

PrCLose shuts down the Printing Manager. Memory used by the Printing Manager and the printer resource file is released. PrClose does not close the Printer Driver. Use PrDrvrClose to close the Printing Manager.

Print Records and Dialogs

```
void    PrintDefault (hPrint)
        THPrint hPrint;
```

PrintDefault puts the default print settings into the appropriate fields of hPrint's print record.

```
Boolean PrValidate (hPrint)
    THPrint hPrint;
```

PrValidate makes sure that the fields of hPrint's print record are compatible with the current version of the Printing Manager and the installed printer. If the print record is okay in its current state, PrValidate returns FALSE. If it's not okay, the print record is adjusted according to the printer default values in the printer resource file. After making these adjustments, PrValidate returns TRUE.

PrValidate also makes whatever changes are needed to hPrint's print record so that it has the current style and job settings. These changes *do not* affect PrValidate's return value.

```
Boolean PrStlDialog (hPrint)
    THPrint hPrint;
```

PrStlDialog activates the style dialog. HPrint's current settings are used as the initial settings for the dialog items. If the user cancels the dialog, the print record remains as it is and PrStlDialog returns FALSE. If the user OK's the dialog, the hPrint's print record is changed so that it contains the user's style selections. In this case, PrStlDialog returns TRUE.

If the print record was originally from a document, the document's print record should also be updated when PrStlDialog returns TRUE.

```
Boolean PrJobDialog (hPrint)
    THPrint hPrint;
```

PrJobDialog activates the job dialog. HPrint's current settings are used as the initial settings for the dialog items. If the user cancels the dialog, the print record remains as it is and PrJobDialog returns FALSE. If the user OK's the dialog, the hPrint's print record and the printer resource file is changed so that it contains the user's selections. PrJobDialog returns TRUE.

If the print record was originally from a document, the document's print record should also be updated when PrJobDialog returns TRUE.

```
void PrJobMerge (hPrintSrc, hPrintDst)
    THPrint hPrintSrc, hPrintDst;
```

PrJobMerge copies the job information (prJob) from hPrintSrc's print record to hPrintDst's print record. Then hPrintDst's printer information, band information, and paper rectangle are updated using information in prJob.

Draft Printing and Spooling

```
TPPrPort PrOpenDoc (hPrint, pPrPort, plOBuf)
     THPrint hPrint;   TPPrPort pPrPort;   Ptr plOBuf;
```

PrOpenDoc initializes a printing port (which becomes the current port) and returns a pointer to the port.

Hprint is a handle to the print record associated with this port. The bJDocLoop field in the print record indicates whether this is to be draft printing or spooling. If spooling is called for, the spool file's name, version, and volume reference number are obtained from hPrint's job subrecord.

PPrPort allows you to indicate where you want to store the printing port and plOBuf lets you indicate where in memory you want the I/O buffer. Using NULL for pPrPort will allocate a new printing port. When plOBuf is NULL the volume buffer is used as the I/O buffer.

```
void PrOpenPage (pPrPort, pPageFrame)
     TPPrPort pPrPort;   TPRect pPageFrame;
```

PrOpenPage starts a new page in pPrPort's print document. The page is printed only if the page number is within the range of pages to be printed.

When spooling, pPageFrame points to the rectangle used as Quickdraw's picture frame for this page. When the page is actually being printed, the rectangle is scaled to match the page rectangle given in the printer information subrecord. If you don't want this scaling to occur, use pPageFrame = NULL, and QuickDraw will use the page rectangle for the picture frame.

```
void PrClosePage (pPrPort)
     TPPrPort pPrPort;
```

PrClosePage tells the Printing Manager where the end of a page is for a document using pPrPort. If this is spooling, the QuickDraw picture for the page is closed. If this is draft printing, a form feed is printed and the user is alerted that a new page needs to be inserted.

```
void PrCloseDoc (pPrPort)
     TPPrPort pPrPort;
```

PrCloseDoc finishes printing (or spooling) the document using pPrPort. For draft printing, a form feed is printed and the printer is reset. For spooling, the spool file is closed if everything went okay. If spooling was unsuccessful the file is deleted.

Spool Printing

```
void PrPicFile (hPrint, pPrPort, pIOBuf, pDevBuf, prStatus)
      THPring  hPrint;    TPPrPort  pPrPort;    Ptr  pIOBuf, pDevBuf;
      TPrStatus prStatus;
```

PrPicFile prints the spooled document.

Handling Errors

```
int PrError ( )
```

PrError returns error codes resulting from Printing Manager functions.


```
void PrSetError (iErr)
      int iErr;
```

PrSetError sets a global variable used by the Printing Manager's iErr. If you use iErr = iPrAbort it will allow you to cancel a print job already in progress.

Low-Level Driver Access

```
void PrDrvrOpen ( )
```
PrDrvrOpen opens the Printer Driver.


```
void PrDrvrClose ( )
```
PrDrvrClose closes the Printer Driver.


```
void PrCtlCall(iWhichCtl, lParam1, lParam2, lParam3)
      int iWhichCtl;    long lParam1, lParam2, lParam3;
```
PrCtlCall calls the current printer driver's control routine.


```
Handle PrDrvrDCE ( )
```
PrDrvrDCE returns a handle to the Printer Driver's DCE (device control entry).


```
int PrDrvrVers ( )
```
PrDrvrVers tells you what version number of the Printer Driver is in the system resource file.

void PrNoPurge ( )
PrNoPurge makes the Printer Driver unpurgeable.

void PrPurge ( )
PrPurge makes the Printer Driver purgeable.

RESOURCE MANAGER

The *Resource Manager* organizes Macintosh resource files. It is seldom called directly, but every Macintosh Toolbox Manager that reads information uses the Resource Manager to retrieve that information from the resource files opened during the course of running an application. The resources it reads includes typefaces, icons, text, dialog templates, window templates, control definitions, drivers, desk accessories, and even an application's code.

The Resource Manager is really a simple database tool. Resources may be found by name or by numeric ID. You might be tempted to use the Resource Manager as a simple database tool in your own applications, but you should avoid doing this except for trivially small databases. The Resource Manager is too slow for most general purpose database uses.

Constants

```
/* Resource Attributes        */
#define resSysRef             0x80
#define resSysHeap            0x40
#define resPurgeable          0x20
#define resLocked             0x10
#define resProtected          0x08
#define resPreload            0x04
#define resChanged            0x02
#define resUser               0x01

/* Resource File Attributes    */
#define mapReadOnly           128
#define mapCompact            64
#define mapChanged            32

/* ResError Result Code Constants */
#define noErr                 0
#define resNotFound           -192
#define resFnotFound          -193
#define addResFailed          -194
#define addRefFailed          -195
#define rmvResFailed          -196
#define rmvRefFailed          -197

#define mapReadOnly           0x80
#define mapCompact            0x40
#define mapChanged            0x20
```

Data Structures

Not applicable.

Functions

Initializing the Resource Manager

        int   InitResources ()

InitResources initializes the Resource Manager, opens the system's resource file, and reads in the file's resource map. The return value is the file's reference number. InitResources is called by the system at startup. Your application should *not* call InitResources.

        void   RsrcZoneInit ()

RsrcZoneInit will initialize the resource map read in from the system resource file. RsrcZoneInit is called by the system (*not* your application) when your application starts up. All open resource files, except for the system resource file, are closed. It then goes through the resource map, giving NULL values to handles that point to the application heap (these are easy to find—they all have 0 (zero) resSysHeap attributes), since the previous application heap is no longer valid.

Opening and Closing Resource Files

        void   CreateResFile (fileName)
                Str255 fileName;

CreateResFile will create a resource file with the given name, provided there is no existing file with the given name.

        int OpenResFile (fileName)
                Str255 fileName;

OpenResFile opens a resource file specified by fileName. The resource map is read in from the file, all resources having a set resPreLoad attribute are read in, the file becomes the current resource file, and a reference number to the file is returned by OpenResFile.
        If the file is already open, the file reference number is returned, but the file does not become the current resource file. If the file cannot be opened, ResError returns an Operating System result code and OpenResFile returns -1.

The system resource file and the application's resource file are already opened. The system resource file has the reference number 0. To find out the reference number of the application resource file, call CurResFile after the application starts up and before any other resource files are opened.

ResError Codes: noErr   no error

```
void    CloseResFile (refNum)
        int refNum;
```

CloseResFile closes the resource file with reference number refNum.

The following events happen when CloseResFile is called: UpdateResFile is called, ReleaseResource is called for each resource in the file, the memory used by the resource map is released, and the resource file is closed.

If refNum is 0 (the system resource file), all file open resource files are closed before this one. If refNum is not a reference number for a resource file, then nothing happens and ResError returns an error code.

All open resource files (except the system resource file) are closed when the application is terminated.

ResError Codes: noErr   no error
                                    resFNotFound   can't find resource file

Checking for Errors

```
int     ResError ()
```

ResError returns the error codes resulting from the last Resource Manager routine.

ResError Codes: noErr   no error
                                      resNotFound   can't find resource
                                      resFnotFound   can't find resource file
                                      addResFailed   couldn't add resource
                                      addRefFailed   couldn't add reference
                                      rmvResFailed   couldn't remove resource
                                      rmvRefFailed   couldn't remove reference

Setting the Current Resource File

```
int     CurResFile ()
```

CurResFile returns the current resource file's reference number. To get the resource file reference number for the application, call CurResFile when the application is started.

When the system resource file is the current resource file, CurResFile returns the actual reference number of the system resource file. Your application can use either this number or 0 when refering to the system resource file.

```
int     HomeResFile (theResource)
        Handle theResource;
```

HomeResFile returns the file reference number of the resource file containing theResource. If an error occurs (theResource isn't a handle to a resource), HomeResFile returns -1.

ResError Codes: noErr   no error
                               resNotFound   resource not found

```
void    UseResFile (refnum)
        int refNum;
```

UseResFile sets the resource file with the given reference number to be the current resource file. Using 0 for refNum will make the system resource file the current resource file.

ResError Codes: noErr   no error
                               resFNotFound   resource file not found

```
int     CountTypes ()
```

CountTypes looks in all the open resource files and returns the total number of resource types that are found.

```
void    GetIndType (theType, index)
        ResType *theType;   int index;
```

GetIndType sets theType equal to the resource type referenced by index. Index should be a number from 1 to the number returned by CountTypes. If index is not in that range, theType is set equal to four NULL (ASCII code = 0) characters.

Getting and Disposing of Resources

```
void    SetResLoad (load)
        Boolean load;
```

SetResLoad affects the routines that return handles to resources. If load is TRUE, then the routines that return handles to resources will also automatically read the resource into memory. If load is FALSE, these routines will not read in the resource and they will return a NULL handle.

The normal state is for resources to be read into memory. Be aware that other Toolbox routines rely on the Resource Manager, and to have these routines work correctly, you should restore the normal state as soon as possible.

```
int CountResources (theType)
        ResType theType;
```

CountResources looks through all open resource files and returns the total number of resources of theType that are found.

```
Handle GetIndResource (theType, index)
        ResType theType;    int index;
```

GetIndResource returns a handle to a resource of the given type. The resource whose handle is returned is determined by the index, where index is a number from 1 to the value returned by CountResources (above).

```
Handle GetResource (theType, theID)
        ResType theType;    int theID;
```

GetResource returns the handle to the resource of theType having theID. If you haven't called SetResLoad (FALSE), GetResource will read the resource into memory.

GetResource will search for the resource starting in the current resource file then go through all resource files opened before the current resource file. If the resource is not found, a NULL handle is returned.

ResError Codes: noErr   no error
                       resNotFound   resource not found

```
Handle GetNamedResource (theType, name)
        ResType theType;    Str255 name;
```

GetNamedResource returns a handle to the resource of theType having the given name. GetNamedResource is the same as GetResource (above), except that it uses a name rather than an ID number.

ResError Codes: noErr   no error
resNotFound   resource not found

```
void    LoadResource (theResource)
        Handle theResource;
```

LoadResource reads theResource into memory. If theResource is already in memory, LoadResource does nothing.

ResError Codes: noErr   no error
resNotFound   resource not found

```
void    ReleaseResource (theResource)
        Handle theResource;
```

ReleaseResource frees the memory occupied by theResource's data and the handle to the resource in the resource map becomes NULL. TheResource can no longer be used as a resource handle. If the resource needs to be read in again, a new handle will be allocated.

ReleaseResource should only be called when your application is completely through with a resource.

ResError Codes: noErr   no error
resNotFound   resource not found

```
void    DetachResource (theResource)
        Handle theResource;
```

This routine removes the resource from the resource map. This has the effect of making the resource manager forget about this resource.

Getting Resource Information

```
int     UniqueID (theType)
        ResType theType;
```

UniqueID will return an ID number for the given resource type (theType) which is not used in any of the open resource files. The ID will be greater than 0, but it may be in the system resource range (0 to 127). Be sure to check that the returned value is greater than 127. If it isn't, you should call UniqueID again.

```
void    GetResInfo (theResource, theID, theType, name)
        Handle theResource;  int *theID;  ResType *theType;  Str255 name;
```

GetResInfo will give you the name, theType and theID of a resource when you provide a handle to a resource. If theResource is not a handle to a resource, GetResInfo does nothing.

ResError Codes: noErr   no error
                      resNotFound   resource not found

```
int     GetResAttrs (theResource)
        Handle theResource;
```

GetResAttrs will return the attributes of the resource whose handle is theResource. If theResource is not a handle to a resource, GetResAttrs will do nothing.

ResError Codes: noErr   no error
                      resNotFound   resource not found

```
long    SizeResource (theResource)
        Handle theResource;
```

SizeResource returns the number of bytes used by theResource's resource in its resource file. If theResource is not a handle to a resource, -1 is returned by SizeResource.

ResError Codes: noErr   no error
                      resNotFound   resource not found

Modifying Resources

```
void    SetResInfo (theResource, theID, name)
        Handle theResource;   int theID;   Str255 name;
```

SetResInfo changes theResource's name and ID number to the those given by name and theID.

SetResInfo makes the specified changes to resource map. To make the changes permanent, call ChangedResource after calling SetResInfo. These changes can become permanent if ChangedResource is called for *any* resource which is in the same resource file (also in the same resource map) as theResource. This is because ChangedResource causes the entire resource map to be written out when the file is updated. If you do not want these changes to become permanent, you must restore the original values before the resource file is updated.

SetResInfo does nothing when:

- theResource is not a handle to a resource. ResError will return resNotFound error.
- the resource is protected (resProtected attribute is set).
- the resource map becomes too large to fit into memory. In this case, an Operating System error code is returned by ResError.
- there is not enough disk space to store the modified resource file. In this case, ResError returns an appropriate Operating System error code.

```
void    SetResAttrs (theResource, attrs)
        Handle theResource;   int attrs;
```

SetResAttrs sets theResource's attributes (in the resource map) to the given attrs. If theResource is not a handle to a resource, SetResAttrs does nothing.

Do not use SetResAttrs for setting the resChanged attribute, this attribute must only be changed by using ChangedResource (see below). The only attribute that will become effective immediately is resProtected. All others become effective next time the resource is read in.

You should follow SetResAttrs with a call to ChangedResource if you want the changes to be permanent. Be aware that calling ChangedResource will cause the entire resource map to be written out when the resource file is updated.

ResError Codes: noErr   no error
                         resNotFound   resource not found

```
void   ChangedResource (theResource)
       Handle theResource;
```

ChangedResource checks to see if there is enough space on the disk to hold the modified resource file. If there is, ChangedResource sets theResource's resChanged attribute in the resource map. If there isn't, the resChanged bit is cleared.

A set resChanged attribute will cause the Resource Manager to:

- write the resource data to the resource file if WriteResource is called or when the resource file is updated.
- write out the entire resource map when theResource's resource file is updated.

ChangedResource does nothing when:

- theResource is not a handle to a resource. In this case, ResError returns the resNotFound code.

- there is not enough space on the disk for the modified resource file. When this happens, an Operating System error is returned by ResError.

When changing resource data for purgeable resources, you must be certain that the resource won't be purged while you are changing it. To do this, make the resource unpurgeable (using Memory Manager's HNoPurge routine). While you are operating on it, write it out once it's been changed, then reset it as being purgeable (using Memory Manager's HPurge routine).

You could accomplish the same thing by calling SetResPurge(TRUE) (see below).

ResError Codes: noErr   no error
                                  resNotFound   resource not found

```
void   AddResource (theData, theType, theID, name)
       Handle theData;   ResType theType;   int theID;   Str255 name;
```

AddResource is used to add a resource to the current resource file by setting the reschanged attribute. TheData is a handle to resource data in memory. If theData is an empty handle, zero-length data will be written out for the resource. The type, ID and name of the resource are given by theType, theID and name. You must provide this resource with a unique ID (see UniqueID), since AddResource does not check for this.

AddResource does nothing when:

- theData is a NULL handle or a handle to a resource. When this happens, ResError will indicate that adding the resource failed.
- there is not enough room for the resource. This can happen if the resource map gets too big to fit in memory or if there won't be enough space on the disk to store the resource. If this is the case, ResError returns the appropriate Operating System result code.

ResError Codes: noErr   no error
                                  addResFailed   resource was not added

```
void   RmveResource (theResource)
       Handle theResource;
```

RmveResource is used to remove a resource from the current resource file. TheResource is a handle to the resource that is to be removed. The resource reference will be removed from the resource map, and the resource data is removed from the resource file when the file is updated.

RmveResource does nothing when:

- theResource is not a handle to a resource in the current resource file.
- the resProtected attribute is set for theResource.

After successfully removing the resource, call the Memory Manager function DisposHandle to free the memory occupied by the resource data.

ResError Codes: noErr   no error
                               rmvResFailed   resource was not removed

```
void    UpdateResFile (refNum)
        int refNum;
```

UpdateResFile updates a resource file according to its resource map. RefNum is the reference number for the resource file. The following activities occur when UpdateResFile is called:

- The data in the file is made current. Here, resource data is added, changed, or removed from the file according to the resource map. WriteResource is called for each resource whose resChanged attribute is set. If a resource's data is larger than before, the data is written at the end of the file.
- Next the file is compacted: vacancies left by moved, or removed resources are closed up.
- If you added, removed or called ChangedResource (successfully), the entire resource map is written out to the resource file in its current form.

UpdateResFile is useful if you want to update a file without closing it. You do not need to call UpdateResFile before closing a file since it is automatically called by CloseResFile.

ResError Codes: noErr   no error
                               resFNotFound   can't find the resource file

```
void    WriteResource (theResource)
        Handle  theResource;
```

WriteResource will write out the resource data for theResource if it's resChanged attribute is set. After writing out the data, the resChanged attribute is cleared. If the resource has been purged, zero-length data is written out. If the resProtected attribute has been set, or if theResource is not a handle to a resource, WriteResource does nothing.

WriteResource does not check if there is enough space on the disk for the the resource, but ChangedResource does. Make sure that ChangedResource was successful before calling WriteResource.

ResError Codes: noErr   no error
                         resNotFound   can't find the resource

    void   SetResPurge (install)
            Boolean install;

SetResPurge can cause the Memory Manager to check with the Resource Manager before it purges data with a handle. The Resource Manager determines whether or not this is a handle to a resource in the application heap. If it is, WriteResource is called if the resChanged attribute is set. This occurs if SetResPurge(TRUE) has been called. SetResPurge(FALSE) restores the normal state— the Memory Manager purges without consulting the Resource Manager.

Advanced Routines

    int   GetResFileAttrs (refNum)
            int refNum;

GetResFileAttrs returns the attributes of the resource file with reference number refNum. If there is no resource file with refNum, then an error code is returned by ResError.

    ResError Codes: noErr   no error
                         resFNotFound   can't find the resource file

    void   SetResFileAttrs (refNum, attrs)
            int refNum, attrs;

SetResFileAttrs sets the file attributes of a resource file. RefNum is the reference number of the resource file; the attributes for this file are set to attrs. You should *not* change the attributes of the system resource file.

    ResError Codes: noErr   no error
                         resFNotFound   can't find the resource file

TOOLBOX UTILITIES

ToolBox Utilities is a grab bag of routines. It contains: fixed point arithmetic, which is considerably faster than floating point, string manipulation, bit-image compression, bit manipulation, longword manipulation and graphics utilities.

Some of the ToolBox Utilities routines, like the bit manipulation routines, are redundant with respect to the capabilities C provides. Others, such as the graphics routines, might be better classified among QuickDraw routines.

Data Structures

```
typedef long Fixed;

struct Int64Bit
{        long  hiLong;
         long  loLong;
};

typedef struct Int64Bit Int64Bit;

typedef Str255 *StringPtr;
typedef Str255 **StringHandle;

typedef struct Cursor *CursPtr;
typedef struct Cursor **CursHandle;

typedef struct Pattern *PatPtr;
typedef struct Pattern **PatHandle;
```

Functions

Fixed-Point Arithmetic

```
Fixed    FixRatio (numer, denom)
         int numer, denom;
```

FixRatio does fixed point division. The value returned by FixRatio is the fixed point value of numer/denom. When denom is 0, FixRatio returns 0x7FFFFFFF plus the sign bit of numer.

```
Fixed    FixMul (a, b)
         Fixed a, b;
```

FixMul does fixed point multiplication. The return value of FixMul is the fixed point value of **a*b**, computed MOD 65536 and truncated.

```
int FixRound (x)
        Fixed x;
```

FixRound rounds the positive fixed point number x to the nearest integer and returns that integer. If x is halfway between to integers, FixRound will round up. The rounded values of negative fixed point numbers are equal to -FixRound(-x).

String Manipulation

```
StringHandle NewString (theString)
        Str255 theString;
```

NewString makes room for theString on the heap and returns a handle to it. NewString does *not* put theString onto the heap, it just sets it up so that your application can put it there.

```
void    SetString (h, theString )
        StringHandle h;    Str255 theString;
```

SetString makes the handle h a handle to theString.

```
StringHandle GetString (stringID)
        int stringID;
```

GetString returns a handle to the string which has resource ID equal to the given stringID. If the string is not already in memory, GetString calls GetResource('STR ',stringID), thus relying on the Resource Manager to read it. An empty handle is returned if the string cannot be read into memory.

```
void    GetIndString (theString, strListID, index)
        Str255 theString;    int strListID, index;
```

GetIndString sets theString equal to the index value of the string in the string list. The string list is specified by strListID. If the string list is not in memory, GetIndString calls GetResource('STR#',strListID), thus using the Resource Manager to read in the string list.

Index must be a number from 1 to the number of strings in the given string list. If index is out of range, or if the string list cannot be read, theString becomes an empty string.

Byte Manipulation

```
long    Munger (h, offset, ptr1, len1, ptr2, len2)
        Handle h;   Ptr ptr1, ptr2;   long offset, len1, len2;
```

Munger (this rhymes with plunger) is a function which can be used for string manipulation. Munger looks through the text (handle h) at a particular starting point (given by offset) and replaces the first occurance of a particular string (given by ptr1 and len1, called the "target string") with another string (given by ptr2 and len2, called the "replacement string").

The value returned by Munger is the position in the text of the character just beyond the replacement string. Munger has other cases:

- If ptr1 is NULL, Munger replaces the string of length len1 at the offset position with the replacement string. The offset of the character just beyond the replacement string is the return value.

- If len1 < 0, then the replacement string is inserted at the given offset and the text is truncated just beyond the replacement string. The offset of the character just beyond the replacement string is the return value.

- If len1=0, the replacement string is inserted at the given offset. No replacement is done. In this case, the return value is the offset of the character just beyond the inserted string.

- If ptr2 is NULL, the text stays the same and Munger returns the offset of the position where the target string was found.

- If len2=0 and ptr2 is not NULL, then the target string is deleted. The return value is the offset where the deletion occurred.

- If the target string is not found in the text, then Munger returns a negative number.

- If the characters from offset to the end of the text match the beginning of the target string, the match is considered good and the replacement is made. The return value is the offset just beyond the last character of the replacement string.

Two points to remember when using Munger:
1. Offset can not be greater than the length of the text, otherwise you will gct unpredictable results.
2. The text is in a relocatable block allocated by the Memory Manager. Munger uses Memory Manager routines to determine the length of the text.

```
void    PackBits (srcPtr,dstPtr, srcBytes)
        Ptr *srcPtr, *dstPtr;   int srcBytes;
```

PackBits compacts data. It does this for srcBytes of data starting at srcPtr and places the compacted data at dstPtr. SrcPtr is then incremented by srcBytes and dstPtr is incremented by the number of bytes that the data was compressed to.

Bytes are compacted whenever there are three or more equal bytes in a row. This condition occurs frequently in Quickdraw images. To compact bit images, call PackBits once for each row in the image. In the worst case, the length of the compacted bytes is one byte longer than the original length. To undo the packing, call UnPackBits (below).

```
void    UnPackBits (srcPtr,dstPtr, dstBytes)
        Ptr *srcPtr, *dstPtr;   int dstBytes;
```

UnpackBits expands the data that was compacted by PackBits (above). The compacted data pointed to by srcPtr gets unpacked to the dstBytes number of bytes pointed to by dstPtr. After the data is expanded, dstPtr is incremented by dstBytes and srcPtr is incremented by the number of bytes that were expanded.

Bit Manipulation

```
Boolean BitTst (bytePtr, bitNum)
        Ptr bytePtr;   long bitNum;
```

BitTst tests whether a given bit is set or clear. If the bit is set, BitTst is TRUE. If the bit is clear, BitTst is FALSE. The bit tested is the bit which offsets bitNum from the high-order bit of the byte pointed to by bytePtr.

```
void    BitSet (bytePtr, bitNum)
        Ptr bytePtr;   long bitNum;
```

BitSet sets the bit which offsets bitNum from the high-order bit of the byte pointed to by bytePtr.

```
void    BitClr (bytePtr, bitNum)
        Ptr bytePtr;   long bitNum;
```

BitClr clears the bit which offsets bitNum from the high-order bit of the byte pointed to by bytePtr.

Logical Operations

```
long    BitAnd (value1, value2)
        long value1, value2;
```

BitAnd returns the result of value1 & value2, where & is C's bitwise AND operator.

```
long    BitOr (value1, value2)
        long value1, value2;
```

BitOr returns the result of value1 | value2, where | is C's bitwise OR operator.

```
long    BitXor (value1, value2)
        long value1, value2;
```

BitXor returns the result of value1 ^ value2, where ^ is C's bitwise exclusive OR operator.

```
long    BitNot (value)
        long value;
```

BitNot returns the result of ~value, where ~ is C's one's complement operator.

```
long    BitShift (value, count)
        long value;   int count;
```

BitShift shifts the bits in the given value. If count is positive, then BitShift returns value << count. If count is negative, value is treated as unsigned and value >> count is returned.

Other Operations on Long Integers

```
int    HiWord (x)
       long x;
```
HiWord returns the high-order word of x.

```
int    LoWord (x)
       long x;
```
LoWord returns the low-order word of x.

```
void    LongMul (a, b, dest)
        long a, b;   Int64Bit *dest;
```
LongMul sets dest equal to a*b.

Graphics Utilities

Handle GetIcon (iconID)
    int iconID;

GetIcon returns a handle to the icon that has the given iconID. If the icon is not in memory, GetIcon calls GetResource('ICON', iconID) to read it in. If the icon cannot be read in, an empty handle is returned.

void   PlotIcon (theRect, theIcon)
    Rect *theRect;   Handle theIcon;

PlotIcon draws theIcon in theRect. TheRect is in the current grafPort, so its coordinates should be in local units. Drawing is done via CopyBits using srcCopy mode (see QuickDraw for information on CopyBits and srcCopy).

PatHandle GetPattern (patID)
    int patID;

GetPattern returns a handle to the pattern having pattern ID equal to patID. If the pattern is not already in memory, GetPattern calls GetResource('PAT ', patID) to read it in. If the pattern cannot be read in, an empty handle is returned.

void   GetIndPattern (thePattern, patListID, index)
    Pattern *thePattern;   int patListID, index;

GetIndPattern sets thePattern equal to a pattern on the pattern list. The pattern list is given by patListID and the particular pattern on the list is specified by index, where index is a number from 1 to the number of patterns on the pattern list. If the pattern list is not in memory, then GetIndPattern calls GetResource('PAT#', patListID) to read it in.

CursHandle GetCursor (cursorID)
    int cursorID;

GetCursor returns a handle to the cursor having the given cursorID.
If the cursor is not already in memory, GetResource('CURS', cursorID) is called to read it in. If the specified cursor cannot be read in, an empty handle is returned.
The system resource file has the following cursors:
```
#define iBeamCursor          1
#define crossCursor          2
#define plusCursor           3
#define watchCursor          4
```

```
void    ShieldCursor (shieldRect, offsetPt)
Rect *shieldRect;    Point offsetPt;
```

ShieldCursor hides the cursor if it is over a rectangle given by shieldRect. You may specify the rectangle in either global or local coordinates. If you use global coordinates for shieldRect, use (0,0) for offsetPt. If you use local coordinates, then use the top left corner of the grafPort's boundary rectangle for offsetPt.

ShieldCursor decrements the cursor level (see Quickdraw routines to find out more about cursor level). It must be balanced by a call to ShowCursor when you no longer wish to have this "shielding" effect.

```
PicHandle GetPicture (pictureID)
int pictureID;
```
GetPicture returns a handle to the picture having the given pictureID. If the picture is not already in memory, GetResource('PICT', pictureID) is called to read it in. If the picture cannot be read in, GetPicture returns an empty handle.

Miscellaneous Utilities

```
long DeltaPoint (ptA, ptB)
Point ptA, ptB;
```

DeltaPoint subtracts ptA from ptB. It returns a long integer whose high-order word is the difference of the vertical coordinates and whose low-order word is the difference of the horizontal coordinates.

```
Fixed SlopeFromAngle (angle)
int angle;
```

SlopeFromAngle returns the slope (slope is dh/dv) of the line which is at the given angle with the y-axis. Angles are measured with 0 degrees at 12 o'clock. Positive degrees are measured clockwise; negative degrees are measured counterclockwise. Angles are treated MOD 180.

```
int AngleFromSlope (slope)
Fixed slope;
```
AngleFromSlope returns the angle between the y-axis and the line having the given slope. As in SlopeFromAngle, angles are measured with 0 degrees at 12 o'clock. Positive degrees are measured clockwise, negative degrees are measured counterclockwise. Angles are treated MOD 180.

DESK MANAGER

The *Desk Manager* opens and closes desk accessories and routes menu commands, editing commands, and events to open desk accessories. The Desk Manager also provides a routine through which desk accessories may be allotted time for periodic actions.

Constants

```
#define undoCmd      0
#define cutCmd       2
#define copyCmd      3
#define pasteCmd     4
#define clearCmd     5
```

Functions

Opening and Closing Desk Accessories

```
int     OpenDeskAcc (theAcc)
        Str255 theAcc;
```

OpenDeskAcc opens the desk accessory whose resource name is specified by theAcc. If theAcc has a window, this window becomes the active window and the display changes accordingly. The Resource Manager is used to read in the desk accessory from the resource file.

If the desk accessory is successfully opened, the return value is the driver reference number. Your application will not need this number, so it can be ignored.

If theAcc cannot be opened the return value is undefined, but that's ok. When this happens, the user already knows that the desk accessory cannot be opened and therefore it won't be displayed. Again, your application can ignore the return value.

Before calling OpenDeskAcc, save the current grafPort using GetPort. Upon return from OpenDeskAcc restore the grafPort with SetPort.

```
void    CloseDeskAcc (refNum)
        int refNum;
```

CloseDeskAcc closes the desk accessory given by refNum. This routine should be used when a system window is active and the user selects close from the file menu. RefNum is the driver reference number for the desk accessory—it is found in the windowKind field of the active window.

If the user clicks a desk accessory's goAway box, the Desk Manager automatically calls CloseDeskAcc. This is not necessary when an application is terminated. When the application heap is released, the desk accessories (which are in the application heap) are also released.

Handling Events in Desk Accessories

```
void     SystemClick (theEvent, theWindow)
         EventRecord *theEvent;    WindowPtr theWindow;
```

SystemClick should be called after determining that a mouse-down event occurred inside a system window. TheWindow is the window where theEvent occurred. SystemClick first determines in which part of the desk accessory the mouse button was pressed.

If theEvent occurred:

- in the content region of an active window, theEvent is passed to the desk accessory which responds appropriately.

- in the content region of an inactive window, theWindow is made the active window.

- in the drag region, the Window Manager function DragWindow is called. DragWindow will drag a gray outline of theWindow across the screen, and then move theWindow when user is done dragging. If theWindow is inactive, DragWindow will make it the active window.

- in the go-away region, the Window Manager function TrackGoAway is called. TrackGoAway will track the mouse until the mouse button is released (TrackGoAway takes care of highlighting). If the button is released in the go-away region, the desk accessory will close itself. If the mouse button is released outside this region, nothing happens.


```
Boolean          SystemEdit (editCmd)
        int editCmd;
```

SystemEdit should be called after determining that the user has selected one of the five standard editing commands from the edit menu. The parameter editCmd inidicates which editing command was chosen. If the edit commands are in the standard arrangement (in ascending order with a gray line between Undo and Cut), then editCmd = menuItem − 1 .

SystemEdit first checks if the active window belongs to a desk accessory. If this is not the case, SystemEdit returns FALSE. It now becomes the application's responsibility to handle this editing. If the active window is a desk accessory, SystemEdit takes care of the event by having the accessory do the right thing. SystemEdit will be TRUE, inidicating that it did what it was supposed to do.

Performing Periodic Actions

> void   SystemTask ( )

SystemTask will cause each open desk accessories to perform whatever predefined periodic action it may have. SystemTask will alert the desk accessory that this action needs to be performed if some specified amount of time has occurred since it was last done.

A desk accessory which has a periodic action is the alarm clock: the displayed time needs to be changed every second (one second = sixty ticks on the Macintosh).

SystemTask should be called at least every sixtieth of a second (this is one tick —the Macintosh's time unit). Calling SystemTask once each time through the event loop will usually meet this specification. If you do a lot of processing in the event loop, you should call SystemTask more often.

Advanced Routines

> Boolean SystemEvent (theEvent)
>   EventRecord *theEvent;

The Toolbox Event Manager routine GetNextEvent calls SystemEvent (SystemEvent is *only* called by GetNextEvent) whenever it gets an event. SystemEvent then determines whether the system intercept can handle this event, or whether theEvent should be passed on to the application. If theEvent is an event that should be handled by the system, then whatever needs to be done to handle theEvent is done, and SystemEvent returns TRUE. If theEvent is an event which should be a handled by the application, then SystemEvent returns FALSE.

SystemEvent will immediately return FALSE for null, abort and mouse-down events. Why FALSE for a mouse-down event? If SystemEvent checked to see if it should handle the mouse-down, it would first have to find out if the event occurred in a system window. This is the same process that it goes through when you call FindWindow. So rather than doing the same calculation twice, it does it once— when you call FindWindow.

If theEvent is a mouse-up or keyboard event, SystemEvent checks if the active window is a desk accessory window capable of handling such an event. If it can, theEvent is passed along to the desk accessory and SystemEvent is TRUE. If it can't, SystemEvent is FALSE and something else has to deal with theEvent.

If theEvent is an activate or update event, SystemEvent checks to see if it occurred in a desk accessory's window. If it did and the desk accessory can handle this event (desk accessories should be set up to do this), the desk accessory is given theEvent and SystemEvent is TRUE. If responsibility to deal with theEvent can't be given to the desk accessory, SystemEvent is FALSE.

If theEvent is a disk-inserted event, SystemEvent calls the File Manager routine MountVol. Some low-level processing takes place here, but SystemEvent returns FALSE, allowing your application the opportunity to take further actions with this event.

```
void    SystemMenu (menuResult)
        long menuResult;
```

SystemMenu is another function that your application should not call—it is used only by the Menu Manager functions MenuSelect and MenuKey. It is called when a item from a desk accessory's menu has been chosen. SystemMenu directs the desk accessory to do the action appropriate for this menu selection. MenuResult has the menu ID as its high-order word and the menu item number as its low-order word. This is the same format used in the return value of MenuSelect and MenuKey

SCRAP MANAGER

The *Scrap Manager* controls access to the desk scrap. The desk scrap is where a piece of "cut" information can be held until it is pasted. The desk scrap is so called because it persists across invocations of Macintosh applications. By writing the desk scrap, your application enables the user to paste material from your application into whatever application he runs next.

Constants

```
#define noTypeErr      -102
```

Data Structures

```
struct   ScrapStuff
{      long   scrapSize;
       Hanle   scrapHandle;
       int   scrapCount;
       int   scrapState;
       StringPtr   scrapName;
};

typedef struct ScrapStuff ScrapStuff;

typedef struct ScrapStuff *PScrapStuff;
```

Functions

Getting Scrap Information

```
PScrapStuff                InfoScrap ( )
```

InfoScrap will give you a ScrapStuff pointer which is where you can find information about the desk scrap. Here is the information you get:

Field Name	Information
scrapSize	size (in bytes) of the desk scrap
scrapHandle	if scrap is in memory, this is a handle to it
	if scrap is on disk, handle is empty

scrapCount	a value that changes each time ZeroScrap is called (see ZeroScrap for details and use)
scrapState	>0 if desk scrap is in memory, 0 if it's on disk
scrapName	pointer to scrap file's name (usually DeskScrap)

Keeping Scrap on the Disk

long   UnloadScrap ( )

UnloadScrap will check first to see if the desk scrap was already written out to the disk. If it was, UnloadScrap does nothing. If this hasn't been done, UnloadScrap writes the desk scrap to the scrap file. If there are no errors, UnloadScrap returns 0, if an error did occur, the return value will be the Operating System error code.

long   LoadScrap ( )

LoadScrap is used to read the desk scrap from the scrap file into memory. It will check first to see if the desk scrap is already in memory. If it's in memory, LoadScrap does nothing—if it is not in memory LoadScrap reads it in. LoadScrap returns 0 if everything went okay. If there were any problems, an Operating System error code will be returned.

Reading from the Scrap

long   GetScrap (hDest, theType, offset)
        Handle hDest;   ResType theType;   long *offset;

GetScrap takes data of theType from the desk scrap and copies it into memory. HDest, which was most likely an empty handle, becomes a handle to the copy. Offset will return the location the data was copied from. The location is given as the number of bytes offset from the start of the desk scrap.

If everything goes according to plan, GetScrap will return the number of bytes you got. If something goes wrong, GetScrap will return an Operating System error or the noTypeErr. The noTypeErr occurs when there is no data of the given type in the desk scrap.

If hDest is NULL, the data will not be read in: this lets you spy on the desk scrap. You can find out if you have data of theType before you allocate a handle for it, or you may just want to find out the size of the data of theType. You can determine the preferred data type of the application that wrote the scrap by calling GetScrap with different types: the type returning offset = 0 is the preferred type (offset 0 tells you this was the first scrap written out).

Writing to the Scrap

long   ZeroScrap ( )

    ZeroScrap clears the desk scrap. The desk scrap must be cleared before it can accept any new scrap from the application, or from a desk accessory. The Operating System error code will be returned if there is an error, otherwise ZeroScrap returns 0.

    ZeroScrap also changes PScrapStuff->scrapCount, indicating that the contents of the desk scrap have been changed. By watching for changes to this field, your application will know if the desk scrap has been changed.

long   PutScrap (length, theType, source)
       long length;   ResType theType;   Ptr source;

    PutScrap writes the data at source to the desk scrap. Length specifies the number of bytes to be written and theType is the data type. If there are no error, then PutScrap will return 0 -- otherwise the Operating System error code will be returned.

    You *must* clear the desk scrap (by calling ZeroScrap) before your first call to PutScrap.

SEGMENT LOADER

The principal job of the *Segment Loader* is to load the segments of an application on demand. If an application is divided into segments when it is created, the Segment Loader will provide a transparent "overlay" mechanism that can leave unused parts of an application on disk until they are used.

The Segment Loader section of the ToolBox also contains some utility routines that can help applications that can handle multiple documents at one time. These routines return information about the documents that were selected when the application was launched. These routines provide roughly the same functionality as the the "argv" argument vector that is conventionally an argument of the "main" routine in a C program.

Constants

```
#define appOpen   0
#define appPrint  1
```

Data Structures

```
struct AppFile
{       int vRefNum;
        OSType fType;
        int versNum;
        Str255 fName;
};

typedef struct AppFile AppFile;
```

Functions

```
void   UnloadSeg (routineAddr)
       Ptr routineAddr;
```

UnloadSeg makes the segment that routineAddr points to relocatable and purgeable. The segment is not purged at this time, but it can be when the Memory Manager needs to do it. The Segment Loader will reload the segment if it needs one of its routines but the segment is not in memory.

```
void   CountAppFiles (message, count)
       int *message, *count;
```

CountAppFiles reads information sent by the Finder to your application.

Count is set to the number of documents selected when your application was started, and message will tell you whether the selected documents are to be opened (message = appOpen) or printed (message = appPrint).

```
void   GetAppFiles (index, theFile)
       int index;   AppFile *theFile;
```

GetAppFiles gets information about a document that was selected when your application started up.

Use index to specify on which document you want information, where index is between 1 and the count returned by CountAppFiles (above). The information is returned in theFile. It includes the volume reference number, file type, version number and file name, and is stored in the AppFile structure (see Data Structures, above).

```
void   ClrAppFiles (index)
       int index;
```

ClrAppFiles indicates to the Finder that your application has processed the file indicated by index. It does this by setting the file type (in the Finder information) to 0.

Call ClrAppFiles after opening or printing a selected document. Doing this will insure correct results from CountAppFiles and GetAppFiles.

```
void   GetAppParms (apName, apRefNum, apParam)
       Str255 apName;   int *apRefNum;   Handle *apParam;
```

GetAppParms gets information about the current application.

ApName is the application's name and apRefNum is the reference number of the application's resource file.

ApParam is a handle to the Finder information (but you may find that using GetAppFiles is an easier way to access the Finder information).

```
void   ExitToShell ( )
```

ExitToShell releases the application heap, then starts up the Finder. Use ExitToShell to exit from your program.

Index

MORE
FROM
SAMS

Understanding Solid State Electronics (4th Edition)
William E. Hafford and Gene W. McWhorter
This book explains complex concepts such as electricity, semiconductor theory, how electronic circuits make decisions, and how integrated circuits are made. It helps you develop a basic knowledge of semiconductors and solid-state electronics. A glossary simplifies technical terms.
ISBN: 0-672-27012-9, $14.95

Understanding Communications Systems (2nd Edition)
Don L. Cannon and Gerald Luecke
This book explores many of the systems that are used every day—AM/FM radio, telephone, TV, data communications by computer, facsimile, and satellite. It explains how information is converted into electrical signals, transmitted to distant locations, and converted back to the original information.
ISBN: 0-672-27016-1, $14.95

Understanding Computer Science (2nd Edition) *Roger S. Walker*
Here is an in-depth look at how people use computers to solve problems. This book covers the fundamentals of hardware and software, programs and languages, input and output, data structures and resource management.
ISBN: 0-672-27011-0, $14.95

Understanding Computer Science Applications *Roger S. Walker*
This book discusses basic computer concepts and how computers communicate with their input/output units and with each other by using parallel communications, serial communications, and computer networking.
ISBN: 0-672-27020-X, $14.95

Understanding Data Communications (2nd Edition) *John L. Fike et al.*
Understand the codes used for data communications, the types of messages, and the transmissions channels—including fiber optics and satellites. Learn how asynchronous modems work and how they interface to the terminal equipment. Find out about protocols, error control, local area and packet networks.
ISBN: 0-672-27019-6, $14.95

Understanding Digital Electronics (2nd Edition) *Gene W. McWhorter*
Learn why digital circuits are used. Discover how AND, OR, and NOT digital circuits make decisions, store information, and convert information into electronic language. Find out how digital integrated circuits are made and how they are used in microwave ovens, gasoline pumps, video games, and cash registers.
ISBN: 0-672-27013-7, $14.95

Understanding Digital Troubleshooting (2nd Edition) *Don L. Cannon*
This book presents the basic principles and troubleshooting techniques required to begin digital equipment repair and maintenance. The book begins with overviews of digital system fundamentals, digital system functions, and troubleshooting fundamentals. It continues with detecting problems in combinational logic, sequential logic, memory, and I/O.
ISBN: 0-672-27015-3, $14.95

Understanding Microprocessors (2nd Edition) *Don L. Cannon and Gerald Luecke*
This book provides insight into basic concepts and fundamentals. It explains actual applications of 4-bit, 8-bit and 16-bit microcomputers, software, programs, programming concepts, and assembly language. The book provides an individualized learning format for the newcomer who wants to know what microprocessors are, what they do, and how they work.
ISBN: 0-672-27010-2, $14.95

Look for these Sams Books at your local bookstore.

To order direct, call 800-428-SAMS or fill out the form below.

- -

Please send me the books whose titles and numbers I have listed below.

_____

_____

_____

_____

_____

Enclosed is a check or money order for $ _____
Include $2.50 postage and handling.
AR, CA, FL, IN, NC, NY, OH, TN, WV residents add local sales tax.

Charge my: ☐ VISA ☐ MC ☐ AE

Account No.

Expiration Date _____

Name *(please print)* _____

Address _____

City _____

State/Zip _____

Signature _____
(required for credit card purchases)

Mail to: Howard W. Sams & Co.
Dept. DM
4300 West 62nd Street
Indianapolis, IN 46268

DC065

SAMS™